新标准 中文本科系列教材

初级中文综合教程 ③

CHUJI ZHONGWEN ZONGHE JIAOCHENG

总主编：张 浩
主 编：葛 娟
编 者（按姓氏笔画排列）：
　　　李立成　施梦泽　葛 娟

北京语言大学出版社
BEIJING LANGUAGE AND CULTURE
UNIVERSITY PRESS

© 2025 北京语言大学出版社，社图号 24161

图书在版编目（CIP）数据

初级中文综合教程. 3 / 葛娟主编；李立成，施梦泽，葛娟编. -- 北京：北京语言大学出版社，2025.4. （新标准中文本科系列教材 / 张浩总主编）. -- ISBN 978-7-5619-6643-3

I. H195.4

中国国家版本馆 CIP 数据核字第 2024SM3263 号

初级中文综合教程 3

CHUJI ZHONGWEN ZONGHE JIAOCHENG 3

排版制作：	北京创艺涵文化发展有限公司
责任印制：	周 燚

出版发行：	北京语言大学出版社
社　　址：	北京市海淀区学院路 15 号，100083
网　　址：	www.blcup.com
电子信箱：	service@blcup.com
电　　话：	编 辑 部 8610-82303395
	国内发行 8610-82303650/3591/3648
	海外发行 8610-82303365/3080/3668
	北语书店 8610-82303653
	网购咨询 8610-82303908
印　　刷：	北京瑞禾彩色印刷有限公司

版　　次：	2025 年 4 月第 1 版	**印　次：**	2025 年 4 月第 1 次印刷
开　　本：	889 毫米 × 1194 毫米 1/16	**印　张：**	17.75
字　　数：	287 千字		
定　　价：	89.00 元		

PRINTED IN CHINA

凡有印装质量问题，本社负责调换。售后 QQ 号 1367565611，电话 010-82303590

总前言

中文作为第二语言教学,其命名从"对外汉语教学"演变为"汉语国际教育",再进一步发展为"国际中文教育",这两次关键性的更名标志着中文教学领域的持续拓宽,彰显了其在全球范围内的普及与影响力的逐步提升。为顺应新时代国际中文教育事业的发展需求,2021年3月,中华人民共和国教育部、国家语言文字工作委员会正式发布了《国际中文教育中文水平等级标准》。该标准创造性地推出了"三等九级"的新范式,同时提出了"等级质量"与"集成创新"的新理念,优化升级了"3 + 5"("3"指言语交际能力、话题任务内容、语言量化指标三个层面,"5"指听、说、读、写、译五种语言技能)规范化新路径。正是在这样的时代背景下,"新标准中文本科系列教材"(以下简称"新标准中文")应运而生。本系列教材旨在以《国际中文教育中文水平等级标准》为参照,更好地满足新标准下本科来华留学生中文教学的需求。

一、适用对象

"新标准中文"主要是为来华攻读汉语言专业本科学历的留学生量身打造的,能够全面满足初、中、高各层次的中文综合课、专业技能课和专业知识课的教学需求;也可用作海内外相关培训课程的中文教材,来华学习中文的长期进修生及中文自学者也可选用。

二、结构规模

"新标准中文"的教材体系与专业课程体系联系紧密,采取综合语言能力培养与听、说、读、写、译专项语言技能训练相融合的教学模式和教材编写模式。此外,还增设了商务、翻译、教学等专业方向的专业语言技能教材和专业知识教材,以满足不同领域的学习需求。全套教材被精心划分为三个层级和两个序列,即初、中、高三个层级,横向和纵向两个序列。横向序列,根据课程性质和专业方向,划分为汉语言技能与知识、文化知识、汉外翻译、商务汉语四大板块,确保学生在各个领域得到全面的学习。纵向序列则以综合课教材为主线,辅以听、说、读、写各分项技能的配套教材，贯穿一至四年级，平衡了一般技能课与各层级专业技能课、知识课的比例，确保学生在各个学习阶段都能获得深入而均衡的学习效果。

三、编写理念

本系列教材深度融汇了第二语言教学理论及学习理论，充分考虑了学习者的个体特征、认知差异以及实际需求。在编写过程中，我们始终秉持语言学习与知识学习相融合的教学理念，旨在全方位提升学习者的汉语言能力及自主学习能力，特别强调对学习者认知能力与跨文化交际能力的双重培养，确保学习者在掌握语言技能的同时，拥有更加宽广的视野和跨文化的沟通素养。

"多元、立体、创新、智能"是本系列教材的基本理念。多元，即对教学法、教学理论、教学大纲及教学材料、训练方式兼容并包；立体，即加强主干教材和配套教学资源的综合开发；创新，即在继承原有成熟的教学理念、教学方式和教材编写研究成果的基础上，对各分系列教材进行整体和局部的特色设计；智能，即在教材研发模式上，依托多媒体数字化平台，以更智能、更灵活的方式服务于课堂内外的教学工作。

四、编写原则

为实现本系列教材的编写理念，本系列教材在编写过程中遵循如下原则：

标准依据　以《国际中文教育中文水平等级标准》为基石，将其核心理念融入教材编写的每个环节。针对各类教材特性，研制与之匹配的教学大纲，确保每部教材独具匠心，同时又能与其他教材形成互补，共同构建完整的教材体系。

结构模式　秉持"结构—功能—文化"三者融合的理念，将语言的结构规则、交际功能以及文化知识结合起来，形成一个全面、系统的教学体系，从而实现语言知识、语言技能与文化认知的协同发展。

话题设计　精选多元话题，从校园生活点滴到当前社会热点，从中华传统文化的深度介绍到现代中国的多维展示。话题设计兼具开放性与包容性，注重跨文化交际的深度解析，旨在增进学习者对中国社会的全面理解，推动不同文明间的交流与互鉴。

语言知识　遵循中文教学与学生认知规律，系统呈现中文基本词汇、语法与汉字知识，多角度展示中文口语与书面语的差异，强调语言要素的语用功能，突出语段与语篇的教学，以此助力学生掌握并灵活运用中文。

技能训练　涵盖听、说、读、写、译五大分项技能，五大技能既各自独立，又相互关联，形成一个完整的技能体系。各分项技能在初级、中级、高级教学阶段逐层递进，实现多层级覆盖，从而精准满足不同层次学习者的实际需求。

专业培养　中文技能培养贯穿本科教学始终，中高级阶段渐进式强化专业技能与专业知识，专业特色鲜明的教材资源帮助学生实现从单一中文能力向"语言＋专业"综合素养的跃升，彰显复合型、多元化的人才培养理念。

五、教学资源

教学资源是确保教材高效利用的关键支撑。为助力教学工作顺利进行，本系列教材配备教师用书、精选教案及教学示范视频等丰富的资源，依托多媒体数字化平台，以智能化、多样化的方式全面服务于课堂内外的教学实践。

六、分工与致谢

本系列教材的编写团队由北京语言大学国际中文学院（原汉语学院）的中青年骨干教师组成。在编写过程中，我们得到了众多支持和指导，对此深表感激！同时，我们也热切期待各位专家、学者、老师及同学们能够不吝赐教，提出宝贵的意见和建议，以使本系列教材日臻完善。

张浩

2024 年 6 月 26 日

编写说明

适用对象

《初级中文综合教程》第 2～4 册适用于有一定中文基础（词汇量 800～1000）的汉语言专业本科一年级留学生，也可供具有同等水平的进修生和其他学习者使用。

培养目标

发展学习者的中文交际能力、中文综合运用能力和专业学习能力，突出认知能力、跨文化交际能力的培养。

编写理念

以切实提升学习者的中文综合运用能力为目标，秉持"结构、功能、文化相结合"的编写理念，以语言结构为纲，以话题为导引，遵循"以学习者为中心"的编写原则。选取具有广泛包容性的话题，课文语料兼具知识性和趣味性，重视跨文化交际能力的培养，满足学习者的认知需求。重视成段表达与写作训练，对话、课文具有一定的长度和深度，旨在加强对学习者中文语篇能力的训练，为其中高级阶段的中文学习打下坚实的基础。

教程体例

每课由本课学习重点、热身、课文、词语、重点词、语法、综合运用、文化小贴士/扩展阅读几大板块组成。

- **本课学习重点**

    以表格的形式直观地呈现当课话题、重点词、重点句、语法、汉字知识、文化小贴士/扩展阅读，便于学习者预习时提前了解课文大致内容以及当课语言学习重点，同时也便于学习者复习时快速回顾上述内容。

- **热身**

    通过与课文话题相关的问题激发学习者的学习兴趣，将学习者引入课文的学习。

- **课文**

    以听前问题来导入，从听力角度训练学习者对于课文主要内容的抓取能力，同时激发学习者对于课文的学习兴趣。课文理解部分细分为三个环节，力求通过环环相扣的进阶式操练，训练学习者的口语表达能力和课文理解能力。第一个环节是根据课文内容回答问题/听课文录音并朗读课文/填写表格，侧重于考查学习者对于课文内容的基本理解；第二个环节是借助关键词、重点句型句式、填空等形式对整篇课文内容进行复述，重在训练学习者的语言技能与思辨能力；第三个环节是"动口与动手"，给出与课文内容紧密相关的话题，让学习者以个人或小组的形式完成相应任务。

● **词语**

第2册和第3册生词以《国际中文教育中文水平等级标准》（以下简称《等级标准》）的二、三级词语为主，第4册生词以《等级标准》的四级词语为主。受课文内容制约，不排除少量超纲词。词语表中标注词语的拼音、词性、英文释义，离合词的拼音在中间加"//"。

● **重点词**

每课从词语表中选出10个左右重点词语进行单独讲解，列出常用搭配和3个典型例句。兼类词根据词性分别给出常用搭配和例句。重点词之后设置"选词填空"练习，便于检测学习者对重点词的掌握情况。

● **语法**

第2册和第3册的语法点以《等级标准》二级和三级语法项目为主，每课设置3～4个语法点；第4册以《等级标准》四级语法项目为主，每课设置2～3个语法点。语法点的阐释多以表格形式呈现，简单明了，便于学习者理解记忆。每个语法点至少列出3个例句，有多个用法的语言点，每个用法单列例句，所给例句皆为典型语境下的典型用法。语法点之后设置练习，练习形式依据该语法点的使用特征而定。比如，常见于口语表达的，尽量采用情景对话练习的形式；常见于书面语表达的，则会在练习的上下文设计上做到语体的协调一致。

● **综合运用**

通过语音练习、汉字知识、口语表达训练三个板块，对当课的内容进行综合性的训练。

其中语音练习主要包括听录音选择正确答案、听句子给画线词语标声调、听绕口令或古诗三种练习题型。汉字知识部分主要介绍汉字的相关知识，帮助学习者初步了解汉字的偏旁部首、结构以及发展历史，以此激发学习者认知汉字、学习汉字的兴趣。口语表达训练围绕当课话题，要求学习者以小组为单位展开社会调查并以表格形式进行记录，或者选取与当课相关的话题进行小组辩论，以此训练学习者的口语表达能力和思辨能力。

● **文化小贴士/扩展阅读**

第2册和第3册的文化小贴士，从不同角度介绍中华古今文化的变迁，帮助学习者更深入地了解中国人的思维方式与生活方式，减少跨文化交际中的误解。第 4 册的扩展阅读，内容与当课话题紧密相关，是主课文的自然延伸。文后配有多种形式的练习，以便及时检测学习者对短文的理解情况。

教程特点

（一）系统性与针对性相结合

作为系列教材的一部分，《初级中文综合教程》第 2～4 册以搭建从初级到中高级的桥梁为编写目标，遵循由易到难、循序渐进的教材编写原则。

系统性主要体现在：（1）生词量的把控方面，第 2 册每课生词量控制在 40 个左右，第 3 册每课生词量控制在 50～60 个，第 4 册每课生词量控制在 70～80 个。（2）语法点的选取方面，涵盖了《等级标准》二级到四级的词类、短语、固定格式、句子成分、句子的类型、强调的方法等语法项目。（3）词语、语法点的复现方面，考虑到遗忘曲线规律，编写时尤其注重词语、语法点的复现。

针对性主要体现在：以学习者为中心，满足学习者的学习需求和目标需求，充分体现"在华"这种现实性的语言环境和语言条件，充分考虑学习者的兴趣点、关注点及其中文水平，并凸显本学科的性质与综合课的特点。除了关注学习者的词汇和语法知识学习之外，加大了对学习者语篇表达能力、阅读能力、听说能力等方面的训练强度和力度。

（二）实用性、趣味性与知识性相结合

课文注重实用性、趣味性和知识性相结合。第 2 册和第 3 册采用"对话（课文一）+ 短文（课文二）"模式，以语言结构要素为依据，以功能为主线设计对话情境，编写对话和课文，满足学习者的语言交际需求和深入了解中国的认知需求。活动场景从校内扩展到校外、社会，知识内容从基本的日常交际扩展到中国传统文化和当代中国。第 4 册课文为叙述体，选自近年的报纸、杂志、书籍等，在尊重原文的基础上根据教学需要进行了改写。课文话题主要涉及校园生活、生活方式、兴趣爱好、自然环境、社会现象、人际 / 社会交往、升学就业、中国传统文化、科技发展、环境保护、中外文化差异等多个方面。

在练习的设置上，根据不同的练习内容设计不同的操练形式。既有选词填空、连词成句、改写句子这样的简单的、封闭性操练；也有根据上下文情景，用指定词语或结构完成句子或对话、看图说话这样的半封闭性进阶操练；还有就某一话题内容进行调查、采访、讨论、汇报等灵活、开放性的表达训练。

（三）创造性设计课后配套练习

课本中的练习具有突破性创新，比如课堂练习的设计比较重视运用和贯彻任务型教学法，大部分练习是需要学习者分组完成的，凸显听、说能力的训练。

（四）多维度引领学习者感知中国、探索世界

教程注重传统与现代的融合，既介绍中国传统文化和生活方式，也全方位展示当下中国人的日常生活、价值观念，帮助学习者更加深入地了解中国和中国文化。与此同时，将当今世界各国关注的热点话题引入教程，如"亲子关系""空巢老人""环境保护""就业与升学"等，以此激发学习者对全球热点问题的探讨与思考。

使用建议

第 2～4 册供汉语言专业本科一年级留学生或同等水平的长期进修生一个学年使用。第一学期学习第 2 册和第 3 册，第二学期学习第 4 册。建议平均 6～8 课时完成一课（每课时 50 分钟）。

目 录

13	快递两三天就可以送到 The express can be delivered in two or three days	1
	话题： Topic:	谈购物 Talk about shopping
	语法： Grammar:	1. 时间副词："就"和"才" Adverbs of time 2. 结果补语 2：动词＋到/住/走 Resultative complement II
	汉字知识： Knowledge of Chinese characters:	1. 独体字 Single-Component Characters 2. 合体字 Multi-Component Characters
	文化小贴士： Cultural tips:	中国的丝绸、刺绣与丝绸之路 Silk, Embroidery and the Silk Road in China

14	小心掉进去 Don't fall in	19
	话题： Topic:	谈秋游 Talk about autumn outing
	语法： Grammar:	1. 趋向补语 1（2）：简单趋向补语（动词＋上/下/进/出/回/起＋宾语） Directional complement I (2): Simple directional complement 2. 趋向补语 2：复合趋向补语 Directional complement II: Compound directional complement
	汉字知识： Knowledge of Chinese characters:	象形字 Pictographic Characters
	文化小贴士： Cultural tips:	中国五岳 The Five Great Mountains of China

15	我本来不太了解京剧，也唱不好 I didn't know much about Peking opera and I couldn't sing well either	37
	话题： Topic:	谈休闲娱乐 Talk about recreation
	语法： Grammar:	1. 可能补语 Potential complement 2. 因果复句 Cause-effect complex sentence （1）由于……，所以 / 因此…… （2）不用关联词语的因果复句
	汉字知识： Knowledge of Chinese characters:	指事字 Self-Explanatory Characters
	文化小贴士： Cultural tips:	中国象棋与围棋 Chinese Chess and Go

16	把其他材料放进去 Put other ingredients in	57
	话题： Topic:	谈美食制作 Talk about gourmet food making
	语法： Grammar:	1."把"字句 1：表处置 把-sentence I: Indicating disposal or settlement （1）主语＋把＋宾语＋动词＋结果补语 / 趋向补语 / 状态补语 （2）主语＋把＋宾语＋动词＋到 / 在＋处所 （3）主语＋把＋宾语1＋动词＋（给）＋宾语2 2. 条件复句：只要……，就…… Conditional complex sentence 3. 承接复句：首先……，然后…… Successive complex sentence
	汉字知识： Knowledge of Chinese characters:	会意字、形声字 Associative Compounds, Pictophonetic Characters
	文化小贴士： Cultural tips:	中国的四大菜系 Four Major Cuisines in China

17	请您把这幅字给我们解释一下吧 Please explain this piece of script to us	78

话题: Topic:	谈传统节日 Talk about traditional festivals
语法: Grammar:	1. 递进复句 Progressive complex sentence 　（1）不光……，而且 / 还…… 　（2）……并且…… 2. "把" 字句 2：表处置 把-sentence II: Indicating disposal or settlement 　（1）主语＋把＋宾语（＋给）＋动词＋了 / 着 　（2）主语＋把＋宾语＋动词（＋一 / 了）＋动词 　（3）主语＋把＋宾语＋动词＋动量补语 / 时量补语
汉字知识: Knowledge of Chinese characters:	假借字 Phonetic Loan Characters
文化小贴士: Cultural tips:	中国四灵——古代吉祥的象征 Four Holy Beasts in China—Ancient Auspicious Symbols

18	养儿防老 Bring up children for the purpose of being looked after in old age	98

话题: Topic:	谈亲子关系 Talk about parent-child relationship
语法: Grammar:	1. 目的复句：为了…… Purposive complex sentence 2. 并列复句：一方面……，一方面…… Coordinate compound sentence 3. 假设复句：……的话，…… Hypothetical complex sentence 4. 条件复句：只有……，才…… Conditional complex sentence
汉字知识: Knowledge of Chinese characters:	多音多义字 Heteronymic Characters
文化小贴士: Cultural tips:	当代中国的人口结构 Demographic Structure of Contemporary China

19	叔叔阿姨看上去真精神！ Auntie and uncle look great!	118

话题： Topic:	谈人际交往 Talk about interpersonal relationships
语法： Grammar:	1. 转折复句：Adversative complex sentence: 　……是……，就是 / 不过…… 2. 选择复句：Alternative complex sentences: 　不是 A，就是 B 3. 递进复句：Progressive complex sentence: 　不仅……，还……
汉字知识： Knowledge of Chinese characters:	同音字 Homophonous Characters
文化小贴士： Cultural tips:	岁寒三友 Three Friends of Winter

20	他被一辆出租车撞了 He was hit by a cab	138

话题： Topic:	谈论一件倒霉事 Talk about a piece of bad luck
语法： Grammar:	1. 被动句 1：Passive sentence I: 　主语 + 被 / 叫 / 让 + 宾语 + 动词（短语）+ 其他成分 2. 被动句 2：Passive sentence II: 　主语 + 被 + 动词 + 其他成分
汉字知识： Knowledge of Chinese characters:	异体字 Variant Characters in Chinese
文化小贴士： Cultural tips:	塞翁失马 A Blessing in Disguise

21	一天到晚就是手机 All day long, nothing but the mobile phone	156
话题： Topic:	谈手机改变生活 Talk about mobile phones changing life	
语法： Grammar:	1. 不用关联词语的假设复句和转折复句 Hypothetical complex sentences and adversative complex sentences without correlatives 2. 动补式离合词：Separable verbs of VC (verb-complement): 　　打开 / 看见 / 离开 / 完成 3. 并列复句：Coordinate compound sentence: 　　一会儿……，一会儿……	
汉字知识： Knowledge of Chinese characters:	形似字 Characters with Similar Shapes	
文化小贴士： Cultural tips:	中国的"新四大发明" The "Four Great New Inventions" in China	

22	买房还是租房？ Buying a house or rent one?	178
话题： Topic:	谈消费 Talk about consumption	
语法： Grammar:	1. 不用关联词语的选择复句 Alternative complex sentences without correlatives 2. 假设复句：Hypothetical complex sentence: 　　要是……，（主语）就…… 3. 紧缩复句：Compressed complex sentence: 　　一……，就…… 4. 固定格式：Fixed pattern: 　　除了……（以外），……还 / 也 / 都……	
汉字知识： Knowledge of Chinese characters:	汉字的字体演变 The Evolution of Chinese Characters	
文化小贴士： Cultural tips:	中国行政区划 Administrative Divisions of China	

23	我一点儿计划都没有 I don't have any plans at all	200

话题： Topic:	谈假期计划 Talk about vacation plans
语法： Grammar:	1. 固定格式：Fixed pattern: 一……也/都+不/没（有）…… 2. 不用关联词语的承接复句 Successive complex sentences without correlatives 3. 疑问代词任指用法（2）：Arbitrary reference of interrogative pronouns II: 疑问代词（+就）+疑问代词
汉字知识： Knowledge of Chinese characters:	中国书法艺术 The Art of Chinese Calligraphy
文化小贴士： Cultural tips:	西南双城记 A Tale of Two Cities in the Southwest

24	你不是要读研究生吗？ Aren't you going to graduate school?	222

话题： Topic:	谈理想 Talk about ideals
语法： Grammar:	1. 强调的方法：Ways to emphasize: （1）用反问句表示强调：不是……吗？／难道……吗？ （2）用"一点儿也不……"表示强调 （3）用"是"表示强调 （4）用"就"表示强调 2. 疑问代词的不定指用法 Indefinite reference of interrogative pronouns 3. 固定格式：Fixed pattern: 越……，越……
汉字知识： Knowledge of Chinese characters:	常见印刷字体 Common Printing Fonts
文化小贴士： Cultural tips:	理想也会变化 Ideals Will Also Change

生词表 Vocabulary list	242

13 快递两三天就可以送到
The express can be delivered in two or three days

本课学习重点

话题 Topic	谈购物 Talk about shopping
重点词 Keywords	故意　按照　打折　迷　立刻　从此　达到　意外　应该
重点句 Key sentences	1. 你怎么这么晚才回来？ 2. 马上就放暑假了，你有什么打算？ 3. 我考完试就回国，我要回去参加我姐姐的婚礼。 4. 假期可能就在北京，我要努力学习，记住学过的每一个词。 5. 正想着要不要买时，别人就买走了那件衣服。
语法 Grammar	1. 时间副词："就"和"才" 　　Adverbs of time 2. 结果补语2：动词 + 到 / 住 / 走 　　Resultative complement Ⅱ
汉字知识 Knowledge of Chinese characters	1. 独体字 Single-Component Characters 2. 合体字 Multi-Component Characters
文化小贴士 Cultural tips	中国的丝绸、刺绣与丝绸之路 Silk, Embroidery and the Silk Road in China

下面是乔治的睡眠记录，乔治是几点睡觉的？几点起床的？你觉得乔治的睡眠时间长吗？ Here is George's sleep log. What time did he go to bed? And what time did he wake up? Do you think he sleeps a lot?

课文 TEXT

课文 1 🎧 13-1

听前问题：大卫暑假有什么打算？

安　琪：你怎么这么晚才回来？

爱　华：对不起，我不是故意的，我在教室里复习的时候睡着了。

安　琪：马上就放暑假了，你有什么打算？

爱　华：我考完试就回国，我要回去参加我姐姐的婚礼。你呢？

安　琪：我刚来北京没多久，假期可能就在北京。我要努力学习，记住学过的每一个词。

爱　华：好学生！不过最近我没有办法努力学习，因为总想着送我姐姐礼物的事。

安　琪：准备礼物很简单，你可以上网啊。我们想买的东西在网上差不多都能买到，只需要动动手指，不一会儿就可以完成。快递两三天就可以送到。

爱　华：你不知道，我的行李太重了，按照规定得多交不少钱呢。

安　琪：那好办。你可以到机场免税店买礼物。

爱　华：好主意！那我要重新考虑一下买什么礼物。

安　琪：机场免税店里有很多名牌烟、酒、手表、化妆品，你可以选一选。

爱　华：但是我姐姐不抽烟，也不喝酒，手表和化妆品也太贵了。

安　琪：那你可以买一些中国传统工艺品，你姐姐一定喜欢。

（在机场免税店）

售货员：您怎么付钱？

爱　华：信用卡。

售货员：今天正好打五折，一共二百九十九元。女士，您的信用卡，请收好。谢谢！

课堂练习

1. 根据课文内容回答问题。Answer the questions based on the text.
   （1）安琪暑假有什么打算？
   （2）爱华最近为什么没办法努力学习？
   （3）机场免税店里有什么？

2. 分角色表演课文。Act out the text in roles.

3. 如果你是课文中的安琪,你会建议爱华买什么礼物?(可参考给出的词语)If you were Angie in the text, what gift would you suggest Aihua buy? (You can refer to the words given)

上网　不一会儿　快递　送到　免税店　名牌　传统工艺品

词语1　🎧 13-2

词语	拼音	词性	英文释义
1. 故意	gùyì	副词	on purpose; deliberately
2. 睡着	shuìzháo		fall asleep
3. 婚礼	hūnlǐ	名词	wedding
4. 动	dòng	动词	move
5. 手指	shǒuzhǐ	名词	finger
6. 不一会儿	bù yíhuìr		a while
7. 完成	wán//chéng	动词	complete; accomplish
8. 快递	kuàidì	名词	express
9. 行李	xíngli	名词	luggage; baggage
10. 重	zhòng	形容词	heavy
11. 按照	ànzhào	介词	according to
12. 规定	guīdìng	名词、动词	specification; stipulate
13. 免税店	miǎnshuìdiàn	名词	duty-free shop
14. 重新	chóngxīn	副词	again
15. 考虑	kǎolǜ	动词	think about; consider
16. 名牌	míngpái	名词	famous brand
17. 烟	yān	名词	cigarette
18. 手表	shǒubiǎo	名词	(wrist) watch
19. 化妆品	huàzhuāngpǐn	名词	cosmetics

20. 抽烟	chōu//yān	动词	smoke
21. 工艺品	gōngyìpǐn	名词	handiwork
22. 付	fù	动词	pay
23. 信用卡	xìnyòngkǎ	名词	credit card
24. 打折	dǎ//zhé	动词	give a discount
25. 收	shōu	动词	keep

重点词

故意

（1）他经常故意做这样的事。

（2）昨天我迟到了，我不是故意的。

（3）他是故意拿走你的词典的。

按照

（1）游戏要按照大家的要求玩儿。

（2）按照老师的计划，这个星期我们会学完第十三课。

（3）面包是按照三元一个卖给他的。

打折

（1）我想买的手机现在打折了。

（2）A：电脑打几折？

　　B：打五折呢！

（3）A：这台电视机还会打折吗？

　　B：不再打折了，因为已经打过折了。

练一练

选词填空。Fill in the blanks with the given words.

> 故意　按照　打折　动　完成　重新　付　收

（1）老师说这周末之前我们得_____作业。

（2）一会儿要下雨了，我们把衣服_____一下吧。

（3）我认为这件事不能让她去，你_____考虑一下吧。

（4）你昨天是_____迟到的吧？

（5）你_____一下手指就能买到很多东西。

（6）A：一共180元，您用什么_____钱呢？

　　　B：信用卡。

（7）A：这双鞋还会便宜吗？

　　　B："双十二"会_____，那时候你再来吧。

（8）爸爸告诉我应该_____自己的计划做事。

课文2 🎧 13-3

听前问题：现在流行什么？

你知道现在流行什么吗？对了！是网上购物。我妈妈就是个"网购迷"。

她第一次网购是买衣服。有一天，妈妈逛商场，忽然看到一件很漂亮的衣服，但是价格有点儿贵，正想着要不要买时，别人就买走了那件衣服。同事提醒她可以试试网购，我妈妈就上网查了一下：同样的衣服，比商场便宜一百元！妈妈立刻就拍了，没两天衣服就送到家了。妈妈左看看右看看，发现和商场里的衣服完全一样。从此，妈妈就开始了自己的"网购生活"，很少再去逛商场了。

13 快递两三天就可以送到

现在网购已经成了现代人生活中不能缺少的一部分。每年11月11日是中国的"双十一"网络购物节。这一天有许多商品都会打折促销，吸引人们购买。2021年11月11日，天猫商城当天的交易额就达到了5403亿元。

今年的"双十一"已经结束了，这几天相信大家都在兴奋地"拆快递"。有一个电影明星晒出了她买的900件商品。还有一个电影明星在整理快递的时候，意外发现她在三个月前买的一件商品还没有收到，着急地问应该怎么办。

网购正改变着我们的生活。它带走了我们不少钱，但是也给我们带来了不少快乐。

课堂练习

1. 根据课文内容回答问题。Answer the questions based on the text.
   （1）妈妈第一次"网购"买的是什么？
   （2）妈妈为什么会选择"网购"？
   （3）中国"双十一"这一天许多商品会怎么样？

2. 根据课文内容填空，并复述课文。Fill in the blanks based on the text and retell it.
   你知道现在流行什么吗？对了！是_____。我妈妈就是个"_____"。
   我妈妈第一次_____是_____。有一天，妈妈逛商场，忽然_____一件很漂亮的_____，但是_____有点儿贵，正想着_____买时，别人就____了那件衣服。同事_____她可以试试网购，我妈妈就上网_____：同样的衣服，比商场_____一百元！妈妈_____就拍了，没两天就送到家了。妈妈左看看右看看，发现和商场里的衣服_____。，妈妈就开始了自己的"网购生活"，很少再去_____了。

现在网购已经成了现代人生活中＿＿＿＿的一部分。每年11月11日是中国的"双十一"＿＿＿＿节。这一天有许多商品都会＿＿＿＿，吸引人们购买。

3. 选用下列提示词语，说说妈妈的网购经历。Choose the following prompt words to talk about Mother's online shopping experience.

| 流行 | 网购 | 迷 | 商场 | 忽然 | 贵 | 提醒 |
| 同样的 | 立刻 | 没两天 | 快递 | 从此 | | |

词语 2 🎧 13-4

	词语	拼音	词性	英文释义
1.	流行	liúxíng	动词	be popular
2.	购物	gòuwù	动词	go shopping
3.	迷	mí	后缀	fan; enthusiast
4.	忽然	hūrán	副词	unexpectedly; all of a sudden; suddenly
5.	价格	jiàgé	名词	price
6.	提醒	tí//xǐng	动词	remind
7.	立刻	lìkè	副词	immediately; right away
8.	拍	pāi	动词	purchase (online)
9.	从此	cóngcǐ	副词	from then on; henceforth
10.	现代	xiàndài	名词	modern times
11.	缺少	quēshǎo	动词	lack; be short of
12.	商品	shāngpǐn	名词	goods; merchandise
13.	促销	cùxiāo	动词	promote sales
14.	购买	gòumǎi	动词	buy; purchase
15.	交易	jiāoyì	名词	transaction

13 快递两三天就可以送到

16. 额	é	后缀	volume; amount
17. 达到	dá//dào	动词	reach; come up to
18. 亿	yì	数词	a hundred million
19. 相信	xiāngxìn	动词	believe
20. 拆	chāi	动词	unpack; unwrap
21. 晒	shài	动词	post online
22. 整理	zhěnglǐ	动词	clear up; sort out
23. 意外	yìwài	形容词、名词	unexpected; accident
24. 应该	yīnggāi	动词	be supposed to; should

专有名词

| 天猫商城 | Tiānmāo Shāngchéng | Tmall |

重点词

迷

（1）我的妈妈是一个"网购迷"。

（2）中国有很多人喜欢打篮球，也有很多篮球迷。

（3）他非常喜欢看电视，是一个电视迷。

立刻

（1）老师进来以后，同学们立刻安静了。

（2）我有事找他，请他立刻来502房间。

（3）看到女朋友，他的脸立刻红了。

从此

（1）听了老师的话，他从此开始认真学习。

（2）那天，她帮助了我，从此我们成了好朋友。

（3）我们分手吧！从此以后，你不要来找我了。

达到

（1）2021年的"双十一"结束了，交易额达到了5000多亿。

（2）经过大家的努力，我们班的成绩达到了年级第一。

（3）她想成为一名翻译，不过她的中文现在还没有达到很高的水平。

意外

（1）我一直以为她家离学校很远，意外发现她就住在学校附近。

（2）马克的学习成绩特别好，这次考了59分，大家都很意外。

（3）他不太喜欢和别人聊天儿，你问他他不说话，我不觉得意外。

（4）这件事是一个意外。

应该

（1）我的手机不见了，我应该怎么办？

（2）我应不应该帮她？

（3）上课时，我们不应该吃东西。

练一练

选词填空。Fill in the blanks with the given words.

> 达到　迷　从此　立刻　购物　意外　提醒　促销

（1）听了大家的想法，他_____改变了自己的主意。

（2）他是一个电影_____，看过很多国内的和国外的电影。

（3）妈妈很喜欢_____，总是在网上买很多东西。

（4）你来看我，我很_____。

（5）经过长时间的努力，我们的成绩_____了优秀。

（6）"双十一"这天，网上的许多商品都会打折_____。

（7）接到妈妈的电话，他_____跑回家了。

（8）快要考试了，老师每天都会_____同学们要认真准备。

语法 GRAMMAR

一、时间副词："就"和"才" Adverbs of time: "就" and "才"

"就""才"在表示时间、数量词语的前后位置不同时，表达的意义有相同点，也有不同。当"就"和"才"在表示时间、数量词语的前面时，"就"和"才"都表示时间短、数量小。如：

"就" and "才" have similarities and differences in meaning when they are placed before and after words indicating time or quantity. When "就" and "才" are placed before words indicating time or quantity, both "就" and "才" mean short time and small quantity. For example:

（1）这次放假就/才1天。（时间短）

（2）这件衣服就/才50块钱。（数量少）

当"就"和"才"在表示时间、数量的词语后面时，"就"表示时间短、数量小、事情发生得早或结束得早；"才"表示时间长、数量大、事情发生得晚。如：

When "就" and "才" are placed after words indicating time or quantity, "就" means short time, small quantity, or that something happens or ends early, while "才" means long time, large quantity, or that something happens late. For example:

（1）这些作业1小时就完成了。（时间短）

（2）这些作业1小时才完成。（时间长）

（3）这件衣服50块钱就可以买到。（数量少）

（4）这件衣服800块钱才买到。（数量大）

（5）大卫今天7：00就来了。（事情发生得早）

（6）玛丽今天9：00才来。（事情发生得晚）

练一练

1. 选词填空。Fill in the blanks with the given words.

> 就　　才

（1）大学毕业五年了，我们_____见过一次面。

（2）A：从重庆到北京需要多久？

　　　B：比去成都远多了，坐飞机三个小时_____到。

（3）对我来说，汉字太难了。我花了一个小时_____记住这些汉字。

（4）他一个月能看完这本小说，但我要五个月_____能看完。

（5）他们谈了一个月恋爱_____结婚了。

（6）他一直玩儿到凌晨（língchén, wee hours）三点_____睡觉。

（7）真便宜！两千元_____买到了华为手机。

（8）虽然中国特别大，但是快递两三天_____能送到家。

2. 用"就"或"才"改写句子。Rewrite the sentences with "就" or "才".

例：他今天凌晨三点睡觉，六点起床。

　　<u>他今天三点才睡觉。</u>

（1）今天他很累，所以晚上九点睡觉，以前他都是晚上十二点多睡觉。

_____

（2）他三个月看完了这本书，我要花半年时间。

_____

（3）周末他花了一上午时间加完了班。

_____

（4）我一分钟喝完了一大瓶水。

_____

（5）我花一万元买了一个衣柜。

_____

二、结果补语2：动词+到／住／走　Resultative complement II: Verb +到／住／走

1. 【动词+到】表示人或物通过动作移动到某处；或表示动作达到了预期目标，有了结果。
Indicating that somebody or something arrives at a certain place through an action; or indicating that an action has achieved its anticipated goal and has a result.

（1）你可以在网上买东西，快递两三天就可以送到。
（2）他已经回到家了。
（3）我去了很多家商店才买到那支钢笔，你买到了吗？
（4）A：同学们打开课本，今天我们学习第20课。
　　　B：老师，我们还没有学到第19课呢。

2. 【动词+住】表示动作结束或使某物固定，也可表示不让次序混乱、不让东西丢失。
Indicating the end of an action or the fixing of something; it can also indicate preventing the order from being confused or preventing something from getting lost.

（1）你说的事情我都记住了。
（2）警察抓（zhuā，catch）住了小偷儿。
（3）他练习了很长时间，但最后还是没有接住球。
（4）电梯最后停住了吗？

3. 【动词+走】表示通过动作使人或物体离开原来的位置。
Indicating making a person or an object away from its original position through an action.

（1）安娜买走了这件衣服。
（2）他骑走了我的自行车。
（3）我从家里离开时，没有拿走我的行李箱。
（4）我打算从学校寄（jì，send）走行李。

练一练

1. 连词成句。String the words together into appropriate sentences.

   （1）我 一直 记 没 词语 住 这些

   _____

   （2）他 飞 周末 了 上海 到

   _____

   （3）住 了 停 吗 汽车

   _____

   （4）词典 小李 本 走 了 那 买

   _____

   （5）到 门口 您 快递 放 给 了

   _____

2. 看图，用括号里的词和"到/住/走"写句子。Look at the pictures and write sentences with the words in the brackets.

   （1）

   _____（拿）

   （2）

   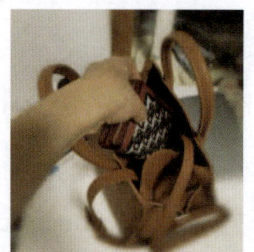

   _____（偷 tōu）

   （3）

   _____（骑）

   （4）

   _____（送）

（5）　　　　　　　　　　　　　（6）

_____（跑）　　　_____（接）

综合运用 COMPREHENSIVE USE

语音练习 🎧 13-5

一、听录音选择正确答案。Listen to the recording and choose the correct answers.

1. A. guīdìng   B. guìdìng   2. A. ānzhào   B. ànzhào
3. A. wánchēng B. wán//chéng   4. A. gùyì   B. gùyì
5. A. cóngxīn   B. chóngxīn   6. A. lìkè   B. líkè
7. A. cóngcí   B. cóngcǐ   8. A. dǎzhē   B. dǎ//zhé
9. A. tí//xǐng B. tīxǐng   10. A. yìwài   B. yīwài

二、听句子给画线词语标声调。Listen to the sentences and mark the tones of the underlined words.

1. 我不是<u>故意</u>的，我在<u>教室</u>里复习的时候<u>睡着</u>了。
2. 马上就<u>放</u>暑假了，你有什么<u>打算</u>？
3. 我要努力学习，<u>记住</u>学过的每一个词。
4. 妈妈逛商场，<u>忽然</u>看到一件很漂亮的衣服，<u>但是</u><u>价格</u>有点儿贵。
5. 天猫商城一天的<u>交易</u>额就<u>达到</u>了 5403 亿元。

三、听一听，读一读。Listen and read.

逢雪宿芙蓉山主人　　　　　Féng Xuě Sù Fúróng Shān Zhǔrén
　　[唐] 刘长卿　　　　　　　　[Táng] Liú Chángqīng
日暮苍山远，天寒白屋贫。　　Rì mù cāngshān yuǎn, tiān hán báiwū pín.
柴门闻犬吠，风雪夜归人。　　Cháimén wén quǎn fèi, fēngxuě yè guī rén.

汉字知识

一、独体字 Single-Component Characters

汉字的形体结构可以分为独体字和合体字两大类。独体字在字形上分解不出两个或两个以上的部件，而只能分解出笔画。例如：日、月、上、木、人、马、手。

The structure of Chinese characters can be divided into two main categories: single-component characters and multi-component characters. Single-component characters cannot be broken down into two or more parts, instead, they can only be divided into strokes. For example: 日 (sun), 月 (moon), 上 (up), 木 (tree), 人 (person), 马 (horse), 手 (hand).

二、合体字 Multi-Component Characters

汉字的字形结构，除了独体字外就是合体字。合体字是由两个或两个以上的部件组合而成的汉字，例如：好、你等。现代汉字多数为合体字，90%左右的合体字是形声字，例如：爸、忙等。还有一部分是会意字，例如：美、家等。

Apart from single-component characters, the structure of Chinese characters also includes multi-component characters. Multi-component characters are formed by combining two or more parts. For example: 好 (good), 你 (you), etc. Most modern Chinese characters are multi-component characters. About 90% of multi-component characters are pictophonetic characters. For example: 爸 (father), 忙 (busy), etc. A portion of them are associative compounds. For example: 美 (beautiful), 家 (home), etc.

口语表达训练

一、你们国家的人一般喜欢在哪儿购物？请简单介绍一下，完成调查表。
Where do people in your country prefer to go shopping? Make a brief introduction and complete the questionnaire.

大学生	已经工作的人	老年人

二、问问你的三位同学：他们喜欢网购吗？他们会在"双十一"网购吗？为什么？请完成下表。Ask three of your classmates if they like online shopping, and if they will shop online on Double Eleven and why? Please complete the table below.

你的购物方式		
你喜欢网购吗？	你会在"双十一"网购吗？	为什么？

中国的丝绸、刺绣与丝绸之路
Silk, Embroidery and the Silk Road in China

中国的丝绸与刺绣有着悠久的历史。丝绸中的云锦、蜀锦、壮锦和宋锦被称为"四大名锦",其中云锦在元、明、清三朝是皇家御用贡品。"刺绣"与"丝绸"密切相关。中国有四大名绣:苏绣、蜀绣、湘绣、粤绣。

中国古代西汉时期,汉武帝派张骞出使西域,开辟了中西交通要道——丝绸之路。丝绸之路的开通,架起了东西方文化交往的桥梁,中国的丝绸等被运往西方,而异域的核桃、音乐等也通过此路来到中国,为整个人类文明做出了重要的贡献。

2013年,中国国家主席习近平先后提出共建"丝绸之路经济带"和"21世纪海上丝绸之路"的重大倡议。在他的亲自谋划、亲自部署、亲自推动下,"一带一路"这个根植于历史厚土、顺应时代大势的重大国际合作倡议走深走实,为各国开拓出了一条通向共同繁荣的机遇之路。

Chinese silk and embroidery have a long history. Among the silks, Yun brocade, Sichuan brocade, Zhuang brocade and Song brocade are known as the "Four Great Brocades". Among them, Yun brocade was an imperial tribute during the Yuan, Ming, and Qing dynasties. "Embroidery" is closely related to "silk". China has four famous embroidery styles: Suzhou embroidery, Sichuan embroidery, Hunan embroidery, and Guangdong embroidery.

During the Western Han Dynasty in ancient China, Emperor Wu sent Zhang Qian as an envoy to the Western Regions, opening up the Silk Road, a vital route for East-West communication. The opening of the Silk Road has built a bridge for cultural exchange between the East and the West. Chinese silk and other goods were transported to the West, while foreign items like walnuts and music were introduced to China through this route, making significant contributions to human civilization.

In 2013, Chinese President Xi Jinping proposed the initiatives to jointly build the "Silk Road Economic Belt" and the "21st Century Maritime Silk Road". Under his personal planning, deployment, and promotion, the "Belt and Road Initiative", an important international cooperation initiative rooted in historical soil and in line with the trend of the times, has made substantial progress. This initiative has opened up a path of opportunity leading to shared prosperity for various countries.

14 小心掉进去
Don't fall in

本课学习重点	
话题 Topic	谈秋游 Talk about autumn outing
重点词 Keywords	至少　弄　朝　进行　由　接近　之一　相互　同时
重点句 Key sentences	1. 等一下，我拿出地图看看。 2. 别跑下去，慢慢走，小心掉进去。 3. 谁能指出来我们学校的位置？
语法 Grammar	1. 趋向补语1（2）：简单趋向补语（动词＋上/下/进/出/回/起＋宾语） 　　Directional complement I (2): Simple directional complement 2. 趋向补语2：复合趋向补语 　　Directional complement II: Compound directional complement
汉字知识 Knowledge of Chinese characters	象形字 Pictographic Characters
文化小贴士 Cultural tips	中国五岳 The Five Great Mountains of China

热身 WARM-UP

秋天到了,你想出去走走吗?请在表格中写下你的秋天出行计划并告诉同学。
It's autumn. Do you want to go out for a walk? Please write down your autumn travel plan in the table and tell your classmates.

时间	地点	活动
周六	八达岭	爬长城

课文 TEXT

课文 1   🎧 14-1

听前问题:他们是怎么去植物园的?

(在去植物园的汽车里)

安琪:快到植物园了吗?

14 小心掉进去

乔治：等一下，我拿出地图看看。

爱华：我已经打开手机地图了，我们至少还要十分钟才能到。

安琪：汽车能开进植物园吗？

乔治：不行。车只能停在植物园门口，下车以后我们还要走一二百米。

安琪：同学们，拿上东西，我们准备下车了。

（在植物园里）

乔治：你们看，下边是一个池塘，我下去看看。

安琪：别跑下去，慢慢走，小心掉进去，我听说这个池塘的水很深。乔治，小心你的鞋别弄湿了！

（爬山的时候）

爱华：我太累了，没办法爬上去了。你们继续爬吧！我就在这儿等你们回来。

乔治：这里有一条近路，爱华，手伸过来，我拉你上来。你看，前边的路好走多了。

安琪：爱华，站起来吧。我从后边推你，乔治在前边拉你，我们一起帮你走上去，等一会儿再吃点儿东西，你就不累了。

爱华：你们这么关心和照顾我，我都不好意思了。好吧！站起来继续爬！

（在山上）

乔治：你们看，从这里朝南看，就能看到北京城。

爱华：谁能指出来我们学校的位置？

安琪：太远了，不过我们学校一定是在那个方向。

课堂练习

1. 根据课文内容回答问题。Answer the questions based on the text.

   （1）看到池塘的时候,乔治做了什么?

   （2）爱华爬山的时候怎么了?大家是怎么做的?

   （3）在山上能看到什么?

2. 分角色表演课文。Act out the text in roles.

3. 假如你是课文中的爱华,请说说你们这次爬山的经历。(可选用下列提示词语) If you were Aihua in the text, please describe your mountain climbing experience. (The following prompt words can be used)

   掉进去　弄湿　伸过来　爬上去　拉上来　站起来　推上去　指出来

词语1  14-2

词语	拼音	词性	英文释义
1. 植物园	zhíwùyuán	名词	botanical garden; arboretum
2. 至少	zhìshǎo	副词	at least
3. 不行	bùxíng	动词	not allow
4. 米	mǐ	量词	meter
5. 池塘	chítáng	名词	pond
6. 下去	xià//qù	动词	go down
7. 小心	xiǎoxīn	动词、形容词	be careful; careful
8. 掉	diào	动词	fall (into)
9. 这个	zhège	代词	this
10. 深	shēn	形容词	deep
11. 鞋	xié	名词	shoe
12. 弄	nòng	动词	make; do

13. 湿	shī	形容词	wet
14. 办法	bànfǎ	名词	way; approach
15. 上去	shàng//qù	动词	go up
16. 回来	huí//lái	动词	come back
17. 近	jìn	形容词	close
18. 手	shǒu	名词	hand
19. 伸	shēn	动词	stretch
20. 过来	guò//lái	动词	come over
21. 上来	shàng//lái	动词	come up
22. 起来	qǐ//lái	动词	stand up
23. 站	zhàn	动词	stand
24. 推	tuī	动词	push; give a hand from behind
25. 关心	guānxīn	动词	care for; be concerned with
26. 照顾	zhàogù	动词	look after
27. 朝	cháo	介词、动词	towards; face
28. 南	nán	名词	south
29. 指	zhǐ	动词	point at; identify
30. 出来	chū//lái	动词	*used after a verb to indicate the completion of an action*
31. 位置	wèizhì	名词	location; place
32. 那个	nàge	代词	that
33. 方向	fāngxiàng	名词	direction

重点词

至少

（1）最近感冒的人特别多，今天我们班至少有5位同学请假。
（2）从学校走到超市至少需要5分钟。
（3）这次考试很简单，我至少能得90分。

弄

（1）我弄错了，你想要的是豆汁儿不是牛奶。
（2）爸爸弄来了很多水果。
（3）这事总得弄出个结果来才成。

朝

（1）从食堂朝西走500米就到图书馆了。
（2）老师朝我点了点头。
（3）大家都喜欢朝南的房子。

练一练

选词填空。Fill in the blanks with the given words.

> 弄　小心　照顾　朝　掉　位置　至少　指

（1）下雨了，出门的时候＿＿＿＿地上的水。
（2）我的手机刚刚＿＿＿＿到地上了，不过没有坏。
（3）去上海旅行，你们＿＿＿＿要准备四五千块钱。
（4）从食堂出发，＿＿＿＿南走两分钟就是超市。
（5）这张照片上谁是你的汉语老师？请＿＿＿＿一下。
（6）爸爸帮我＿＿＿＿好了电脑，我特别开心。

（7）您好，我可不可以跟您换一下_____？

（8）我小时候，爸爸妈妈工作特别忙，一直是奶奶_____我的。

课文 2　🎧 14-3

听前问题："一日游"是什么意思？

上个周末，我们学校组织了一次特别的秋游，来自不同国家的留学生和中国学生进行了一次"北京植物园一日游"活动。

北京植物园在北京的西北部，离北京市中心比较远，离香山公园很近。导游介绍说，植物园由植物展览区、名胜古迹区、自然保护区和科学研究区组成，里边种的植物接近一万种。

我们去的时候，植物园里正在举办菊花展览。由南门到卧佛寺的路上全都是菊花，颜色有红的、黄的、白的，特别好看。导游说，菊花在中国是一种常见的花，也是一年中开得最晚的花，它还是北京的市花之一。

我特别喜欢这次秋游活动。因为它增加了中国学生和外国留学生的相互了解，同时，也让我们留学生对中国文化有了新的理解和认识。

课堂练习

1. 根据课文内容回答问题。Answer the questions based on the text.

（1）植物园由哪几个区组成？

（2）导游是怎么介绍菊花的？

（3）"我"觉得这次秋游活动怎么样？

2. 根据课文内容填空，并复述课文。Fill in the blanks based on the text and retell it.

北京植物园在北京的_____，离北京市_____比较远，离香山公园很近。导游介绍说，植物园由植物展览区、_____区、自然保护区和_____区组成，里边种的植物_____一万多种。我们去的时候，植物园里正在_____菊花展览。导游说，菊花是一种_____的花，也是一年中_____的花，还是北京的市花_____。

我很喜欢这次活动。它增加了中国学生和外国留学生的_____了解，同时，也让我们留学生对中国文化有了新的理解和_____。

3. 选用下列提示词语，介绍你理想的秋游活动。Choose the following prompt words to describe your ideal autumn outing.

> 秋游　组织　进行　由　接近　同时　增加　了解

词语 2　🎧 14-4

词语	拼音	词性	英文释义
1. 组织	zǔzhī	动词、名词	organize; organization
2. 秋游	qiūyóu	动词	autumn outing
3. 进行	jìnxíng	动词	conduct; carry on
4. 游	yóu	动词	go visiting; tour; go sightseeing
5. 部	bù	名词	part; region
6. 中心	zhōngxīn	名词	center; hub
7. 导游	dǎoyóu	名词	tour guide
8. 由	yóu	介词	by
9. 展览	zhǎnlǎn	动词、名词	exhibit; exhibition
10. 区	qū	名词	section; area; zone
11. 自然	zìrán	名词	nature
12. 保护	bǎohù	动词	protect; preserve
13. 科学	kēxué	名词	science
14. 研究	yánjiū	动词	research

15. 组成	zǔchéng	动词		form; compose; constitute
16. 接近	jiējìn	动词		approach; be close to; approximate
17. 菊花	júhuā	名词		chrysanthemum
18. 常见	cháng jiàn			common
19. 市花	shìhuā	名词		city flower
20. 之一	zhīyī	名词		one of
21. 增加	zēngjiā	动词		increase
22. 相互	xiānghù	副词		mutually
23. 同时	tóngshí	连词、名词		meanwhile; same time
24. 理解	lǐjiě	动词		understand; comprehend

专有名词

1. 香山	Xiāng Shān	Fragrant Hill
2. 卧佛寺	Wòfó Sì	Temple of the Reclining Buddha

重点词

进行

（1）我们正在进行考试，请不要说话。

（2）我们学校和那所学校的篮球比赛正在进行中，还没结束。

（3）HSKK是怎么进行的呢？你能给我介绍一下吗？

由

（1）我们班的汉语课由王老师负责。

（2）"明"字由"日"和"月"组成。

（3）妈妈，今天的晚饭由我来做吧！

接近

（1）已经接近12点，爸爸妈妈一定已经休息了。
（2）我们上周已经分手了，你不要再接近我了，好不好？
（3）火车越来越接近北京了，孩子们也越来越兴奋。

之一

（1）她是我们班最认真的学生之一。
（2）北京是我最喜欢的城市之一。
（3）豆汁儿是我最喜欢的老北京小吃之一。

相互

（1）他们相互认识吗？
（2）他们说，有一样爱好的人，会相互接近。
（3）我们要相互帮助，相互学习，这样才能有进步。

同时

（1）他是一位老师，同时也是一位妈妈。
（2）我们同时说出了"分手吧"！
（3）我们认真学习的同时，也要多做一些运动。

练一练

选词填空。Fill in the blanks with the given words.

| 进行　由　接近　同时　组织　之一　相互　常见 |

（1）这次考试，我们班有20位同学的成绩_____95分。

（2）请你再等一会儿吧！里面的汉语比赛还正在_____着呢。

（3）他学习不认真，看书的_____还在玩儿手机。

（4）昆明是我最喜欢的中国城市_____。

（5）如果你们能_____理解，那么大事也会变成小事。

（6）我们学校的食堂很大，_____五层楼组成，我最喜欢食堂三层的饭菜。

（7）学习汉语的时候，留学生们_____的问题是口语和听力不太好。

（8）老师_____我们一起去参观植物园，然后再一起回学校。

语法 GRAMMAR

一、趋向补语1（2）：简单趋向补语（动词+上/下/进/出/回/起+宾语） Directional complement I (2): Simple directional complement (Verb + 上/下/进/出/回/起 + Object)

趋向补语用在动词之后，描述动作的方向，表示人或事物运动、位移的方向，趋向补语的基本意义就是趋向动词本身所表示的意义，即方向意义。

Directional complements are used after verbs to describe the direction of an action, to indicate the direction of movement or displacement of somebody or something. The basic meaning of a directional complement is the meaning of the directional verb itself, i.e. the meaning of direction.

上册中已经学过"动词+来/去"的用法，例如：

In the previous volume, we have already learned the usage of "verb + 来/去", for example:

（1）他向这边走来了。

（2）你给他带去吧！

（3）明天我带一本汉语书来。

（4）昨天他拿来了一本词典。

本册所学的简单趋向补语有"上、下、进、出、回、起"，宾语需放在趋向补语的后面。

Simple directional complements to be learned in this volume are "上, 下, 进, 出, 回, 起", where the object should be placed after the directional complement.

基本格式：动词＋上／下／进／出／回／起＋宾语，例如：

The basic form is "verb＋上／下／进／出／回／起＋object", for example:

（1）你爬上十楼了没有？
（2）汽车能开进动物园吗？
（3）我走回三楼，从书包里拿出一本杂志。
（4）王老师从桌子上拿起那本书，接着又放下了。

二、趋向补语2：复合趋向补语　Directional complement II: Compound directional complement

复合趋向补语由两组简单趋向补语组合而成，其基本意义仍是趋向补语本身所表示的意义，即方向意义。如：

A compound directional complement is formed by combining two simple directional complements, and its basic meaning is still the meaning of the directional complements, i.e., the meaning of direction. For example:

	出	过	回	进	起	上	下
来	出来	过来	回来	进来	起来	上来	下来
去	出去	过去	回去	进去	×	上去	下去

基本格式：动词+出来/出去等复合趋向补语。动词的宾语如果是表示事物的名词，宾语的位置可在复合趋向补语的后面或者在"来""去"的前面；如果宾语是表示地点的名词，只能放在"来""去"的前面。例如：

The basic form is verb +compound directional complements such as 'come out' and 'come in'. If the object of the verb is a noun representing something, the object can be placed after the compound directional complement or before the "来" or "去" in the compound directional complement; if the object is a noun representing a place, it can only be placed before "来" or "去". For example:

（1）请你站起来。
（2）你的电脑从楼下拿上来了吗？
（3）他从二楼走下来了。
（4）他从书包里拿出来一本书。

（5）他从书包里拿出一本书来。
（6）他慢慢地走出教室去了。
（7）他忽然跑上三楼去了。
（8）他已经飞回上海去了。

练一练

1. 改错句。Correct the erroneous sentences.

（1）放学后，男孩儿开心地跑来家。

（2）为拿上来书架上的那本词典，李娜搬去了一把椅子。

（3）姐姐从桌子上拿下一本杂志看了一会儿。

（4）王奶奶住在一楼，我从楼上拿上去一些水果送给她。

（5）外边下雨了，妈妈拿去一把雨伞就出来了。

（6）老师走进去教室了，同学们马上拿进书和笔。

2. 请选择正确的趋向补语填空。Fill in the blanks with the correct directional complements.

出来　进来　上来　下去　过去　过来

（1）孩子慢慢地向我们走了_____。
（2）听到楼下有人叫我，我马上跑_____了。
（3）下课时间到了，同学们的作业快点儿交_____吧！
（4）请等一下，桌子我还没有搬_____呢。
（5）你在那个路口等几分钟，车一会儿就开_____了。
（6）今天太冷了，妈妈从衣柜里给我拿_____一件大衣。

综合运用 COMPREHENSIVE USE

语音练习 14-5

一、听录音选择正确答案。Listen to the recording and choose the correct answers.

1. A. chítáng　　B. cítáng　　　2. A. kēxué　　B. kèxué
3. A. zhìshǎo　　B. zìshǎo　　　4. A. yánjiū　　B. yānjiū
5. A. jiějìn　　　B. jiējìn　　　6. A. jínxíng　　B. jìnxíng
7. A. zǔzhī　　　B. zhǔzhī　　　8. A. zìrán　　B. zīrán
9. A. cháng jiàn　B. chǎng jiàn　10. A. tóngshí　B. tóngshì

二、听句子给画线词语标声调。Listen to the sentences and mark the tones of the underlined words.

1. 不好！我的鞋弄湿了。
2. 你们这么关心照顾我，我都不好意思了。
3. 植物园里正在举办菊花展览。
4. 谁能指出来我们学校的位置？
5. 这次活动增加了中国学生和外国留学生的相互了解。

三、听一听，读一读。Listen and read.

　　　望月怀远　　　　　　　Wàng Yuè Huáiyuǎn

　　［唐］张九龄　　　　　　[Táng] Zhāng Jiǔlíng

海上生明月，天涯共此时。　Hǎi shàng shēng míngyuè, tiānyá gòng cǐshí.
情人怨遥夜，竟夕起相思。　Qíngrén yuàn yáoyè, jìngxī qǐ xiāngsī.
灭烛怜光满，披衣觉露滋。　Miè zhú lián guāng mǎn, pī yī jué lù zī.
不堪盈手赠，还寝梦佳期。　Bù kān yíng shǒu zèng, huán qǐn mèng jiāqī.

象形字 Pictographic Characters

　　象形是通过描绘物体的形状来表示字义，是汉字的"六书"之一，也是最原始的造字法。用这种方法所造的字叫作象形字。作为一种书写符号，象形字脱胎于图画，但又与图画有着本质的不同。

　　象形字大多是独体字，是构成其他汉字的基础，但用象形法造字，局限性很大，因为有些复杂的事物和抽象的概念是很难画出来的。因此，后来又在象形字的基础上产生了指事、会意、形声等其他的造字方法。

　　象形字为数不多，《说文解字》里只有300多个。汉代以后，1000多年来只造了"伞、凹、凸"等少数几个象形字。后来的合体字有相当一部分是用象形字构成的。例如"人"是"你、们、企"等字的构字成分，"贝"是"财、贸、狈"等字的构字成分，"马"是"驴、驾、妈、骂"等字的构字成分。因此，从字源上了解象形字的形、义、音，可以帮助我们掌握一大批现代通用汉字的字义和读音。

　　Pictograph represents meaning by depicting the shape of objects. It is one of the "Six Principles" of Chinese character formation and is the most primitive method of creating characters. Characters created using this method are called pictographic characters. As a kind of written symbol, pictographic characters evolved from drawings but are fundamentally different from them.

　　Most pictographic characters are single-component characters and serve as the foundation for other Chinese characters. However, the method of creating characters through pictograph has significant limitations because it is difficult to draw complex objects and abstract concepts. Therefore, other methods of character formation, such as self-explanatory characters, associative compounds, and pictophonetic characters, were later developed based on pictographic characters.

　　There are not many pictographic characters; the *Shuowen Jiezi* dictionary lists only about 300. After the Han Dynasty, for over a thousand years, only a few pictographic characters like "伞" (umbrella), "凹" (concave), and "凸" (convex) have been created. Later, many multi-component characters are formed using pictographic characters. For example: "人" (person) is a component in characters like "你" (you), "们" (a plural suffix), and "企" (enterprise). "贝" (shell, ancient currency) is a component in characters like "财" (wealth), "贸" (trade), and

"犭" (a type of wild dog). "马" (horse) is a component in characters like "驴" (donkey), "驾" (drive), "妈" (mother), and "骂" (scold).

Therefore, understanding the form, meaning, and sound of pictographic characters from their origins can help us grasp the meanings and pronunciations of a large number of modern Chinese characters.

口语表达训练

一、找三位同学，问问他们的爬山计划，完成下表。Find three of your classmates and ask them about their mountain climbing plans and complete the table below.

姓名	去哪儿	什么时候去	怎么安排

二、如果学校组织一次秋游，你最想去哪儿？为什么？问问你身边的几位同学，完成下表。If the school organizes an autumn outing, where would you like to go the most? Why? Ask some of your classmates around you and complete the table below.

姓名	最想去哪儿	为什么

文化小贴士 CULTURAL TIPS

中国五岳
The Five Great Mountains of China

五岳，中华传统文化中五大名山的总称，分别是东岳泰山、西岳华山、南岳衡山、北岳恒山、中岳嵩山。

泰山坐落在山东省中部，为中国五岳之首，主峰海拔1532.7米，高度居五岳第三位，泰山在中国的政治、文化、历史上占有很高的地位；华山位于陕西省华阴市，主峰海拔2154.9米，以险峻著称，有"奇险天下第一山"之称；衡山位于湖南省中部，主峰海拔1300.2米，以风景秀丽著称；恒山位于山西省大同市，主峰海拔2016.1米；嵩山位于河南省登封市，主峰海拔1491.7米，嵩山东端的中岳庙是中国最早的道教庙宇之一。

俗语说"五岳归来不看山"，五岳风景各异，是中国古代帝王拜天之地，也是现在中国的国家级风景区。

The Five Great Mountains is a collective term for the five most famous mountains in traditional Chinese culture. They are:

1. East Great Mountain: Mount Tai (Tài Shān, 泰山)
   - Location: Central Shandong Province
   - Height: 1,532.7 meters
   - Significance: Mount Tai is the most revered of the Five Great Mountains and the third in height, and holds a high position in China's political, cultural, and historical landscape.

2. West Great Mountain: Mount Hua (Huà Shān, 华山)
   - Location: Huayin City, Shaanxi Province
   - Height: 2,154.9 meters
   - Significance: Mount Hua is known for its steep and dangerous paths, and is often referred to as the "most precipitous mountain under heaven".

3. South Great Mountain: Mount Heng (Héng Shān, 衡山)
   - Location: Central Hunan Province

- Height: 1,300.2 meters
- Significance: Mount Heng renowned for its beautiful scenery.

4. North Great Mountain: Mount Heng (Héng Shān, 恒山)
   - Location: Datong City, Shanxi Province
   - Height: 2,016.1 meters

5. Central Great Mountain: Mount Song (Sōng Shān, 嵩山)
   - Location: Dengfeng City, Henan Province
   - Height: 1,491.7 meters
   - Significance: The Eastern Peak of Mount Song is home to the Zhongyue Temple, one of the earliest Taoist temples in China.

The saying goes, "After seeing the Five Great Mountains, one need not look at other mountains." Each of these mountains offers unique landscapes and has been a place of worship for ancient emperors. Today, they are designated as national scenic areas in China.

15 我本来不太了解京剧，也唱不好
I didn't know much about Peking opera and I couldn't sing well either

本课学习重点	
话题 Topic	谈休闲娱乐 Talk about recreation
重点词 Keywords	从没　自从　看来　光　受不了　原来　麻烦 本来　不一定
重点句 Key sentences	1. 我唱不好，还是听你唱吧。 2. 由于我妈妈是中国人，以前她总教我中国古诗，因此我从小就特别喜欢诗词里的那些自然形象。 3. 由于妈妈对你的影响很大，所以你学得会汉语，也听得懂古诗。 4. 我本来不太了解京剧，也唱不了，但是爷爷对我的影响不小，现在我也唱得了一小段了。
语法 Grammar	1. 可能补语 Potential complement 2. 因果复句 Cause-effect complex sentence （1）由于……，所以/因此…… （2）不用关联词语的因果复句
汉字知识 Knowledge of Chinese characters	指事字 Self-Explanatory Characters
文化小贴士 Cultural tips	中国象棋与围棋 Chinese Chess and Go

热身 WARM-UP

📝 说一说，写一写：他们周末都做什么了？你呢？ Talk and write: What did they do on the weekend? What about you?

课文 TEXT

课文 1 🎧 15-1

听前问题：今天晚上有什么电视节目？

爱华：第三期《中国好声音》马上就要开始了，不知道今天的歌手会带来哪些好听的歌。野田，一起来看吧！

野田：我对唱歌不太感兴趣，不看了。最近你又学会什么新歌了啊？

爱华：《给你的歌》。

野田：什么？给我的歌？

爱华：不是给你的歌，是歌的名字叫《给你的歌》。（哼唱）"希望一直在等着，从没离开过……"

野田：不错啊。

爱华：怎么样？好听吧？我来教你。

野田：不行不行，我唱不好，还是听你唱吧。我发现自从你开始唱歌，你的汉语水平就越来越高了，看来唱歌对你帮助很大啊。

爱华：哪里啊！我跟你比差远了。你喜欢看的《中国诗词大会》，我完全看不懂。你怎么会对古代诗词那么感兴趣？

野田：由于我妈妈是中国人，以前她总教我中国古诗，因此我从小就特别喜欢诗词里的那些自然形象。

爱华：明白了。由于妈妈对你的影响很大，所以你学得会汉语，也听得懂古诗。

野田：我的汉语还差得远呢！接下来，我要挑战一下中国的电视剧。不过，我始终不太喜欢看电视剧，光一件小事就要演好几集，太长了，让人受不了。

爱华：不过你这个办法对学习汉语一定有帮助，我也要试试。《中国好声音》开始了，我戴上耳机看。

> 课堂练习

1. 根据课文内容回答问题。Answer the questions based on the text.

   （1）爱华又学会了什么新歌？

   （2）爱华喜欢看哪个中国节目？野田呢？

   （3）野田的汉语水平怎么样？为什么他的汉语水平是这样的？

2. 分角色表演课文。Act out the text in roles.

3. 如果你是课文中的爱华，请根据课文内容向大家介绍下野田喜欢什么电视节目并说明原因，谈谈他对其他节目的看法。（可选用下列提示词语）If you were Aihua in the text, please give us an introduction on what TV program Noda enjoys watching and why, and talk about what he thinks about other programs according to the text. (The following prompt words can be used)

   中国诗词大会　由于　影响　因此　自然形象　电视剧　始终　受不了

词语 1   🎧 15-2

词语	拼音	词性	英文释义
1. 期	qī	量词	*referring to things done periodically*
2. 歌手	gēshǒu	名词	singer
3. 哪些	nǎxiē	代词	which
4. 好听	hǎotīng	形容词	easy on the ear
5. 哼	hēng	动词	hum; croon
6. 从没	cóng méi		never ever
7. 离开	lí//kāi	动词	leave
8. 自从	zìcóng	介词	since
9. 看来	kànlái	动词	it looks; it seems
10. 古代	gǔdài	名词	ancient times

11.	由于	yóuyú	连词、介词	since; because of
12.	古诗	gǔshī	名词	ancient poetry
13.	因此	yīncǐ	连词	therefore; thus
14.	里	lǐ	名词	inside
15.	那些	nàxiē	代词	those
16.	形象	xíngxiàng	名词	image; imagery
17.	接下来	jiē xiàlái		next; then; after that
18.	挑战	tiǎo//zhàn	动词	challenge
19.	始终	shǐzhōng	副词	always; from beginning to end
20.	光	guāng	副词	only
21.	演	yǎn	动词	play; act; perform
22.	集	jí	量词	episode
23.	让	ràng	动词	let
24.	受不了	shòubuliǎo	动词	can't stand; can't take it anymore
25.	试	shì	动词	try
26.	戴	dài	动词	wear
27.	耳机	ěrjī	名词	earphone; headset

专有名词

1.	《中国好声音》	《Zhōngguó Hǎo Shēngyīn》	*The Voice of China*
2.	《中国诗词大会》	《Zhōngguó Shīcí Dàhuì》	*Chinese Poetry Conference*

重点词

从没

（1）我还从没看过中国电影呢！

（2）我们从没去过北京,所以非常想去看看。

（3）他从没说要和我们一起去听音乐会,一定是你记错了。

自从

（1）自从那件事以后,我再也不去那家超市了。

（2）自从我开始每天运动以后,我的身体好多了。

（3）自从上大学后,我再也没有见过他。

看来

（1）他的脸红红的,头一直低着,看来很紧张。

（2）九点了,他还没来,看来他今天不会来了。

（3）在我看来,他做得很好。

光

（1）今天早上我起床起晚了,光吃了一个面包,就去上学了。

（2）我们一下午光看了一个电影,别的什么都没做。

（3）弟弟光想着出去玩儿,到现在还没写完作业呢。

受不了

（1）我的这份麻辣烫太辣了,我受不了了。

（2）今天太热了,我快受不了了。

（3）我受不了你一直说自己的事情,我也有想说的事情。

15 我本来不太了解京剧，也唱不好

练一练

选词填空。Fill in the blanks with the given words.

> 因此　始终　自从　从没　接下来　看来　挑战　受不了　光

（1）在他_____，大卫的中文说得很好。

（2）他_____说不做，所以我们都不喜欢他。

（3）我喜欢干净，_____房间里这个样子。

（4）大卫最近学习很努力，_____这次考试他考得不错。

（5）今天我想要_____用中文接中国人的电话。

（6）我_____不知道这个工艺品是怎么做的。

（7）_____妹妹留学回来以后，我们家越来越热闹了。

（8）我_____离开过家，这次一个人去法国旅游还挺害怕的。

（9）你先把菜洗干净，_____等妈妈来做饭。

课文 2　🎧 15-3

听前问题：京剧票友是什么意思？

京剧也叫京戏，是中国的传统艺术，有好几百年的历史了，2010年列入联合国教科文组织非物质文化遗产名录。

以前没有其他娱乐方式，听戏看戏就是最大的享受了。但是，现在可不一样了。由于好玩儿的东西太多了，例如电影、电视、卡拉OK、电子游戏吸引了大量的年轻人，因此喜欢京剧的年轻人也就越来越少了，会演唱京剧的年轻人就更少了。可是老年人不一样，他们小时候是看着京剧长大的，因此，现在还有很多老年人喜欢京剧，有一些退休的老年人常常在公园里唱京剧。他们有的拉京胡，有的敲锣鼓，有的唱戏，还有人拿着音响来伴奏，自娱自乐，人们叫他们京剧

票友。

　　我爷爷就是一个京剧票友。原来他就很喜欢京剧，现在每天都要去一个公园，和一群票友唱京剧。如果有一天去不了，他就会觉得全身不舒服。虽然那个公园离家有点儿远，但他不觉得麻烦。我本来不太了解京剧，也唱不了，但是爷爷对我的影响不小，现在我也唱得了一小段了。爷爷说京剧唱得好唱不好不一定是最重要的，能常和一群跟自己有共同兴趣的人在一起才是最让人快乐的事情。

课堂练习

1. 根据课文内容回答问题。Answer the questions based on the text.
   （1）为什么喜欢京剧的年轻人越来越少了？
   （2）老年人为什么喜欢京剧？他们经常做什么？
   （3）"我"爷爷是"票友"吗？他常做什么？

2. 根据课文内容填空，并复述课文。Fill in the blanks based on the text and retell it.
   　　京剧也叫_____，是中国的_____，有_____年的历史了，2010年列入_____组织非物质文化遗产名录。

   　　以前没有其他_____，听戏看戏就是最大的_____了。但是，现在可不一样了。由于_____太多了，例如电影、电视、卡拉OK、电子游戏吸引了大量的_____，因此喜欢京剧的年轻人也就_____了，会_____的年轻人就更少了。可是老年人不一样，他们小时候是看着京剧_____，因此，现在还有很多老年人喜欢京剧。有一些退休的老年人常常在_____唱京剧。他们有的拉_____，有的_____，有的_____，还有人拿着音响来_____，自娱自乐，人们叫他们_____。

   　　我爷爷就是一个京剧票友。_____他就很喜欢京剧，现在每天都要去一个公园，和_____票友唱京剧。如果有一天_____，他就会觉得_____。虽然那个公园离家有点儿远，但他不觉得_____。我本来

15 我本来不太了解京剧，也唱不好

_____京剧，也_____，但是爷爷对我的_____不小，现在我也_____一小段了。爷爷说京剧_____不一定是_____的，能常和一群跟自己有_____兴趣的人在一起才是最让人_____的事情。

3. 根据课文内容，选用下列提示词语和句型，介绍一些中国老年人喜欢的娱乐方式。Based on the text, choose the following prompt words and sentence patterns to introduce some ways of entertainment favored by the elderly in China.

> 享受　演唱　有的……，有的……　票友　由于……，因此……
> 原来　本来　不一定

词语 2　🎧 15-4

	词语	拼音	词性	英文释义
1.	京戏	jīngxì	名词	Peking/Beijing opera
2.	艺术	yìshù	名词	art
3.	列入	lièrù	动词	be included/listed in
4.	非物质文化遗产	fēiwùzhì wénhuà yíchǎn		intangible cultural heritage
5.	名录	mínglù	名词	list; directory
6.	娱乐	yúlè	名词、动词	recreation and entertainment; amuse
7.	戏	xì	名词	traditional Chinese opera
8.	享受	xiǎngshòu	名词、动词	enjoyment; enjoy
9.	可	kě	副词	*used for emphasis*
10.	例如	lìrú	动词	take for example
11.	电子	diànzǐ	名词	electron
12.	演唱	yǎnchàng	动词	sing; chant
13.	长大	zhǎngdà		grow up
14.	退休	tuì//xiū	动词	retire

15. 京胡	jīnghú	名词	*jinghu*
16. 敲	qiāo	动词	knock; beat
17. 锣鼓	luógǔ	名词	gongs and drums
18. 音响	yīnxiǎng	名词	stereo equipment
19. 伴奏	bànzòu	动词	musical accompaniment
20. 自娱自乐	zìyú-zìlè		amuse oneself
21. 票友	piàoyǒu	名词	amateur performer
22. 原来	yuánlái	名词、形容词、副词	the past; original, former; originally
23. 天	tiān	名词	day
24. 群	qún	量词	cluster; group; flock
25. 全身	quánshēn	名词	whole body
26. 麻烦	máfan	形容词、动词	troublesome; trouble
27. 本来	běnlái	副词	originally; at first
28. 小	xiǎo	形容词	small
29. 段	duàn	量词	used to indicate time/distance
30. 不一定	bùyídìng	副词	not certainly

专有名词

| 联合国教科文组织 | Liánhéguó Jiào-kē-wén Zǔzhī | United Nations Educational, Scientific and Cultural Organization (UNESCO) |

重点词

原来

（1）原来我不喜欢北京小吃，现在我觉得还不错。

（2）我们还住在原来的地方，没有搬家。

（3）原来是你啊！我一直以为是小李呢。

15 我本来不太了解京剧,也唱不好

麻烦

(1)你们带着这么小的孩子去旅行,是很麻烦的。
(2)帮你搬家,我不觉得麻烦。
(3)麻烦你告诉我一下王老师的电话号码。

本来

(1)他本来身体很不好,不过,现在好多了。
(2)本来,我不想出去,可是妈妈很想让我和她一起下楼走走。
(3)A:这种小事我们最好不去麻烦别人。
　　B:本来嘛,这些事情我们要学会自己去解决。

不一定

(1)你最好问问老王,他不一定想让你去帮助他。
(2)他能不能上大学现在还不一定呢!
(3)看来他不一定知道这件事。

练一练

选词填空。Fill in the blanks with the given words.

麻烦　本来　娱乐　享受　不一定　演唱　原来　退休

(1)我们_____要去爬山的,但是现在外面下雨了,去不了了。
(2)_____以后,你想过什么样的生活?
(3)这是你_____的房间,我们哪儿都没动过。
(4)我要和爸妈一起,好好_____春节带给我们的快乐。
(5)公园里,有一个女孩儿在_____中文歌。
(6)你现在回去拿多_____啊!

（7）我爸爸在一家_____公司工作。

（8）去中国还是去法国旅行还_____呢。

语法 GRAMMAR

一、可能补语 Potential complement

在结果补语或趋向补语和中心语之间插入"得/不"，表示主观条件或客观条件是否能实现（某种结果或趋向）。

Between the head word and the resultative or directional complement, "得" or "不" is inserted to indicate whether the subjective or objective condition allows the realization (of a certain result or tendency) or not.

1.【动词 + 得 / 不 + 动词 / 形容词】

肯定形式：【主语 + 动词 + 得 + 动词 / 形容词】Affirmative form: [Subject + Verb + 得 + Verb/Adjective]

主语（S）	谓语（P）		
	动词	得	动词 / 形容词
这些作业	写	得	完。
那件衣服	洗	得	干净。
手机号码	看	得	清楚。
京剧	听	得	懂。

否定形式：【主语 + 动词 + 不 + 动词 / 形容词】Negative form: [Subject + Verb + 不 + Verb/Adjective]

主语（S）	谓语（P）		
	动词	不	动词 / 形容词
这些作业	写	不	完。
这件衣服	洗	不	干净。
京剧	听	不	懂。

疑问形式1：【主语+动词+得+动词/形容词+吗】Interrogative form I: [Subject + Verb + 得 + Verb/Adjective + 吗]

主语（S）	谓语（P）			
	动词	得	动词/形容词	吗
你们	听	得	懂	吗？
你的书包	找	得	到	吗？
这台电脑	买	得	起	吗？
黑板上的字	看	得	清楚	吗？

疑问形式2：【肯定式+否定式】Interrogative form II: [Affirmative form + Negative form]

主语（S）	肯定式	否定式
你们	听得懂	听不懂？
你的书包	找得到	找不到？
这台电脑	买得起	买不起？
黑板上的字	看得清楚	看不清楚？

2.【动词+得/不+了（liǎo）+名词】[Verb + 得/不 + 了 + Noun]

表示主客观条件是否容许实现（某种动作或者变化）。

Indicating whether the subjective or objective condition allows the realization (of a certain action or change) or not.

主语（S）	谓语（P）				
	动词	得/不	了	名词	助词
今天	去	得	了	故宫。	
我今天	上	得	了	课。	
弟弟	走	不	了	路	了。

练一练

1. 看图,用"可能补语"完成句子。Look at the pictures and complete the sentences with potential complements.

这些菜太多了,我_____。　　黑板上的字太小了,我_____。

这件衣服太贵了,我_____。　　教室坐_____五十个人吗?

2. 改错句。Correct the erroneous sentences.

(1)30个饺子太多了,我吃不好。

_____

(2)弟弟总是那么吵,我受得不了。

_____

(3)这是我的书包,谁也不拿走。

_____

(4)这个书包很大,装进去这么多书。

_____

(5)你说慢点儿,太快了,我记得不住。

_____

二、因果复句　Cause-effect complex sentence

【由于……，所以 / 因此……】"由于"引出事情的原因，"所以 / 因此"强调结果。

"由于" is used to introduce the cause of something and "所以 / 因此" stresses the result.

（1）由于艾丽很喜欢看中国电影，所以她的口语能力提高得很快。

（2）由于小明起晚了，所以今天上班迟到了。

（3）由于天气不好，因此我们不能按照原来的计划出去了。

（4）由于父母平时工作非常忙，因此都是他来照顾弟弟妹妹的。

有时候有因果关系的两个分句之间可以不用关联词。

Sometimes there can be no correlatives between two clauses that have a cause-effect relationship.

（5）我唱不好，还是听你唱吧。

（6）他参加过学校组织的很多活动，认识了很多朋友。

（7）山本今天回国，他妈妈特别高兴。

练一练

1. 连线。Match the columns.

（1）由于最近爸爸去国外工作了，　　　身体特别健康。

（2）弟弟昨天睡得很早，　　　因此今天没来上课。

（3）由于杰克感冒了，　　　所以没听见老师说了什么。

（4）爷爷总是去运动，　　　今天很早就起床了。

（5）由于大家都在玩儿手机，　　　因此这段时间都是妈妈送我去上学。

2. 用"由于……，所以/因此……"改写句子。Rewrite the sentences with "由于……，所以 / 因此……".

（1）他经常帮助我。我们成了好朋友。

_____

（2）安娜家里有事。安娜下个星期打算回国。

_____

（3）这件衣服太贵了。我只好买那件便宜点儿的。

（4）今天妈妈工作很忙。妈妈没有时间给我做晚饭了。

（5）去年他出国了。我们很少联系了。

综合运用 COMPREHENSIVE USE

语音练习 🎧 15-5

一、听录音选择正确答案。Listen to the recording and choose the correct answers.

1. A. gēshǒu   B. gēshóu   2. A. zìcóng   B. zìchóng
3. A. kànlai   B. kànlái   4. A. xínxiàng B. xíngxiàng
5. A. shǐzhōng B. shǐzōng   6. A. ěrjì   B. ěrjī
7. A. yìshù   B. yìsù   8. A. mínglù   B. mínlù
9. A. yǎnchàng B. yǎnchàn   10. A. tuīxiū   B. tuì//xiū

二、听句子给画线词语标声调。Listen to the sentences and mark the tones of the underlined words.

1. 我发现<u>自从</u>你开始唱歌，你的汉语水平就<u>越来越</u>高了。

2.（哼唱）希望一直在等着，<u>从没离开</u>。

3. <u>接下来</u>，我要挑战一下中国的电视剧。

4. 以前没有其他<u>娱乐</u>方式，听戏看戏就是最大的<u>享受</u>了。

5. 他们有的拉<u>京胡</u>，有的敲<u>锣鼓</u>，有的唱戏，还有人拿着<u>音响</u>来伴奏，自娱自乐。

三、听一听，读一读。Listen and read.

送杜少府之任蜀州　　　　　　　Sòng Dù Shàofǔ Zhī Rèn Shǔ Zhōu
　　[唐]　王勃　　　　　　　　　　[Táng]　Wáng Bó
城阙辅三秦，风烟望五津。　　　　Chéngquè fǔ sān qín, fēngyān wàng wǔ jīn.
与君离别意，同是宦游人。　　　　Yǔ jūn líbié yì, tóng shì huànyóurén.
海内存知己，天涯若比邻。　　　　Hǎinèi cún zhījǐ, tiānyá ruò bǐlín.
无为在歧路，儿女共沾巾。　　　　Wúwéi zài qílù, érnǚ gòng zhān jīn.

 汉字知识

指事字 Self-Explanatory Characters

指事字是用象征性抽象符号表示汉字的意义或者在象形字上加上提示符号来表示意义的汉字。指事字有两种。一种是用象征性抽象符号组成的，例如："一、二、三、十、廿、上、下"等，这种指事字很少。另一类是在象形字的基础上增加提示性符号，例如"刃"，是在"刀"上加一点，表示刀口；"甘"，是在"口"中加一点，表示口中有甘美的食物；"本"，是在"木"的下面加一横，表示树根；"末"，是在"木"的上面加一横，表示树梢。

Self-explanatory characters are characters that use symbolic, abstract symbols to represent the meaning of Chinese characters, or add indicative symbols to pictographic characters to convey meaning. There are two types of self-explanatory characters:

1. Symbolic Abstract Characters:
   - These characters are composed of symbolic, abstract symbols. Examples include:
     一 (yī, one), 二 (èr, two), 三 (sān, three), 十 (shí, ten), 廿 (niàn, twenty), 上 (shàng, up), 下 (xià, down).

   This type of self-explanatory character is relatively rare.

2. Pictographic Characters with Added Indicative Symbols:
   - These characters are formed by adding indicative symbols to pictographic characters. Examples include:
     刃 (rèn, blade): A dot is added to the character 刀 (dāo, knife) to represent the knife's edge.

甘 (gān, sweet): A dot is added inside the character 口 (kǒu, mouth) to represent something sweet and refreshing in the mouth.

本 (běn, root): A horizontal line is added below the character 木 (mù, tree) to represent the tree's root.

末 (mò, end): A horizontal line is added above the character 木 (mù, tree) to represent the treetop.

口语表达训练

一、问问你的家人喜欢什么电视节目，并请他们简单说说为什么。Ask your family what their favorite TV programs are and ask them to briefly explain why.

家人	喜欢的电视节目	为什么

二、采访三位同学，看看他们喜欢什么娱乐方式，为什么会喜欢这种娱乐方式，并完成下表。Interview three of your classmates to see what types of entertainment they enjoy and why they enjoy those, and complete the table below.

同学	喜欢的娱乐方式	为什么

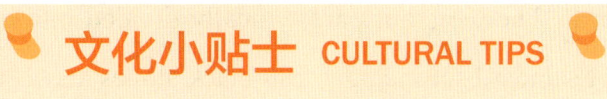

文化小贴士 CULTURAL TIPS

中国象棋与围棋
Chinese Chess and Go

中国象棋定型于北宋末南宋初，象棋有棋盘和棋子。棋盘由九条竖线和十条横线交叉形成，中间划定楚河汉界，盘上一共有九十个交点，棋子是放在交点上的。一副象棋共有三十二个棋子，分为红、黑两组，各有十六个，由下棋的双方各拿一组。黑红双方各有将（帅）一，士（仕）、象（相）、车、马、炮各二，卒（兵）五，各子走法不同。将与帅、士与仕、象与相、卒与兵，其走法和作用是一样的，之所以写法不同，只是为了区分是红方还是黑方。

围棋是一种策略（cèlüè）型两人棋类游戏，中国古代称"弈（yì）"，西方称"Go"。围棋起源于中国，棋具分为棋子、棋盘、棋钟和棋谱。棋子分黑白两色，多为扁圆形，它的数量以黑白子各180个为宜。棋盘的盘面有纵、横（zòng、héng）各十九条等距离、垂直交叉的平行线，共构成361（19×19）个交叉点。棋钟也叫计时器，在正式的比赛中可以使用计时器对选手的时间进行限制。棋谱是记录棋局的工具，通常以笔记本的形式出现。

Chinese chess took its current form during the late Northern Song and early Southern Song dynasties. It consists of a chessboard and chess pieces. The chessboard is formed by nine vertical lines and ten horizontal lines, with the *river* in the middle, creating a grid with a total of 90 intersections. The pieces are placed on these intersections. A set of Chinese chess has 32 pieces, divided into red and black, with each side having 16 pieces. The pieces for each side include: 1 General (Jiàng for red, Shuài for black), 2 Advisors (Shì), 2 Elephants (Xiàng), 2 Chariots (Jū), 2 Horses (Mǎ), 2 Cannons (Pào) and 5 Soldiers (Bīng for red, Zú for black). Each type of piece has a unique way of moving. The General, Advisors, Elephants, and Soldiers on both sides have the same movement and function, but their names differ to distinguish between the red and black sides.

Go is a strategic board game for two players, known as "Yì" in ancient China and "Go" in the West. Originating in China, the game's equipment includes Go stones, a Go board, a

Go clock, and Go records. The Go stones are typically divided into black and white, with a flattened round shape. A standard set includes 180 black stones and 180 white stones. The Go board has a grid of 19 vertical and 19 horizontal lines, creating 361 intersections where the stones are placed. The Go clock is also known as a timer, it is used in official competitions to limit the players' time. The Go records are tools for recording the game, usually in the form of a notebook.

16 把其他材料放进去
Put other ingredients in

本课学习重点	
话题 Topic	谈美食制作 Talk about gourmet food making
重点词 Keywords	仅仅　赶紧　帮忙　随便　合适　尽量　讲究　明显 却　化
重点句 Key sentences	1. 今天我把做菜的材料都准备好了。 2. 我把材料放在桌子上。 3. 赶紧过来给我帮忙，把那个碗给我。 4. 我只输入"鱼香"两个字，就查出来了好多种做法。 5. 首先把肉放到锅里，炒一会儿，然后把其他材料放进去，继续炒，最后把鱼香汁倒进去。
语法 Grammar	1. "把"字句1：表处置 把-sentence I: Indicating disposal or settlement 　（1）主语＋把＋宾语＋动词＋结果补语/趋向补语/状态补语 　（2）主语＋把＋宾语＋动词＋到/在＋处所 　（3）主语＋把＋宾语1＋动词（＋给）＋宾语2 2. 条件复句：只要……，就…… 　Conditional complex sentence 3. 承接复句：首先……，然后…… 　Successive complex sentence
汉字知识 Knowledge of Chinese characters	会意字 Associative Compounds、形声字 Pictophonetic Characters
文化小贴士 Cultural tips	中国的四大菜系 Four Major Cuisines in China

热 身 WARM-UP

我们一起做早餐——草莓（cǎoméi, strawberry）面包片吧。Let's make breakfast together—strawberry bread slices.

面包　盘子　奶油　草莓（cǎoméi, strawberry）

第一步，把_____放在_____上；
第二步，把_____涂（tú, apply）
　　　　在_____上；
第三步，把_____放在_____上；
第四步，你可以吃它了！

课 文 TEXT

课文 1　🎧 16-1

听前问题：王东他们想做什么呢？

王东：你们一直说，想学学怎么做鱼香肉丝这个菜，今天我把做菜的材料都准备好了，咱们可以做一下。

乔治：太好了。以前我仅仅吃过这个菜，今天我要亲自学学怎么做这个菜。

安琪：对。仅仅会吃还不够，还要会做才行。

王东：我把材料放在桌子上，你们也别闲着。安琪，上网查查鱼香肉丝的做法。乔治，赶紧过来给我帮忙，把那个碗给我。

16 把其他材料放进去

安琪：我只输入"鱼香"两个字，就查出来了好多种做法，哪一种才是正宗做法啊？

王东：都差不多。只要是鱼香肉丝的做法，随便选一种就行。

安琪：这里说"盐少许"，还有"辣椒适量"。"少许"是多少？"适量"又是多少？

王东："少许"就是"一点儿"，"适量"就是"合适的数量"。

乔治：那"一点儿"是多少？"多少"算合适呢？这怎么计算啊？

王东：中国菜就是这样，一个人一个做法，没有统一的标准。你喜欢甜的，就多放一点儿糖；他喜欢酸的，就多放一点儿醋。我们今天尽量按照菜谱上说的去做。

乔治：快做吧！我都饿了。

王东：好，我开始炒菜了。首先把肉放到锅里，炒一会儿，然后把其他材料放进去，继续炒，最后把鱼香汁倒进去。

课堂练习

1. 根据课文内容回答问题。Answer the questions based on the text.

（1）乔治以前吃过鱼香肉丝吗？

（2）他们是怎么知道鱼香肉丝的做法的呢？

（3）王东认为中国菜的做法怎么样？

2. 分角色表演课文。Act out the text in roles.

3. 乔治他们已经学会做鱼香肉丝了，你会做什么菜？请给大家介绍一下吧！（可参考给出的词语和句型）George and his friends have learned to cook Yu-Shiang Shredded Pork now. What kind of dishes can you cook? Please introduce it to everyone! (You can refer to the words and sentence patterns given)

> 首先……，然后……，最后……　肉　锅　其他材料　炒
> 放　倒　把……放……　把……倒……　少许　适量

词语 1　🎧 16-2

词语	拼音	词性	英文释义
1. 鱼香肉丝	yúxiāng ròusī		Shredded Pork with Garlic Sauce
2. 把	bǎ	介词	used to put the object before the verb
3. 材料	cáiliào	名词	material; ingredient
4. 仅仅	jǐnjǐn	副词	just; only
5. 亲自	qīnzì	副词	in person; personally
6. 放	fàng	动词	put
7. 闲	xián	形容词	idle
8. 做法	zuòfǎ	名词	way of doing sth.
9. 赶紧	gǎnjǐn	副词	without delay; as soon as possible
10. 帮忙	bāng//máng	动词	help
11. 碗	wǎn	名词	bowl
12. 输入	shūrù	动词	input
13. 正宗	zhèngzōng	形容词	authentic and original
14. 只要	zhǐyào	连词	as long as; if only
15. 随便	suíbiàn	形容词、动词	at random; do as one pleases
16. 盐	yán	名词	salt
17. 少许	shǎoxǔ	形容词	a little; a bit

18. 辣椒	làjiāo	名词	chilli
19. 适量	shìliàng	形容词	just proper in amount; appropriate; moderate
20. 合适	héshì	形容词	suitable; appropriate
21. 计算	jìsuàn	动词	calculate; measure
22. 统一	tǒngyī	形容词、动词	uniform; unify
23. 甜	tián	形容词	sweet
24. 醋	cù	名词	vinegar
25. 尽量	jǐnliàng	副词	as... as possible
26. 菜谱	càipǔ	名词	recipe; cookbook
27. 炒	chǎo	动词	stir fry
28. 首先	shǒuxiān	副词	first
29. 锅	guō	名词	pot; pan
30. 汁	zhī	名词	sauce; gravy
31. 倒	dào	动词	pour

重点词

仅仅

（1）我早上仅仅吃了一个苹果，现在很饿。

（2）我的中文还不行，仅仅会说"你好"。

（3）这不仅仅是一件简单的事情，还是一件很重要的事情。

赶紧

（1）车来了，你赶紧走吧。

（2）她不爱你，你赶紧把她忘了吧。

（3）快开学了，你还不赶紧写作业？

帮忙

（1）明天我需要你来帮忙。

（2）上个星期我搬家，小王帮了我大忙。

（3）你能不能帮我一个忙？

随便

（1）这道题不重要，你随便写写吧。

（2）去不去，随你的便。

（3）你一句随随便便的话，我开心了一天。

合适

（1）我们找一个合适的地方学习吧！

（2）我觉得咱们俩不太合适。

（3）你看这件衣服合适不合适？

尽量

（1）我们的作业很多，但是尽量今天写完吧。

（2）汉语太重要了，我们要尽量学好它。

（3）请大家尽量不要去人多的地方。

练一练

选词填空。Fill in the blanks with the given words.

仅仅　统一　随便　闲　合适　适量　赶紧　输入　帮忙　尽量

（1）中学生们每天要穿学校_____的校服进学校。

（2）学习汉语，_____会说是不行的，还要多多练习听和写。

（3）我会做的菜不多，但是我会_____把这个菜做好。

（4）我只想_____看看，现在还不知道要买什么。

（5）太晚了，_____回家吧。

（6）妈妈的商店关了，最近她总是很_____。

（7）姐姐让我去给她_____一下_____。

（8）每天喝_____的咖啡，对身体有好处。

（9）请你把名字_____进去。

（10）这么晚了，你还在房间里唱歌，你觉得_____吗？

课文 2 🎧 16-3

听前问题：上个星期，"我们"聚餐的时候聊了什么呢？

上个星期，王东教我们做了几个中国菜。我们一边吃着自己做的菜，一边讨论中国和西方的不同。我发现，中国人做菜最常用的方式是炒，西方人最常用的方式是烤。做菜的时候，中国人讲究艺术，把菜的颜色、味道和形状看得很重要；西方人重视科学，讲究菜的营养和热量。

饮料方面也有比较明显的不同。中国人爱喝茶，西方人爱喝咖啡。咖啡有很多种类，很多中国人分不清楚；中国茶也有很多种类，光绿茶就有几十种，很多西方人也常把它们弄错。很多人总是把咖啡和牛奶放在一起喝，有些地方也把牛奶加到茶里，这就成了奶茶。中国人传统的喝茶方式是不加牛奶的。可是，很有意思的是，现在中国却有很多奶茶店，年轻人很喜欢喝奶茶。

这是一个全球化的时代。在中国可以吃到肯德基、麦当劳，可以喝到星巴克、可口可乐；在西方到处都有中餐馆，可以吃到炒菜和饺子。今后，中国和西方的不同也会越来越少。

> 课堂练习

1. 根据课文内容回答问题。Answer the questions based on the text.

   （1）中国和西方的做菜方式有什么不一样？

   （2）在饮料方面，中国和西方有什么不同？

   （3）中国和西方的饮食差别为什么会越来越小？

2. 根据课文内容填空，并复述课文。Fill in the blanks based on the text and retell it.

   上个星期，王东教我们做了几个_____。我们一边吃着自己做的菜，一边讨论中国和西方的_____。我发现，中国人做菜最常用的方式是_____，西方人最常用的方式是_____。做菜的时候，中国人讲究_____，把菜的颜色、_____和形状看得很重要；西方人重视_____，讲究菜的_____和_____。

   饮料方面也有比较_____的不同。中国人爱_____，西方人爱_____。咖啡有很多种类，很多中国人_____；中国茶也有很多种类，光绿茶就有_____种，很多西方人也常把它们_____。很多人总是把咖啡和牛奶_____喝，有些人也把牛奶加到_____，这就成了奶茶。中国人传统的喝茶方式是不加牛奶的。可是，很有意思的是，现在中国却有很多奶茶店，年轻人很喜欢_____。

   这是一个_____的时代。在中国可以吃到肯德基、麦当劳，可以喝到星巴克、可口可乐；在西方到处都有_____，可以吃到_____和饺子。今后，中国和西方的不同会越来越少。

3. 选用下列提示词语，试着说一说中国和你的国家的饮食有哪些不同。Choose the following prompt words and try to talk about the differences between the diet in China and that in your country.

炒	艺术	颜色	味道	形状	饮料	茶	烤
重视	科学	营养	热量	咖啡	牛奶		

词语 2　🎧 16-4

词语	拼音	词性	英文释义
1. 讨论	tǎolùn	动词	discuss
2. 西方	Xīfāng	名词	the West
3. 常用	cháng yòng		frequently used; in common use
4. 烤	kǎo	动词	roast
5. 讲究	jiǎngjiu	动词、形容词	be particular about; tasteful
6. 形状	xíngzhuàng	名词	shape
7. 营养	yíngyǎng	名词	nutrition
8. 饮料	yǐnliào	名词	drink; beverage
9. 明显	míngxiǎn	形容词	obvious; distinct
10. 种类	zhǒnglèi	名词	class; kind; category
11. 分	fēn	动词	tell... from...; distinguish
12. 绿茶	lǜchá	名词	green tea
13. 加	jiā	动词	add
14. 奶茶	nǎichá	名词	milk tea
15. 却	què	副词	however
16. 全球	quánqiú	名词	whole world
17. 化	huà	后缀	*used as a suffix to turn a noun or an adjective into a verb*
18. 时代	shídài	名词	time; era; age
19. 中餐馆	zhōngcānguǎn	名词	Chinese restaurant
20. 今后	jīnhòu	名词	future; days to come

专有名词

1. 肯德基	Kěndéjī		KFC
2. 麦当劳	Màidāngláo		McDonald's

| 3. 星巴克 | Xīngbākè | Starbucks |
| 4. 可口可乐 | Kěkǒu Kělè | Coca-Cola |

重点词

讲究

（1）学习中文，要讲究方法。
（2）爱华是一个讲究的人。
（3）大卫对饮食比较随便，不是太讲究。

明显

（1）你明显瘦了很多，快说说你的减肥方法是什么。
（2）你看，她明显不太喜欢喝咖啡。
（3）很明显，他对京剧不感兴趣。

却

（1）大家都想去北京，你却想去上海。
（2）我以前不喜欢吃中国菜，但是现在却每天都吃。
（3）她不喜欢跑步，却比我们跑得都快。

化

（1）现在的世界越来越全球化了。
（2）来到中国以后，我发现中国真的特别现代化。
（3）小孩子每天吃的食物要多样化，不能只吃一两种。

练一练

选词填空。Fill in the blanks with the given words.

> 常用　化　分　讲究　时代　发明　加　明显　却

（1）妹妹开始减肥了，她最近吃喝很_____。

（2）我们现在还不知道巧克力是谁_____的。

（3）很_____这件事不是他做的。

（4）今天我们要学习一些_____的词语。

（5）在这杯茶里_____进去一些牛奶，就是一杯好喝的奶茶了。

（6）我觉得现在就是最好的_____。

（7）"巳"和"已"我总是_____不清楚。

（8）妈妈天天早早起来给孩子做早餐，孩子_____不喜欢吃。

（9）全球_____的世界，需要各个国家相互帮助、共同发展。

语法 GRAMMAR

一、"把"字句1：表处置　把-sentence I: Indicating disposal or settlement

"把"字句表示处置。"把"与名词或代词构成介词短语，在句中充当状语的句子就叫作"把"字句。"把"字句可以表示处置，表示对介词"把"的宾语所表示的人或事物加以处置，使之发生一定的变化，如位置的变化、所属关系的转移或者形态的变化等。

The 把-sentence indicates disposal or settlement. A sentence in which the character "把" forms a prepositional phrase with a noun or a pronoun that serves as the adverbial is called a 把-sentence. The 把-sentence can be used to indicate disposal or settlement, which means to dispose or settle the person or thing represented by the object to let him/her/it undergo a certain change, such as a change in position, a change in ownership, or a change in form.

1. 【主语 + 把 + 宾语 + 动词 + 结果补语 / 趋向补语 / 状态补语】[Subject + 把 + Object + Verb + Resultative/Directional/State complement]

表示形态的变化 Indicating a change in form

主语（S）	谓语（P）					
	状语	把	宾语	动词	结果补语 / 趋向补语 / 状态补语	助词
我们	应该	把	作业	写	完。	
安琪	没（有）	把	茶	喝	光。	
爱华		把	手	举	起来	了。
丽美		把	杯子	洗	得很干净	吗？

2. 【主语 + 把 + 宾语 + 动词 + 到 / 在 + 处所】[Subject + 把 + Object + Verb + 到 / 在 + Location]

表示位置的变化 Indicating a change in position

主语（S）	谓语（P）						
	状语	把	宾语	动词	到 / 在	处所	助词
他	想	把	面包	带	到	教室。	
安娜		把	牛奶	倒	到	杯子里	了。
乔治		把	笔	放	到	书包里	了？
妈妈	没（有）	把	水果	放	在	桌子上。	

3. 【主语 + 把 + 宾语1 + 动词（+ 给）+ 宾语2】[Subject + 把 + Object 1+ Verb (+ 给) + Object 2]

表示所属关系的变化 Indicating a change in ownership

主语（S）	谓语（P）					
	状语	把	宾语1	动词（+ 给）	宾语2	助词
老师	没（有）	把	作业	发（给）	我们。	
我		把	礼物	送（给）	妈妈	了。
你	也	把	钱	交给	爸爸	吗？
姐姐		把	巧克力	拿给	妹妹	了。

16 把其他材料放进去

> 练一练

1. 看图，用"把"字句回答括号中的问题。Look at the pictures and write sentences according to the questions in the brackets.

（他做了什么？）

_____

（他做了什么？）

_____

（她做了什么？）

_____

（她做了什么？）

_____

2. 明天是爱华的生日，"我们"要给爱华准备一个生日晚会，请大家布置一下教室。用本课学过的"把"字句式说说准备的过程。It's Aihua's birthday tomorrow and we're going to prepare a birthday party for her. Let's decorate the classroom a little bit. Use the 把-sentence learned in this lesson to talk about the preparation process.

二、条件复句：只要……，就……　Conditional complex sentence: 只要……，就……

条件复句"只要……，就……"用来表示达到某种条件就会出现某种结果。可以用来表达想法、讨论学习和工作等。

The conditional complex sentence "只要……，就……" is used to indicate that if some condition is met, a certain result will occur. It can be used to express ideas, discuss study and work, etc.

（1）只要多练习，你的中文就会有进步。

（2）只要认真运动，你就会变瘦。

（3）只要明天不下雨，我们就去跑步。

（4）老师只要留作业，我就会赶紧写完。

练一练

1. 连词成句。String the words together into appropriate sentences.

（1）好好　只要　学习　，　你　开心　就　妈妈　会。

_____

（2）到　中国　只要　，　中餐　很多　吃　就　我们　可以。

_____

（3）中国　乔治　来　只要　，　带　他　我　就　故宫　去。

_____

（4）起床　早点儿　明天　你　只要　，　开车　你　就　来　我　接。

_____

2. 请用"只要……，就……"完成句子。Complete the sentences with "只要……，就……".

（1）乔治很喜欢锻炼，_____。

（2）丽美的口语不好，王东告诉她："_____。"

（3）安琪很喜欢购物，_____。

（4）妈妈最近在学习做饭，_____。

（5）长城很有名，_____。

三、承接复句：首先……，然后…… Successive complex sentence: 首先……，然后……

承接复句"首先……，然后……"用来连接具有承接关系的分句，按照顺序叙述连续发生的动作或情况。

The successive complex sentence "首先……，然后……" is used to join clauses that have a successive relationship, describing actions or situations that happen successively in a sequential order.

（1）首先把肉放到锅里，炒一会儿，然后把其他材料放进去。

（2）每天我回家以后，首先做作业，然后听音乐。

（3）放假后，我首先去上海旅游，然后再回国。

练一练

用"首先……，然后……"完成对话。Complete the conversations with "首先……，然后……".

（1）A：今天晚上你打算做什么？
　　　B：_____。

（2）A：这个周末玛丽的生日，她计划怎么过？
　　　B：_____。

（3）A：你知道意大利面怎么做吗？
　　　B：_____。

（4）A：如果你来中国，你打算去哪儿玩儿？
　　　B：_____。

综合运用 COMPREHENSIVE USE

语音练习　🎧 16-5

一、听录音选择正确答案。Listen to the recording and choose the correct answers.

1. A. cáiliào　　　B. cháiliào　　　2. A. zuòfǎ　　　B. zhuòfǎ

3. A. shūrù	B. shūlù	4. A. zèngzōng	B. zhèngzōng
5. A. jìsuàn	B. qìsuàn	6. A. gǎnjǐn	B. gǎnjìn
7. A. cháng yòng	B. cháng yòn	8. A. jiǎngjiu	B. jiǎngqiú
9. A. juànqiú	B. quánqiú	10. A. shídài	B. sídài

二、听句子给画线词语标声调。Listen to the sentences and mark the tones of the underlined words.

1. 以前我<u>仅仅</u>吃过这个菜，今天我要<u>亲自</u>学学怎么做这个菜了。

2. <u>赶紧</u>过来<u>给</u>我帮忙，把那个碗给我。

3. 这里说"<u>盐少许</u>"，还有"辣椒<u>适量</u>"。

4. 西方人重视科学，讲究菜的<u>营养</u>和<u>热量</u>。

5. 中国茶也有很多<u>种类</u>，光<u>绿茶</u>就有几十种。

三、听一听，读一读。Listen and read.

<table>
<tr><td align="center">画</td><td align="center">Huà</td></tr>
<tr><td align="center">［唐］ 王维</td><td align="center">[Táng]　Wáng Wéi</td></tr>
<tr><td>远看山有色，近听水无声。</td><td>Yuǎn kàn shān yǒu sè, jìn tīng shuǐ wú shēng.</td></tr>
<tr><td>春去花还在，人来鸟不惊。</td><td>Chūn qù huā hái zài, rén lái niǎo bù jīng.</td></tr>
</table>

汉字知识

会意字 Associative Compounds

用两个或两个以上的部件合成一个字，将这些部件的意义合成为新字的意义，这种造字法叫作会意。用会意法造的字就是会意字。会意字包括"以形会意"和"以义会意"。"以形会意"指通过字符的形象合起来表意（如"步"，像双脚一前一后走路，表示步行），"以义会意"指通过字符的字义合起来表意（如山高为"嵩"）。

用会意的方法造字开辟了合体造字的新路，突破了象形、指事两种造字法的局限，组合形式灵活多样，表意方法更加丰富，是汉字发展史上的巨大进步。会意字也有不能表音的缺点，记录语言仍然不够方便，造字量方面虽然较象形、指事大幅增加，但也有一定的限度。

甲骨文　　　金文　　　大篆　　　小篆　　　隶书　　　楷书

Associative compounds are characters formed by combining two or more parts. The meaning of the new character comes from the meanings of these parts. This method of creating characters is called "associative compounding". Characters created this way are called associative compounds. There are two types of associative compounds, namely "form-based associative compounds" and "meaning-based associative compounds". Form-based associative compounds use the shapes of the parts to represent meaning. For example, the character "步" looks like two feet, one in front of the other, representing walking. Meaning-based associative compounds use the meanings of the parts to represent meaning. For example, the character "嵩" combines the meanings of "mountain" and "high".

Using associative compounds to create characters opened up a new way to form characters. It went beyond the limitations of pictographic and self-explanatory characters, offering more flexible combinations and richer ways to represent meaning. This was a big step forward in the history of the development of Chinese characters. However, associative compounds also have a downside: they can't indicate pronunciation, making it less convenient to record language. While the number of characters created this way is larger than with pictographic and self-explanatory methods, it still has its limits.

形声字 Pictophonetic Characters

形声字是由表示汉字意义的形旁和表示汉字读音（dúyīn）的声旁组成的汉字。在现代常用汉字中，形声字超过80%。形声字中声旁和形旁的组合方式有很多种，最主要的有下面六种：

左形右声：妈、吧、快、请、啊、饭
左声右形：歌、和、领、故、功、战
上形下声：零、花、景、草、爸、字
上声下形：您、华、想、忘、架、背

内形外声：闻、闷、问、闵

外形内声：园、厅、历

Pictophonetic characters are characters made up of a semantic part (形旁, xíngpáng) that indicates the meaning and a phonetic part (声旁, shēngpáng) that indicates the pronunciation. In commonly used modern Chinese characters, pictophonetic characters make up over 80%. There are various ways to combine the semantic and phonetic parts, mainly including the following six:

1. Left semantic, right phonetic: 妈 (mā), 吧 (bā), 快 (kuài), 请 (qǐng), 啊 (ā), 饭 (fàn).
2. Left phonetic, right semantic: 歌 (gē), 和 (hé), 领 (lǐng), 故 (gù), 功 (gōng), 战 (zhàn).
3. Top semantic, bottom phonetic: 零 (líng), 花 (huā), 景 (jǐng), 草 (cǎo), 爸 (bà), 字 (zì).
4. Top phonetic, bottom semantic: 您 (nín), 华 (huá), 想 (xiǎng), 忘 (wàng), 架 (jià), 背 (bèi).
5. Inner semantic, outer phonetic: 闻 (wén), 闷 (mèn), 问 (wèn), 闵 (mǐn).
6. Outer semantic, inner phonetic: 园 (yuán), 厅 (tīng), 历 (lì).

口语表达训练

一、你们国家都有什么有名的菜？它们是怎么做的呢？快和我们说说吧！ What are the famous dishes in your country and how are they made? Tell us about it!

国家	菜名	做法

二、中国不同的地方有不同的美食。请进行一次小调查，看看中国的北京、上海、广州这三个城市各有哪些美食，并完成下面的表格。Different parts of China have different cuisines. Please conduct a small survey to see what kind of cuisines there are in each of the three cities in China, namely Beijing, Shanghai and Guangzhou, and complete the table below.

城市	地方美食
北京	
上海	
广州	

中国的四大菜系
Four Major Cuisines in China

　　我们总说，中国有"四大菜系"。这"四大菜系"是指"四大传统菜系"。它们分别是鲁菜、川菜、粤菜和淮扬菜。

　　鲁菜是中国最古老的菜系，北京烤鸭就受到了鲁菜的影响。木须肉是鲁菜的代表。木须肉的做法是：首先将适量盐、胡椒粉和酱油与切好的肉进行搅拌，然后再加入适量的淀粉抓匀腌制，油热后煸炒，将木耳与胡萝卜切好并焯水，将鸡蛋液倒入热好的油中炒好，再将木耳、胡萝卜和黄瓜倒入锅中搅拌，加入酱汁调味，即可出锅。

　　川菜是四大菜系中最大的菜系，也是"百姓菜"。鱼香肉丝就是川菜的代表。川菜还有水煮鱼、麻婆豆腐等。麻婆豆腐的做法是：将切好的豆腐块焯水，锅中倒油，油热了之后放入酱料、豆腐，再加入适量的水，最后加入一小碗淀粉水，稍等片刻就可以食用了。

　　粤菜也就是广东菜。油而不腻是粤菜的一大特点。粤菜的代表菜有白切鸡、菠萝咕噜肉和烧鹅等。菠萝咕噜肉的做法是：在切成小块的猪肉中加入盐、料酒、鸡蛋黄、白胡椒粉腌制，然后加入红薯淀粉，拌好后下油锅炸至变色捞出，并复炸一遍。菠萝切小块。热锅中放底油，加入葱、姜、蒜炒香，然后放入青红椒炒匀，再放入糖醋汁烧开，最后放入炸肉和菠萝块，根据个人口味加入适量盐调味。

淮扬菜非常精美。典型代表有盐水鸭、红烧肉等。红烧肉的做法是：将五花肉、葱和姜切好，将五花肉焯水，然后将五花肉放到蒸锅中，并放入葱和姜，再倒入适量的生抽、白糖等调味料，蒸煮三十分钟即可。

We always say that there are "four major cuisines" in China, which refer to the "four traditional cuisines". These are Lu cuisine, Sichuan cuisine, Cantonese cuisine, and Huaiyang cuisine.

Lu cuisine is one of the oldest cuisines in China. Beijing Roast Duck is influenced by Lu cuisine. A representative dish of Lu cuisine is "Moo Shu Pork" (Sautéed Sliced Pork, Eggs and Black Fungus). Here's how to make it:

1. First, mix an appropriate amount of salt, pepper, and soy sauce with sliced meat.

2. Add some starch and mix well to marinate.

3. Heat oil in a pan and stir-fry the meat.

4. Cut wood ear mushrooms and carrots into small pieces and blanch them.

5. Pour beaten egg into the hot oil and stir-fry.

6. Add the wood ear mushrooms, carrots, and cucumber to the pan and stir-fry.

7. Add sauce for flavoring, and it's ready to serve.

Sichuan cuisine is the largest among the four major cuisines and is known as the "people's cuisine". A representative dish is "Shredded Pork with Garlic Sauce". Other famous Sichuan dishes include Fish Filets in Hot Chili Oil and Mapo Tofu. Here's how to make Mapo Tofu:

1. Cut tofu into blocks and blanch them.

2. Heat oil in a pan and add sauce and tofu.

3. Add an appropriate amount of water to the pan.

4. Finally, add a small bowl of starch water and let it simmer for a moment before serving.

Cantonese cuisine, also known as Guangdong cuisine, is characterized by being rich but not greasy. Representative dishes include Boiled Chicken with Sauce, Gulaorou (Sweet and Sour Pork with Fat), and Roast Goose. Here's how to make Gulaorou:

16 把其他材料放进去

1. Cut pork into small pieces and marinate with salt, cooking wine, egg yolk, and white pepper.
2. Coat the pork pieces with sweet potato starch and deep-fry until golden. Then deep-fry again.
3. Cut pineapple into small pieces.
4. Heat oil in a pan and add onion, ginger, and garlic. Stir-fry until fragrant.
5. Add green and red peppers and stir-fry.
6. Add sugar and vinegar sauce and bring to a boil.
7. Finally, add the fried pork and pineapple pieces. Season with salt to taste.

Huaiyang cuisine is known for its elegance. Typical dishes include Salted Duck and Braised Pork. Here's how to make Braised Pork:

1. Cut pork belly, onion, and ginger into pieces.
2. Blanch the pork belly.
3. Place the pork belly in a steamer with onion and ginger.
4. Add soy sauce, sugar, and other seasonings.
5. Steam for about 30 minutes, and it's ready to serve.

麻婆豆腐（川菜）

红烧肉（淮扬菜）

17 请您把这幅字给我们解释一下吧
Please explain this piece of script to us

本课学习重点

话题 Topic	谈传统节日 Talk about traditional festivals
重点词 Keywords	愿望　圆满　实现　补　商量　庆祝　举行　所有　临时
重点句 Key sentences	1. 那天我不光吃了月饼，而且还跟朋友一起赏月了呢。 2. 不过，我还是把它吃了。 3. 同学们都很高兴，商量组织一次聚会庆祝一下。 4. 上个周末，同学们在学校的一家饭馆举行了聚会，并且把陈老师也请来了。 5. 请您把这幅字给我们解释一下吧。 6. 汉克又把那幅字读了读。
语法 Grammar	1. 递进复句 Progressive complex sentence 　（1）不光……，而且/还……　（2）……并且…… 2. "把"字句 2：表处置 把-sentence II: Indicating disposal or settlement 　（1）主语＋把＋宾语（＋给）＋动词＋了/着 　（2）主语＋把＋宾语＋动词（＋一/了）＋动词 　（3）主语＋把＋宾语＋动词＋动量补语/时量补语
汉字知识 Knowledge of Chinese characters	假借字 Phonetic Loan Characters
文化小贴士 Cultural tips	中国四灵——古代吉祥的象征 Four Holy Beasts in China—Ancient Auspicious Symbols

17 请您把这幅字给我们解释一下吧

热 身 WARM-UP

连一连。Match up.

春节   中秋节   端午节

课 文 TEXT

课文 1   🎧 17-1

听前问题：为什么这个星期六要上课？

大卫：好消息，下个星期一和星期二不上课，放假。

爱华：这是什么节日啊？

李娜：中秋节！中国的传统节日。

爱华：去年我是在南方过的中秋节。那天我不光吃了月饼，而且还跟朋友一起赏月了呢。

大卫：我还是第一次过中秋节呢。李娜，中国人怎么过中秋节啊？

李娜：中国很大，每个地方过中秋节的风俗也不完全一样。不过，吃月饼和赏月的风俗是全国一样的。

大卫：月饼好吃吗？我还没吃过呢。

爱华：我吃过广式月饼，里面的馅儿是一个鸭蛋黄。我觉得那个月饼不光太甜，而且太油腻了。不过，我还是把它吃了。

李娜：月饼有很多种类，下星期食堂里一定有月饼。等你亲自尝一尝，就知道好吃不好吃了。

大卫：中秋节为什么要吃月饼呢？

李娜：中秋节的时候，秋天已经过了一半的时间，这一天月亮很圆。月饼也是圆的。中国人有很多愿望，不光希望生活圆满，而且希望家庭、事业都圆满。人们觉得吃了月饼，这些愿望就会实现。

大卫：我明白了。不过，还有一个坏消息，这个星期六要上课，要把下星期一的课补一补。

课堂练习

1. 根据课文内容回答问题。Answer the questions based on the text.
  （1）爱华去年在哪里过的中秋节？那天她都做了些什么？
  （2）中国各地相同的中秋节习俗是什么？
  （3）中国人中秋节为什么要吃月饼？

2. 分角色表演课文。Act out the text in roles.

3. 如果你是课文中的爱华,请根据课文内容向大家介绍你是怎么过中秋节的。(可参考给出的词语和句型)If you were Aihua in the text, please tell us how you celebrated the Mid-Autumn Festival according to the text. (You can refer to the words and sentence pattern given)

> 吃月饼　赏月　广式月饼　风俗　愿望　不光……,而且……

词语 1 🎧 17-2

词语	拼音	词性	英文释义
1. 消息	xiāoxi	名词	news
2. 去年	qùnián	名词	last year
3. 不光	bùguāng	连词	not only
4. 月饼	yuèbing	名词	moon cake
5. 赏	shǎng	动词	appreciate; enjoy; admire
6. 风俗	fēngsú	名词	custom
7. 全国	quánguó	名词	whole country
8. 广式月饼	Guǎngshì Yuèbing		Cantonese-style moon cake
9. 里面	lǐmiàn	名词	inside
10. 馅儿	xiànr	名词	filling; stuffing
11. 鸭蛋黄	yādànhuáng		duck's egg yolk
12. 油腻	yóunì	形容词	oily; greasy
13. 尝	cháng	动词	taste
14. 月亮	yuèliang	名词	moon
15. 圆	yuán	形容词	round
16. 愿望	yuànwàng	名词	wish; dream; aspiration
17. 圆满	yuánmǎn	形容词	perfect; satisfactory

18. 实现	shíxiàn	动词	realize
19. 坏	huài	形容词	bad
20. 补	bǔ	动词	make up for

专有名词

| 中秋节 | Zhōngqiū Jié | Mid-Autumn Festival |

重点词

愿望

（1）我有两个愿望：一个是有机会去全世界旅行，还有一个是能找到一个好工作。

（2）我最大的愿望是可以去北京学习中文。

（3）快想想你的生日愿望吧！我们一起帮你实现它。

圆满

（1）上个星期，中国举办的杭州亚运会圆满结束了。

（2）他特别优秀，总能圆满地完成经理安排给他的所有工作。

（3）这次大会取得了圆满成功。

实现

（1）我今年已经五十多岁了，还有好几个人生的愿望没有实现。

（2）你的这种想法很难实现。

（3）今年我的计划已经一一实现了。

17 请您把这幅字给我们解释一下吧

补

（1）大夫说我的牙坏了，需要补一补。
（2）安娜，下个星期我们需要补课吗？
（3）奶奶说她已经补好了我的那件衣服。

练一练

选词填空。Fill in the blanks with the given words.

实现　消息　风俗　圆满　愿望　坏　补　赏

（1）听说洛阳（Luòyáng, a city in China）的牡丹（mǔdan, peony）特别有名，下个星期我们要坐火车去那儿_____花。
（2）老师刚刚告诉了我们一个坏_____：下周要考试。
（3）爸爸妈妈都希望自己的孩子有_____的一生。
（4）我的_____是成为一名中文翻译，所以我要好好学习中文。
（5）真让人着急！我的电脑早上_____了，今天我怎么工作啊？
（6）昨天晚上我没睡好，今天我要好好_____个觉。
（7）新的一年里，希望我的愿望都能_____。
（8）中国各地的_____都不太一样，所以你去以前要先了解一下才行。

课文2　🎧 17-3

听前问题：包间墙上挂的那幅字的内容是什么？

期中考试结束了，同学们都很高兴，商量组织一次聚会庆祝一下。上个周末，同学们在学校的一家饭馆举行了聚会，并且把陈老师也请来了。

那家饭馆很有特点，门口挂着两个红灯笼，并且墙上还挂着一些字画。吃饭的时候，我们发现了一幅字——家和万事兴。大家看了半天这几个字，其中有两个字谁都不认识。汉克说："陈老师，请您把这幅字给我们解释一下吧。"

陈老师扶了扶眼镜，看了看那几个字，说："第三个字是'万'的繁体字，一万两万的'万'。最后一个字是'兴'的繁体字，这个字有两个读音，在'高兴'里读第四声，在这里是第一声。'家和万事兴'的意思是，在一个家庭里，大家的关系要好，这样所有的事情才能越来越好。'和'是中国传统文化里的一个重要观念。我们都希望家庭好，世界和平。"

乔治把手机举了起来："我们国家也有这样的说法。我要把它拍下来，发给我妈妈看看。"

汉克又把那幅字读了读，说："我们班就是一个临时的大家庭，我们要相互学习，相互帮助。我们也要做到'家和万事兴'！"

课堂练习

1. 根据课文内容回答问题。Answer the questions based on the text.

   （1）同学们为什么举行聚会？

   （2）大家不认识哪两个字？那两个字是什么意思？

   （3）如何理解"家和万事兴"？说说你的看法。

2. 根据课文内容填空，并复述课文。Fill in the blanks based on the text and retell it.

   期中考试结束了，同学们都很高兴，商量组织一次聚会_____一下。上个周末，同学们在学校的一家饭馆_____聚会，并且把陈老师也请来了。

   这家饭馆很有_____，门口挂着两个_____，并且墙上还挂着一些_____。吃饭的时候，我们发现了一幅字——_____，有两个字大家都不认识，汉克说："陈老师，请您把这幅字给我们_____一下吧。"

17 请您把这幅字给我们解释一下吧

陈老师_____眼镜，看了看那几个字，说："第三个字是'万'的繁体字，一万两万的'万'。最后一个字是'兴'的_____。'家和万事兴'的意思是，在一个家庭里，大家的关系要好，这样_____的事情才能越来越好。'和'是中国传统文化里的一个重要观念。我们都希望_____、世界_____。"

乔治把手机_____起来："我们国家也有这样的说法。我要把它_____，发给我妈妈看看。"

汉克又把那幅字读了读，说："我们班就是一个_____大家庭，我们要相互学习，相互帮助。我们也要做到'家和万事兴'！"

3. 选用下列提示词语，解释一下"家和万事兴"的意思。你们国家有"家和万事兴"这样的说法吗？请你跟大家分享一下吧！Choose the following prompt words to explain the meaning of "家和万事兴". Do you have similar sayings in your country? Please share them with us!

> 传统文化　观念　家庭　所有　越来越　和平

词语 2　　🎧 17-4

词语	拼音	词性	英文释义
1. 期中	qīzhōng	名词	midterm
2. 商量	shāngliang	动词	talk over; discuss
3. 聚会	jùhuì	名词、动词	gathering; get together
4. 庆祝	qìngzhù	动词	celebrate
5. 家	jiā	量词	*used of families/enterprises*
6. 举行	jǔxíng	动词	hold
7. 并且	bìngqiě	连词	and; what's more
8. 陈	Chén	名词	a surname
9. 特点	tèdiǎn	名词	distinguishing feature; characteristic

85

10. 挂	guà	动词	hang
11. 红	hóng	形容词	red
12. 灯笼	dēnglong	名词	lantern
13. 墙	qiáng	名词	wall
14. 字画	zìhuà	名词	calligraphy and painting
15. 幅	fú	量词	used for cloth, pictures, scrolls, etc.
16. 家和万事兴	jiā hé wànshì xīng		harmony in the family leads to success in everything
和	hé	形容词	harmonious
17. 半天	bàntiān	数量词	quite a while
18. 解释	jiěshì	动词	explain
19. 扶	fú	动词	adjust; support with the hand
20. 眼镜	yǎnjìng	名词	spectacles; glasses
21. 万	wàn	数词	ten thousand
22. 繁体字	fántǐzì	名词	traditional Chinese character
23. 读音	dúyīn	名词	pronunciation
24. 声	shēng	名词、量词	tone; used for sounds
25. 意思	yìsi	名词	meaning
26. 关系	guānxì	名词、动词	relationship; concern
27. 所有	suǒyǒu	形容词	all
28. 重要	zhòngyào	形容词	important
29. 观念	guānniàn	名词	idea; concept
30. 和平	hépíng	名词	peace
31. 举	jǔ	动词	raise; hold up
32. 说法	shuōfǎ	名词	expression; saying
33. 临时	línshí	形容词、副词	temporary; at the last moment

重点词

商量

（1）你们商量一下，看看明天中午去哪儿玩儿。

（2）这件事需要一家人一起商量商量。

（3）这件事就这么定了，不需要再跟你商量了。

庆祝

（1）下周是中秋节，你们要去哪里庆祝？

（2）我考完试了，我们出去庆祝庆祝吧！

（3）你生日的时候，家人一般会怎么给你庆祝呢？

举行

（1）今天下午，学校要举行一场篮球比赛。

（2）有一个坏消息：因为下雨了，校园演唱会不能举行了。

（3）周二下午，我们班要举行一场考试。

所有

（1）今天所有的学生都来上课了，也没有人迟到。

（2）今天所有的电影都是中文电影。

（3）不是所有的中国人都喜欢吃饺子，我就不喜欢。

临时

（1）今天上课的时候，我忘带书了，临时用了老师的书。

（2）朋友有事出门了，我成了她女儿的临时"妈妈"。

（3）请临时帮我照顾一下这个孩子。

练一练

选词填空。Fill in the blanks with the given words.

> 举行　和平　临时　所有　举　挂　解释　特点　庆祝　商量

（1）出国留学是大事，我觉得你应该和父母_____一下。

（2）弟弟要去北京上大学了，全家人要_____一下：我们出国旅游一周。

（3）没有带书的同学，请把手_____起来。

（4）我不喜欢这道菜，它的_____是辣和油腻。

（5）请你把这幅画儿_____在你房间的墙上。

（6）下个星期我们学校要_____一次大学生演唱会。

（7）你为什么又迟到了？请你给我_____一下。

（8）不是_____人都喜欢吃北京小吃。

（9）他_____有事，不能参加这次聚会了。

（10）我们这里的每一个人都希望世界_____。

语法 GRAMMAR

一、递进复句　Progressive complex sentence

1. 不光……，而且/还……

多用于书面语，表示除此之外，还有更进一层的意思。可以连接两个小句。主语相同时，"不光"放在主语后；主语不同时，"不光"放在主语前；"而且"或"还"分别连接第二个小分句，都表示进一步说明，"而且"要用在第二个分句前，"还"一般要放在第二个分句的主语后面；"而且"与"还"也可以连用。

It is mostly used in written Chinese to indicate "besides that" and the meaning of a further level beyond that. It can join two clauses. When the subjects are the same, "不光" is placed after the subject; when the subjects are different, "不光" is placed before the subject; "而且" or "还" connects the second clause respectively, both of which indicate further explanation, "而且" is placed before the second clause, while "还" is generally placed after the subject of the second clause; "而且" and "还" can also be used concurrently.

（1）他不光没写作业，而且没来上课。

（2）结婚以后，我不光学会了做饭，还学会了说中文。

（3）不光我父母会网购，而且我爷爷奶奶也会网购。

（4）她不光会说汉语，而且还会说法语。

2. ……并且……

用于书面语，表示几个动作同时进行或几种性质同时存在，还有更进一层的意思。

It is used in written Chinese to indicate that several actions are going on simultaneously or that several properties exist simultaneously, as well as the meaning of a further level.

（1）这次聚会同学们都来了，并且老师们也都来了。

（2）大家对这个问题进行了讨论，并且找到了一个不错的解决办法。

（3）他这么说了，并且也这么做了。

（4）今天下午妈妈要来学校看我，并且还会带来我最爱吃的食物。

练一练

1. 请补全句子。Complete the sentences.

（1）这种花我们家也有，并且_____。

（2）学校食堂的饭菜不光_____，而且_____。

（3）网上的衣服不光_____，而且_____。

（4）我不光_____，而且_____。

（5）他给出了答案，并且_____。

2. 请用括号里的关联词语改写句子。Rewrite the sentences with the correlatives in the brackets.

（1）王老师是我的汉语老师，也是我的朋友。（不光……，而且……）

_____

（2）我弟弟喜欢唱歌，也喜欢游泳。（不光……，还……）

_____

（3）中国的月饼种类很多，都很好吃。（并且）

_____

（4）学做中国美食的时候，我上网找了很多视频（shìpín, video）学习，还请教 (qǐngjiào, consult) 了一些中国朋友。（不光……，而且……）

_____

（5）麦克是一位友好、热情而且优秀的老师。（并且）

_____

二、"把"字句2：表处置　把-sentence II: Indicating disposal or settlement

"把"字句是由"把"字构成的介词短语做状语的动词谓语句，通常句中的谓语动词与"把"字后面的宾语存在动宾关系。"把"字句的结构和用法较为复杂，除了要有"把"字后面的宾语、谓语动词外，动词后还会有补语等其他成分。

The 把-sentence is a sentence with a verbal predicate in which the prepositional phrase formed by "把" serves as the adverbial, usually the object after "把" has a verb-object relationship with the predicate verb in the sentence. The structure and usage of the 把-sentence is rather complicated, in addition to the object and the predicate verb after "把", there are also other components after the verb, such as complements and so on.

1. 【主语+状语+把+宾语（+给）+动词+了/着】[Subject + Adverbial +把+ Object (+给) + Verb + 了/着]

S	状语	把	O	（给）	V	了/着
他	没（有）	把	车票	（给）	带	着。
老师		把	补课的事	（给）	忘	了？
他	应该	把	借的钱	（给）	还	了。

2.【主语＋状语＋把＋宾语＋动词（＋一／了）＋动词】[Subject + Adverbial + 把 + Object + Verb (+ 一／了) +Verb]

S	状语	把	O	V	（一／了）	V
我		把	眼镜	扶	了	扶。
汉克		把	房间	扫	了	扫。
她	想	把	衣服	洗	一	洗。

3.【主语＋状语＋把＋宾语＋动词＋（了＋）动量补语／时量补语】[Subject + 把 + Object + Verb +（了＋）]

S	状语	把	O	V	（了）	Action-measure/Time-measure Complement
我们	要	把	上节课的内容	复习		一下。
我		把	生词	写	了	十遍。
他		把	这个问题	想	了	一天。

练一练

1. 看图，用本课所学的"把"字句式及括号里的词语写句子。Look at the pictures and write sentences with the 把-sentence learned in this lesson and the words in the brackets.

＿＿＿＿＿＿＿＿＿＿（一下）　　＿＿＿＿＿＿＿＿＿＿（一遍）

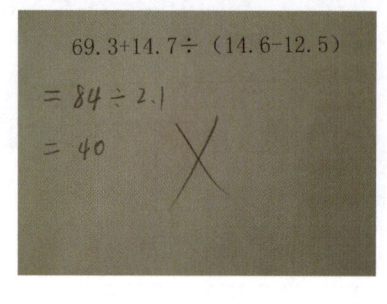

_____（算）　　　　　_____（看）

2. 用"把"字句描述你的一天。Describe your day with the 把-sentence.

综合运用 COMPREHENSIVE USE

语音练习 17-5

一、听录音选择正确答案。Listen to the recording and choose the correct answers.

1. A. fēngsú   B. fēnsú   2. A. xiāoxi   B. xiāoxī
3. A. xiànr   B. xiàn ér   4. A. yǒunǐ   B. yóunì
5. A. shāngliang B. shāngliàng   6. A. tèdiǎn   B. tàdiǎn
7. A. yuánmǎn   B. yuànmǎn   8. A. shuōfǎ   B. suōfǎ
9. A. línshí   B. língshí   10. A. yǎnjīng   B. yǎnjìng

二、听句子给画线词语标声调。Listen to the sentences and mark the tones of the underlined words.

1. 那天我<u>不光</u>吃了<u>月饼</u>，而且还跟朋友一起<u>赏月</u>了呢。

2. 中国人有很多<u>愿望</u>，不光希望生活<u>圆满</u>，而且希望家庭、事业都圆满。

3. 还有一个坏消息：这个星期六要上课，要把下星期一的课<u>补一补</u>。

4. 门口挂着两个红灯笼，并且墙上还挂着一些字画。

5. 陈老师，请您把这幅字给我们解释一下吧。

三、听一听，唱一唱。Listen and sing.

水调歌头

［宋］ 苏轼

明月几时有？把酒问青天。

不知天上宫阙，今夕是何年。

我欲乘风归去，又恐琼楼玉宇，高处不胜寒。

起舞弄清影，何似在人间。

转朱阁，低绮户，照无眠。

不应有恨，何事长向别时圆？

人有悲欢离合，月有阴晴圆缺，此事古难全。

但愿人长久，千里共婵娟。

Shuǐdiào Gētóu

[Sòng] Sū Shì

Míngyuè jǐshí yǒu? Bǎ jiǔ wèn qīngtiān.

Bù zhī tiānshang gōngquè, jīnxī shì hé nián.

Wǒ yù chéng fēng guīqù, yòu kǒng qiónglóu-yùyǔ, gāochù búshèng hán.

Qǐwǔ nòng qīngyǐng, hésì zài rénjiān.

Zhuǎn zhūgé, dī qǐhù, zhào wúmián.

Bù yīng yǒu hèn, héshì cháng xiàng biéshí yuán?

Rén yǒu bēihuān-líhé, yuè yǒu yīnqíng-yuánquē, cǐ shì gǔ nán quán.

Dàn yuàn rén chángjiǔ, qiān lǐ gòng chánjuān.

汉字知识

假借字 Phonetic Loan Characters

假借不是造字的方法，而是用字的方法，即用同音字代替。假借有两种情况。一种是本无其字的假借。语言中有些词的意思比较抽象，不太容易使用象形、指事、会意、形声等方法造字，于是就借用已有的同音字来代替表达这个词义。例如第一人称代词"我"，就是借用表示"武器"义的"我"；"难"和"易"不好造字，于是前者就借用了同音字"难"，这是一种鸟的名字；后者借用了同音字"易"，这是一种小动物的名字。另一种是本有其字的假借。语言中已经有了专用的汉字，但是不太流行，一段时间内人们仍然使用另一个同音字。这种情况在古代是常见的、可接受的，但是现在不可以。现在如果使用别的同音字来代替一个字，属于用字错误。

Phonetic loan characters are not a method of creating new characters, but rather a way of using existing ones. This involves using a character that sounds the same as the intended character. There are two scenarios for phonetic loan characters:

1. No Original Character: Some words in the language have abstract meanings that are difficult to represent using methods like pictographic characters, self-explanatory characters, associative compounds, and pictophonetic characters. In these cases, an existing character with the same sound is borrowed to represent the meaning. For example, the first-person pronoun "我" (wǒ, meaning "I") originally represented a weapon, but it was borrowed to mean "I". Similarly, it's difficult to create new characters to represent the meaning of "难" (nán, meaning "difficult") and "易" (yì, meaning "easy"), so the former borrowed the same-sounding character "难" which indicates the name of a bird, and the latter borrowed the same-sounding character "易" which indicates the name of an animal.

2. Existing but Less Common Character: Sometimes, there is already a specific character for a meaning in the language, but it is not widely used. During certain periods, people continue to use a different character with the same sound. This practice was common and acceptable in ancient times but is not acceptable today. If someone uses a different character with the same sound to replace the correct one, it is considered a mistake.

口语表达训练

一、你知道中国的重阳节吗？上网查询相关资料，四人一组完成一份手抄报。要求包括下面的内容。Have you heard of the Double Ninth Festival in China? Search the Internet for relevant information and make a handwritten newspaper in groups of four. The following contents should be covered.

1. 日期
2. 习俗（饮食、活动）
3. 意义

二、你喜欢中国的哪个节日？采访三位同学，问问他们喜欢中国的哪个节日以及原因，并完成下表。Which traditional Chinese festival do you like? Interview three of your classmates, ask them which Chinese festival they like and why, and complete the table below.

同学姓名	喜欢的节日	原因

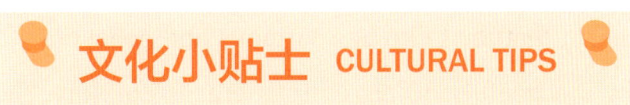

中国四灵——古代吉祥的象征
Four Holy Beasts in China—Ancient Auspicious Symbols

早在中国周代的时候，人们就把麟、凤、龙、龟称为四灵，并且把它们看作是吉祥的象征。这四种动物，除了龟之外，其他三种都是传说中的动物，现实生活中并不存在。它们的历史意义非常深远,反映了中华民族追求幸福、长寿、和平、吉祥的心理。

麟,也就是麒麟,它的身子像鹿,脚像马蹄,尾像牛尾。传说麒麟是有德行的仁兽,皇帝把它看作是太平盛世的象征。民间也有"麒麟送子"的说法,表示早生贵子、子孙繁荣。

凤,也就是凤凰。它头顶美丽的凤冠,身上拥有五彩斑斓的羽毛,是传说中的鸟中之王。凤凰形象高贵,在古代只有皇家才能使用。后来随着时代的发展,民间也开始使用凤凰的形象,尤其在中国的传统婚礼上,凤凰会出现在新娘的头饰和礼服上,表示喜庆和吉祥。现在更是有"龙凤呈祥""望女成凤"的说法。

龙,它的形象非常雄伟,是众多动物的合身。在中国古代,龙的形象也只有皇家才能使用,在一些宫殿、寺庙以及皇家的用具上都刻画着龙,来显示他们至高无上的地位。然而现在,我们大家都可以使用龙的形象来表示吉祥。还有一些活动,比如"赛龙舟""舞龙灯",都表达了中国人对于龙的喜爱。人们常用"望子成龙"表示父母希望孩子长大以后能够出人头地。

龟,是四灵中唯一在现实生活中可以看到的动物,象征健康长寿。龟的寿命很长,人们认为它能够预知未来。因此古代许多祭祀卜辞的活动,大家都会用龟甲来占卜。为了表示对龟的尊重,人们雕刻了许多龟的石雕或者铜雕,将它们放在寺庙或者皇宫庭院里。现在我们也有"龟龄"的说法。

As early as the Zhou Dynasty in China, people revered the Qilin, Phoenix, Loong, and Tortoise as the Four Holy Beasts, considering them auspicious symbols. Except for the tortoise, the other three are mythical creatures that do not exist in reality. Their historical significance is profound, reflecting the Chinese people's pursuit of happiness, longevity, peace, and good fortune.

1. Qilin (麟 or 麒麟): The Qilin has the body of a deer, the hooves of a horse, and the tail of an ox. Legend has it that the Qilin is a virtuous and benevolent creature, the emperors took it as a symbol for a peaceful and prosperous era. In folklore, there is a saying "Qilin sends a son", which expresses the wish for an honorable offspring and a thriving family.

2. Phoenix (凤 or 凤凰): The Phoenix is adorned with a beautiful crown and colorful feathers, making it the mythical king of birds. Its image is noble, and in ancient times, only the imperial family could use it. Over time, the image of the Phoenix was used in folk culture, especially in traditional Chinese weddings, where it appears on the bride's headdress and gown, symbolizing joy and good fortune. Today, there are phrases like "Loong and Phoenix

bring good fortune" and "hoping one's daughter become a Phoenix".

3. Loong (龙): The Loong is a majestic creature, combining features of various animals. In ancient China, the Loong's image was exclusively used by the imperial family, appearing on palaces, temples, and royal artifacts to signify their supreme status. Today, everyone can use the Loong's image to represent good fortune. Activities like Loong boat racing and Loong dancing reflect the Chinese people's love for the Loong. The phrase "hoping one's son become a Loong" is commonly used to express parents' aspirations for their children's success.

4. Tortoise (龟): The Tortoise is the only animal that can be seen in real life among the Four Holy Beasts, symbolizing health and longevity. Tortoises have long lifespans, and people believe they can foresee the future. Therefore, in ancient times, tortoise shells were used for divination in sacrificial rituals. To show respect for the Tortoise, people carved tortoise statues from stone or bronze and placed them in temples or imperial courts. Today, we have the phrase "tortoise age".

18 养儿防老
Bring up children for the purpose of being looked after in old age

本课学习重点	
话题 Topic	谈亲子关系 Talk about parent-child relationship
重点词 Keywords	根本　赶快　代表　把握　靠　不得不　保持　千万
重点句 Key sentences	1. 为了孩子，有的妈妈不再去社会上工作，在家当了全职太太。 2. 她们一方面要管孩子的日常生活，一方面还要关注他们的学习情况。 3. 父母常以为孩子学习成绩好的话，以后就会有成就。 4. 只有实力和能力都提高了，才能更好地把握自己的命运。 5. 我们打算在外工作的话，千万要多想想家中的父母。
语法 Grammar	1. 目的复句：为了…… 　　Purposive complex sentence 2. 并列复句：一方面……，一方面…… 　　Coordinate compound sentence 3. 假设复句：……的话，…… 　　Hypothetical complex sentence 4. 条件复句：只有……，才…… 　　Conditional complex sentence
汉字知识 Knowledge of Chinese characters	多音多义字 Heteronymic Characters
文化小贴士 Cultural tips	当代中国的人口结构 Demographic Structure of Contemporary China

18 养儿防老

热身 WARM-UP

给下面的图片选择对应的词语填空。Choose the corresponding words for the pictures below and fill in the blanks.

全职太太　成绩　夫妻　子女　进步　调查　空巢老人

　　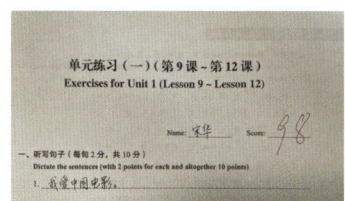　　

_____　　_____　　_____

_____　_____　_____　_____

课文 TEXT

课文 1　🎧 18-1

听前问题：好多父母关心孩子的什么问题？

乔治：我发现好多父母很关心子女的成长问题。

王东：是啊！为了孩子，有的妈妈不再去社会上工作，在家当了全职太太。

乔治：这可不轻松啊！

王东：可不是！她们一方面要管孩子的日常生活，一方面还要关注他们的学习情况，根本没有太多属于自己的时间。

乔治：教育孩子，总是会让很多父母头疼。

王东：是啊！不少孩子平时听到最多的一句话就是"赶快去学习"，因此就以为父母只关心他们的学习成绩。

乔治：而事实是父母很爱孩子。

王东：可是不少孩子并不是真的理解自己的父母。

乔治：因为父母和孩子的很多观念都不太一样，所以亲子关系经常会弄得很紧张。

王东：对。父母常以为孩子学习成绩好的话，以后就会有成就，所以总是特别关注学习成绩的高低。

乔治：可是成绩高并不代表解决问题的能力就强啊！只有实力和能力都提高了，才能更好地把握自己的命运。

课堂练习

1. 根据课文内容回答问题。Answer the questions based on the text.
   （1）全职太太的生活轻松吗？为什么？
   （2）孩子为什么觉得父母只关心学习成绩？事实是什么？
   （3）父母和孩子的观念一样吗？有什么不同？

2. 分角色表演课文。Act out the text in roles.

3. 如果你是课文中提到的孩子，请根据课文内容向大家介绍你和父母的关系。（可参考给出的词语和句型）If you were the kid in the text, please tell us about your relationship with your parents based on the text. (You can refer to the words and sentence patterns given)

> 全职太太　日常生活　学习　情况　成绩　理解　观念
> 紧张　成就　解决问题　实力　能力　把握　命运
> 为了……，……　一方面……，一方面……　……的话，……
> 只有……，才……

词语 1 🎧 18-2

词语	拼音	词性	英文释义
1. 子女	zǐnǚ	名词	sons and daughters; children; offspring
2. 成长	chéngzhǎng	动词	grow
3. 为了	wèile	介词	for; so as to
4. 不再	búzài	动词	no more
5. 社会	shèhuì	名词	society
6. 全职	quánzhí	形容词	full-time
7. 太太	tàitai	名词	wife
8. 可不是	kěbúshi	副词	exactly
9. 一方面	yì fāngmiàn		on the one hand
10. 管	guǎn	动词	take care of
11. 日常	rìcháng	形容词	day-to-day; daily
12. 关注	guānzhù	动词	pay attention to; concern
13. 情况	qíngkuàng	名词	situation; circumstances
14. 根本	gēnběn	副词、名词	at all; base
15. 教育	jiàoyù	动词、名词	educate; education

16. 不少	bù shǎo		quite a few
17. 听到	tīngdào		hear
18. 句	jù	量词	used of language
19. 话	huà	名词	words
20. 赶快	gǎnkuài	副词	hurriedly; at once
21. 事实	shìshí	名词	fact
22. 真的	zhēn de		real
23. 亲子	qīnzǐ	名词	parent-child
24. 的话	dehuà	助词	used at the end of a conditional clause
25. 成就	chéngjiù	名词、动词	achievement; accomplish
26. 高低	gāodī	名词	height
27. 高	gāo	形容词	high; above average
28. 代表	dàibiǎo	动词、名词	mean; stand for; representative
29. 能力	nénglì	名词	capability; competence
30. 强	qiáng	形容词	strong; high-standard
31. 只有	zhǐyǒu	连词	only
32. 实力	shílì	名词	strength; power; competence
33. 把握	bǎwò	动词、名词	grasp; seize; assurance
34. 命运	mìngyùn	名词	fate; destiny; fortune

重点词

根本

（1）看这次的考试成绩，就知道你平时根本没有努力学习。

（2）黑板上的字太小了，我根本看不清楚。

（3）这是解决这个问题的根本。

赶快

（1）请大家赶快上车，车马上就要开了。

（2）你去还是不去，请赶快想好。

（3）赶快回家，马上要下雨了。

代表

（1）成绩高不代表说汉语的水平就高。

（2）他已经18岁了，你能代表他的想法吗？

（3）这次运动会安娜是我们班的代表。

把握

（1）这次，你一定要把握好这个机会！

（2）我们要把握好自己的命运！

（3）今天的课文有点儿难，我没有把握学好它。

练一练

选词填空。Fill in the blanks with the given words.

> 根本 把握 代表 赶快 命运 教育 成就 关注

（1）最近，我一直在_____中国男篮的比赛。

（2）大卫一个人不能_____所有同学。

（3）现在的问题就是我们_____不知道他在哪儿。

（4）你这一天去哪儿玩儿了？_____去洗手，马上要吃饭了。

（5）很多父母总是_____孩子要好好学习，很少去听孩子的心里话。

（6）父母都希望自己的孩子以后有_____。

（7）这次机会，你一定要好好_____。

（8）其实我们每个人的_____都不太一样。

课文 2 🎧 18-3

听前问题："空巢老人"是哪些人？

我们一般把那些身边没有子女照顾，一个人或者夫妻共同居住的老人称为"空巢老人"。一项社会调查显示，到2030年，中国的空巢老人数量会达到两亿。

"养儿防老"是中国的一个传统观念，意思是说父母老了的时候，可以靠子女生活。而现在，时代已经变化，越来越多的年轻人为了实现更好的发展，不得不离开故乡，到别的城市或国外去工作。大多数人平时工作忙，生活压力大，也只有在春节或者其他假期才能回一次家，因此真正陪父母的时间总是非常少。

大部分的"空巢老人"一方面要适应子女长期不在身边的情况，一方面还要合理地安排退休后的生活，让身体始终保持健康，这些都是他们要面对的问题。因为他们知道，只有自己身体健康了，子女在外才会放心。为让孩子能好好地工作和生活，很多父母并不会告诉孩子他们遇到的那些麻烦和困难。但是我们要明白，父母不说，并不代表他们不需要我们。

我们打算在外工作的话，千万要多想想家中的父母。对父母来说，我们的一个电话、几句问候，往往会比送他们礼物或者钱更让他们开心。

18 养儿防老

课堂练习

1. 根据课文内容回答问题。Answer the questions based on the text.

   （1）"养儿防老"是什么意思？

   （2）"空巢老人"会面临什么问题？

   （3）孩子如果打算在外工作的话，怎么做会让父母更开心？

2. 根据课文内容填空，并复述课文。Fill in the blanks based on the text and retell it.

   　　我们_____把那些身边没有子女照顾，_____或者_____共同居住的老人_____"空巢老人"。一_____社会调查_____，到2030年，中国的空巢老人数量会达到_____。

   　　"养儿防老"是中国的一个传统观念，_____是说父母老了的时候，可以靠子女生活。而现在，时代_____变化，越来越多的年轻人为了实现更好的发展，_____离开故乡，到别的城市或国外工作。大多数人_____工作忙，生活压力大，也只有在春节或者其他假期_____能回一次家，因此真正陪父母的时间总是非常少。

   　　大部分的空巢老人一方面要_____子女长期不在身边的情况，一方面还要_____地安排退休后的生活，让身体始终_____，这些都是他们要面对的问题。因为他们知道，_____自己身体健康了，子女在外_____会放心。_____让孩子能好好地工作和生活，很多父母并不会告诉孩子他们遇到的那些麻烦和困难。_____我们要明白，父母不说，并不代表他们不需要我们。

   　　我们打算在外工作的话，_____要多想想家中的父母。_____，我们的一个电话、几句问候，往往会比送他们礼物或者钱更让他们开心。

3. 选用下列提示词语和句型，说说你会让自己的父母成为"空巢老人"吗。为什么？Choose the following prompt words and sentence pattern to talk about whether you would let your parents become "empty nesters"? Why?

   | 观念　靠　变化　发展　压力　不得不　的话 |
   | 为了　亲人　长期　保持　千万　只有……，才…… |

词语 2  18-4

词语	拼音	词性	英文释义
1. 夫妻	fūqī	名词	wife and husband; couple
2. 称为	chēngwéi		be called as
3. 空巢老人	kōngcháo lǎorén		empty nester
4. 项	xiàng	量词	used of itemized things
5. 调查	diàochá	名词、动词	survey; investigate
6. 显示	xiǎnshì	动词	reveal; show
7. 养	yǎng	动词	raise
8. 儿	ér	名词	son; child
9. 防	fáng	动词	prepare for; prevent
10. 老	lǎo	形容词	old
11. 靠	kào	动词	rely on; count on
12. 变化	biànhuà	动词、名词	change
13. 发展	fāzhǎn	名词、动词	development; develop
14. 不得不	bùdébù		have to; cannot but
15. 故乡	gùxiāng	名词	hometown
16. 大多数	dàduōshù	名词	vast majority
17. 压力	yālì	名词	pressure; stress
18. 适应	shìyìng	动词	adjust to; adapt; fit
19. 长期	chángqī	名词	long term; a long period of time
20. 合理	hélǐ	形容词	sensible; reasonable
21. 保持	bǎochí	动词	keep
22. 放心	fàng//xīn	动词	feel relieved; rest assured; be relaxed
23. 遇到	yùdào		come across; encounter

| 24. 千万 | qiānwàn | 副词 | must; be sure to |
| 25. 问候 | wènhòu | 动词 | send one's regards to |

重点词

靠

（1）过去中国人认为，父母老了，可以靠子女生活。
（2）想要学好汉语，不能只靠老师，还要靠自己的努力。
（3）中国人常说："在家靠父母，出门靠朋友。"

不得不

（1）孩子已经长大了，不得不离开父母，一个人生活了。
（2）为了一家人的生活，爸爸不得不努力工作。
（3）我刚刚发现自己没带书，现在不得不回家去拿。

保持

（1）这次考试，你考得不错，要保持住。
（2）女孩子们保持身材并不容易。
（3）我认为保持开心和健康是最重要的事情。

千万

（1）考试的时候千万别紧张。
（2）爸爸，你千万不要忘记，明天是妈妈的生日。
（3）在中国，千万不能酒驾。

练一练

选词填空。Fill in the blanks with the given words.

> 显示　靠　不得不　保持　千万　适应　调查　压力

（1）我_____说，你的汉语进步很大。

（2）你一个人去旅行时，可_____要小心。

（3）一项_____显示，女孩子在夏天会更重视自己的身材变化。

（4）马上要考试了，老师和学生的_____都很大。

（5）乔治学习汉语非常认真，一直_____着第一名的好成绩。

（6）来到中国一年了，我已经_____了这里的生活。

（7）中国人_____自己努力取得了今天的成就。

（8）我的手表怎么不_____时间了？

语法 GRAMMAR

一、目的复句：为了……　Purposive complex sentence: 为了……

引出动作行为的目的，常常放在句子开头。一般有较强的正式语体的意味。

It is used to introduce the purpose of an action or behavior and is often placed at the beginning of a sentence. Generally, it has a strong formal style of speech.

【为了+VP/小句，S+VP/小句】[为了+VP/Clause, Subject + VP/Clause]

为了+VP/Clause	S+VP/Clause
为了实现去中国的梦想，	我努力学习汉语。
为了取得好成绩，	我天天去图书馆学习。
为了照顾孩子，	有的妈妈当了全职太太。

> 练一练

1. 请补全句子。Complete the sentences.

（1）为了＿＿＿＿＿＿＿＿＿＿＿＿＿＿＿＿，我努力学习汉语。

（2）为了＿＿＿＿＿＿＿＿＿＿＿＿＿＿＿＿，妈妈跟着抖音（Dǒuyīn, name of an APP）学习做饭。

（3）为了写好汉字，他＿＿＿＿＿＿＿＿＿＿＿＿＿＿＿＿。

（4）为了去长城，＿＿＿＿＿＿＿＿＿＿＿＿＿＿＿＿。

（5）为了买到机票，＿＿＿＿＿＿＿＿＿＿＿＿＿＿＿＿。

2. 小采访。A brief interview.

请问一问你周围的同学，为了实现自己的目标、理想或者愿望，他们都做了哪些努力。Chat with the classmates around you. Ask them what efforts they have made to achieve their goals, dreams or wishes.

序号	为了……，	S+VP/Clause
1		
2		
3		
4		
5		

二、并列复句：一方面……，一方面…… Coordinate compound sentence: 一方面……，一方面……

用于列举一个事物的两个对等方面。两个"一方面"分别连接两个分句。

It is used to list two equivalent aspects of something. The two "一方面" join two clauses respectively.

（1）妈妈一方面要管孩子的日常生活，一方面还要关注他们的学习情况。

（2）这个周末我一方面要复习汉语，一方面要在家照顾妈妈。

（3）我觉得他很优秀，一方面是由于他工作很努力，一方面是因为他确实很有能力。

> 练一练

1. 请补全句子。Complete the sentences.

（1）妈妈很忙，一方面_____，一方面_____
   _____。

（2）周末的时候，我们一方面要_____，一方面要_____
   _____。

（3）学习汉语时，一方面_____，一方面_____
   _____。

（4）我喜欢旅游，一方面可以_____，一方面可以_____
   _____。

（5）考试没考好，一方面是因为_____，一方面是因为_____
   _____。

2. 请用"一方面……，一方面……"给大家介绍一下你的五个朋友或同学。Give a brief introduction of five of your friends or classmates with "一方面……，一方面……".

例：丽丽很忙，一方面要照顾孩子，一方面还要学习汉语。

（1）_____
（2）_____
（3）_____
（4）_____
（5）_____

三、假设复句：……的话，……　　Hypothetical complex sentence: ……的话

"……的话"用来假设一个条件，后面的小句用来交代结果。"……的话"前面也常常加"如果 / 要是"，以"如果 / 要是……的话，……"形式出现。

"……的话" is used to hypothesize a condition, and the following clause is used to dicate the result. "……的话" is also often preceded by "如果 / 要是" and appears in the form of "如果 / 要是……的话，……".

【……的话，小句】[……的话, Clause]

……的话，	Clause
我们打算在外工作的话，	千万要多想想家中的父母。
如果你不认真准备的话，	可能会考不好。
你要是去中国的话，	你的父母怎么办呢？

练一练

1. 请补全句子。Complete the sentences.

（1）要是_____的话，我马上去报名。

（2）天气太热的话，_____。

（3）如果你不想去的话，_____。

（4）_____的话，我一定去你的生日晚会。

（5）_____的话，我再也不理（lǐ, talk to）你了。

2. 用"……的话，……"谈一谈你的周末计划或者假期计划。Talk about your weekend plans or vacation plans with "……的话，……".

例：要是放假的话，我打算去颐和园看一看。

（1）_____

（2）_____

（3）_____

（4）_____

（5）_____

四、条件复句：只有……，才…… Conditional complex sentence: 只有……, 才……

表示条件唯一。"才"后面的内容要实现，就必须满足"只有"后面的条件，且这个条件往往是唯一的。

Indicating that the condition is an exclusive one. In order to realize what follows "才", the condition following "只有" must be fulfilled, and the condition is often an exclusive one.

【只有 A，才 B】

只有 A，	才 B
只有拿出学生卡，	才能进图书馆。
只有努力学习，	才能取得好成绩。
只有妈妈来了，	才能带走弟弟。

练一练

1. 请补全句子。Complete the sentences.

（1）只有_____，才能考出好成绩。

（2）只有每天锻炼，才_____。

（3）只有_____，才能在中国生活得更好。

（4）只有_____，才能更好地把握自己的命运。

（5）只有我们把自己照顾好了，父母才_____。

2. 请用"只有……，才……"回答问题。Answer the questions with "只有……，才……".

（1）大家要怎么做才可以取得好成绩？
_____

（2）在哪里可以吃到正宗的鱼香肉丝？
_____

（3）你做什么事爸爸妈妈才会满意？
_____

（4）你打算什么时候出国？
_____

18 养儿防老

综合运用 COMPREHENSIVE USE

语音练习 18-5

一、听录音选择正确答案。Listen to the recording and choose the correct answers.

1. A. jiāoyù B. jiàoyù
2. A. kōngcháo B. kōngcáo
3. A. tàitai B. tàitài
4. A. shèhuì B. sèhuì
5. A. gēnběn B. gēngběn
6. A. gǎnkuài B. gǎngkuài
7. A. fàng//xīn B. fànxīn
8. A. fǎnlǎo B. fánglǎo
9. A. chènwéi B. chēngwéi
10. A. xiǎnshì B. xiǎnsì

二、听句子给画线词语标声调。Listen to the sentences and mark the tones of the underlined words.

1. 她们一方面要<u>管</u>孩子的<u>日常</u>生活，一方面还要<u>关注</u>他们的学习<u>情况</u>。
2. 可是成绩高并<u>不代表</u>解决问题的<u>能力</u>就<u>强</u>啊！
3. 越来越多的年轻人为了实现更好的<u>发展</u>，<u>不得不</u>离开<u>故乡</u>，到别的城市或国外去工作。
4. 一方面要<u>适应</u>子女<u>长期</u>不在身边的情况，一方面还要<u>合理地</u>安排退休后的生活。
5. 为了让孩子能好好地<u>工作</u>和生活，很多父母并不会告诉孩子他们遇到的那些<u>麻烦和困难</u>。

三、听一听，读一读。Listen and read.

游子吟	Yóuzǐ Yín
[唐] 孟郊	[Táng] Mèng Jiāo
慈母手中线，游子身上衣。	Címǔ shǒu zhōng xiàn, yóuzǐ shēnshang yī.
临行密密缝，意恐迟迟归。	Lín xíng mìmì féng, yì kǒng chíchí guī.
谁言寸草心，报得三春晖。	Shuí yán cùncǎo xīn, bào dé sān chūn huī.

汉字知识

多音多义字　Heteronymic Characters

汉语中有些字有不同的读音，表示不同的意思，这样的字称为多音多义字。多音多义字的形成有不同的原因。有些字的意思发生了分化，形成了不同读音。例如在"人的后背"中"背"读 bèi，在"背着书包"中"背"读 bēi，意思和用法都不一样。有的是口语和书面语的不同，例如在"薄弱"这个词中，"薄"读 bó，是书面语的读法；在"一张薄纸"中，"薄"读 báo，是口语的读法。有的是简化汉字导致的。例如副词"只 zhǐ"和量词"只（隻）zhī"原来是两个不同的字，简化后都使用"只"这个字形，"只"就有了两个读音。有的是用汉字记录外来词而形成的多音多义现象，例如动词"打"读 dǎ，表示"12个是一打"时，"打"读 dá，来自对英语"dozen"的翻译。

"一打（dá）羽毛球"
"一筒 12 只（zhī）"

In Chinese, some characters have different pronunciations which represent different meanings, known as heteronymic characters. The formation of these characters can be attributed to various reasons: Some characters have undergone a division in meaning, leading to different pronunciations. For example: In "人的后背" (rén de hòubèi), meaning "a person's back", "背" is pronounced as bèi. In "背着书包" (bēizhe shūbāo), meaning "carrying a schoolbag", "背" is pronounced as bēi. Here, both the meaning and usage of "背" differ. Some characters have different pronunciations in spoken and written language. For example: In "薄弱" (bóruò), meaning "weak", "薄" is pronounced as bó, which is the literary reading. In "一张薄纸" (yì zhāng báo zhǐ), meaning "a thin piece of paper", "薄" is pronounced as báo, which is the colloquial reading. Some result from the simplification of Chinese characters. For example: The adverb "只" (zhǐ) and the measure word "只" (zhī, simplified form of "隻") originally are two different characters. After simplification, they both take the form of "只", leading to two pronunciations for this character. Some are heteronymic phenomena that arise from using Chinese characters to transcribe foreign words. For example: The verb "打" (dǎ) is pronounced as dǎ, when it indicates "a dozen", it is pronounced as dá, derived from the English word "dozen".

口语表达训练

一、请三位同学介绍一下他们国家对亲子关系的看法，完成调查表。Ask three of your classmates to describe the views on the parent-child relationship in their country and complete the questionnaire.

同学姓名	国家	对亲子关系的看法

二、你觉得以下行为或观念正确吗？对此你有什么想法？Do you think the following behaviors are correct? What are your ideas on these?

行为或观念	对/错	想法
妈妈说的都是对的，所有的事情都要按照妈妈说的话去做。		
父母身体很好，不需要我关心他们。		
只要有时间，我就愿意回家看看父母。		

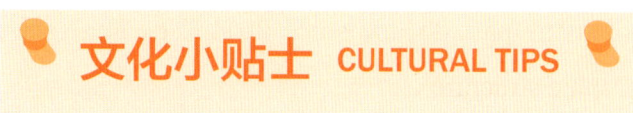

当代中国的人口结构
Demographic Structure of Contemporary China

中国是一个人口基数很大的国家。2023年，中国有14亿多人口，约占世界总人口（约80亿）的17.5%。中国的人口数量与人口结构也在不断地发生变化。最近一次人口普查，即2020年的第七次全国人口普查（"七人普"）对2011—2020年10年间中国的人口变化进行了总结。

"七人普"从6个方面对当代中国自2011年以来10年间的人口结构进行了分析。

一、中国年龄高于65岁的老年人的数量仍在增加，当代中国离"深度老龄化"越来越近。

二、当代中国的新生儿出生数量在减少，少子化趋势增强。现在受教育、社会等方面的影响，很多年轻人选择晚一点儿结婚、晚一点儿生子，甚至部分年轻人选择不结婚。

三、人口性别结构方面，年龄在65岁以下的，女性的数量少于男性的数量，中国社会甚至出现了"剩男"现象，而年龄在65岁及以上的女性的数量多于男性的数量。

四、人口城乡结构方面，近年来中国社会不断发展，中国人的生活水平也不断提高，越来越多的乡村人口加入城市，城镇化水平不断提升。

五、人口学历结构方面，中国很早就有重视教育的传统，过去10年，中国人口的整体文化素质有非常明显的提高。

六、人口民族结构方面，中国是一个多民族国家，有56个民族。近10年来，中国各民族的人口一直在增长。

在各个方面，中国都在不断地发展，人口结构也在不断向更好的方向改变。

China is a country with a very large population base. As of 2023, China has over 1.4 billion people, accounting for approximately 17.5% of the world's total population (around 8 billion). Both the size and structure of China's population are constantly changing. The most recent census, the Seventh National Population Census conducted in 2020, summarized the changes in China's population over the decade from 2011 to 2020.

The Seventh National Population Census analyzed the demographic structure of contemporary China over the past decade since 2011. The analysis covers six aspects of China's current demographic structure:

1. The number of elderly people aged 65 and above continues to increase, bringing contemporary China closer to "deep aging".

2. The number of newborns is decreasing, and the trend of having fewer children is strengthening. Influenced by education, society, etc., many young people are choosing to marry and have children later, and some of them are even choosing not to marry at all.

3. Gender structure: Among those under 65, the number of males is greater than the number of females, leading to the phenomenon of "leftover men" in Chinese society. However, among those aged 65 and above, the number of females is greater than the number of males.

4. Urban-rural structure: With the continuous development of Chinese society, the living standards of the Chinese people have been improving. More and more rural residents are moving to cities, leading to a continuous increase in the level of urbanization.

5. Educational structure: China has a long tradition of valuing education. Over the past decade, the overall cultural quality of the Chinese population has improved significantly.

6. Ethnic structure: China is a multi-ethnic country with 56 ethnic groups. Over the past decade, the population of each ethnic group has been increasing.

In all these aspects, China is continuously developing, and its demographic structure is evolving in a positive direction.

19 叔叔阿姨看上去真精神！
Auntie and uncle look great!

本课学习重点	
话题 Topic	谈人际交往 Talk about interpersonal relationships
重点词 Keywords	终于　一切　看上去　精神　看起来　通过　反正　能够 相当　大大
重点句 Key sentences	1. 习惯是习惯了，就是有时会想家。 2. 叔叔阿姨看上去真精神！ 3. 他们每天不是去唱京剧就是去跳广场舞，身体基本没大毛病。 4. 你们家这套房子不仅阳光好，布置得还特别漂亮。 5. 想是想，不过我并不觉得难过。
语法 Grammar	1. 转折复句：……是……，就是/不过…… 　　Adversative complex sentence 2. 选择复句：不是A，就是B 　　Alternative complex sentence 3. 递进复句：不仅……，还…… 　　Progressive complex sentence
汉字知识 Knowledge of Chinese characters	同音字 Homophonous Characters
文化小贴士 Cultural tips	岁寒三友 Three Friends of Winter

19 叔叔阿姨看上去真精神！

热 身 WARM-UP

说一说，在你们国家去别人家做客会带什么礼物？见了面要说什么呢？ What gifts do you bring when visiting someone in your country? What do you say when you meet?

果汁　红酒　蛋糕　……

您好！_____
_____
_____

课 文 TEXT

课文 1　🎧 19-1

听前问题：安琪来中国多久了？

（敲门声）

李娜：来了！

（李娜开门）

安　　琪：李娜，你好！

李　　娜：欢迎！快请进！

　　　　　来，先换双拖鞋吧！

安　　琪：谢谢！

李　　娜：不客气。安琪，这是我爱人张林，这两位是我父亲和母亲。

安　　琪：叔叔阿姨好！张林你好！我叫安琪。

安琪母亲：我们早就听说你啦！这次终于见到了。别站着了，赶紧请坐吧！

安　　琪：谢谢阿姨。

张　　林：想喝点儿什么？红茶还是果汁？

安　　琪：随便，什么都行。我给你们带了一瓶法国红酒。

安琪父亲：谢谢你啊！

安　　琪：不谢，只是一个小礼物，希望你们喜欢。

安琪母亲：来中国多久了？

安　　琪：我是年初来的，到明年一月份就来了整一年了。

安琪父亲：习惯这里的一切了吗？

安　　琪：习惯是习惯了，就是有时会想家。

李　　娜：想家的时候就来我家吧！我们给你做又营养又好吃的东北菜。

安　　琪：好。叔叔阿姨看上去真精神！

李　　娜：他们每天不是去唱京剧就是去跳广场舞，身体基本没大毛病。

安　　琪：身体好是最幸运的事情。李娜，你们家这套房子不仅阳光好，布置得还特别漂亮。

李　　娜：这个房子最大的优点就是朝南，阳光好。房间都是我妈布置的。我们平时工作忙，没时间弄。

安　　琪：这套房子看起来真不错。

19 叔叔阿姨看上去真精神！

李　　娜：房子好是好，不过缺点是房租太贵了。

安琪母亲：来，咱们吃饭了。

课堂练习

1. 根据课文内容回答问题。Answer the questions based on the text.
   （1）安琪给李娜的父母带了什么礼物？
   （2）李娜的父母身体好吗？看上去怎么样？他们每天都做什么？
   （3）安琪觉得李娜家的房子怎么样？

2. 分角色表演课文。Act out the text in roles.

3. 如果你是课文中的安琪，请根据课文内容向大家介绍一下你去李娜家都聊了什么。（可参考给出的词语和句型）If you were Angie in the text, please tell us what you talked about when you went to Li Na's house based on the text. (You can refer to the words and sentence patterns given)

> 红酒　礼物　年初　想家　精神　房子　房租
> 不是……，就是……　不仅……，还……

词语1 🎧 19-2

	词语	拼音	词性	英文释义
1.	欢迎	huānyíng	动词	welcome
2.	请进	qǐng jìn		please come in
3.	双	shuāng	量词	pair
4.	拖鞋	tuōxié	名词	slippers
5.	爱人	àiren	名词	my love; sweetheart; spouse
6.	父亲	fùqīn	名词	father
7.	母亲	mǔqīn	名词	mother

8. 阿姨	āyí	名词	auntie
9. 啦	la	助词	combination of 了 and 啊, expressing exclamation, interrogation, etc.
10. 终于	zhōngyú	副词	finally; eventually; in the end
11. 见到	jiàndào		meet
12. 请坐	qǐng zuò		please take a seat
13. 红茶	hóngchá	名词	black tea
14. 果汁	guǒzhī	名词	juice
15. 随便	suíbiàn	动词	do at one's convenience
16. 红酒	hóngjiǔ	名词	red wine
17. 年初	niánchū	名词	beginning of the year
18. 明年	míngnián	名词	next year
19. 月份	yuèfèn	名词	month
20. 整	zhěng	形容词	whole; complete
21. 一切	yíqiè	代词	everything; all
22. 有时	yǒushí	副词	sometimes
23. 东北菜	dōngběicài	名词	Northeastern Chinese cuisine
24. 看上去	kàn shàngqù		it seems
25. 精神	jīngshen	形容词、名词	energetic; energy
26. 跳舞	tiào//wǔ	动词	dance
27. 广场	guǎngchǎng	名词	square
28. 基本	jīběn	副词、形容词	almost; by and large; on the whole; basic
29. 毛病	máobìng	名词	health problem; disease
30. 幸运	xìngyùn	形容词	lucky; fortunate
31. 套	tào	量词	used of series/sets of things
32. 不仅	bùjǐn	连词	not only
33. 阳光	yángguāng	名词	sunshine

34. 优点	yōudiǎn	名词	advantage
35. 看起来	kàn qǐlái		it looks
36. 缺点	quēdiǎn	名词	disadvantage
37. 房租	fángzū	名词	rent

专有名词

张林　　　　　　Zhāng Lín　　　　　　Zhang Lin

重点词

终于

（1）大雨下了三天三夜，终于停了。
（2）你终于来了，我们等你一个小时了。
（3）用了一个多月时间，我终于看完了这本书。

一切

（1）这一切都是他做的吗？
（2）我刚到北京，我还不习惯这里的一切呢。
（3）我还记得他为我提供的一切帮助。

看上去

（1）这双拖鞋看上去不错。
（2）这家的北京小吃看上去很好吃。
（3）你看上去很累，怎么了？

精神

（1）你昨晚不是一点才睡吗？怎么看起来这么精神？

（2）刚喝完一杯咖啡，我现在精神得很。

（3）听说明天要考试，班上的同学马上都精神了。

看起来

（1）看起来要下雨了，你带伞了吗？

（2）乔治看起来并不知道你要回国这件事情。

（3）今天老师看起来很不开心。

练一练

选词填空。Fill in the blanks with the given words.

> 一切　优点　看上去　欢迎　精神　幸运　终于　看起来

（1）已经八点多了，_____她今天不会来了。

（2）我为什么和他分手？他说如果我爱他，就应该爱他的_____。

（3）爸爸今天_____不太高兴，是不是因为工作的事情？

（4）出去旅游总是能收到一条"_____你到……来！"的短信。

（5）你对我太好了，认识你是我的_____！

（6）我是一个普通人，有很多缺点，但我也不是没有_____呀！

（7）春节到了，全家人_____又可以见面了。

（8）昨晚睡太晚了，今天上班没有_____。

课文 2 🎧 19-3

听前问题:"我"的男房东和"我"有什么共同的爱好?

我是一名意大利留学生,通过朋友介绍,找到了一个寄宿家庭。房东是一对中年夫妻,人很热情,对我也非常友好。不仅全年的房租给我打了九折,还常陪我去逛街,有时也会带我去看电影、听音乐会。

男主人和我都是球迷。我俩在一起不是看足球、打网球,就是一整天都在说"球",反正我们相处得非常不错。上个月他还送给我一双球鞋呢!当然,有时我也会送给他们一些我从意大利带来的小礼物。能够碰到这么好的房东,我觉得自己是相当幸运的。

出国前,我的汉语水平不高,口语也不怎么样,但是自从和他们住在一起以后,我的汉语水平就大大提高了,因为平时我们之间只用中文交流。现在走在大街上,我终于敢跟中国人说话了。

在国外留学,我也常想念父母。想是想,不过我并不觉得难过。因为身边有那么多热情友好的中国朋友,让我觉得自己的留学生活挺不错的。

课堂练习

1. 根据课文内容回答问题。Answer the questions based on the text.
   (1)"我"怎么找到寄宿家庭的?
   (2)"我"和男主人关系怎么样?我们都一起做什么?
   (3)"我"的汉语水平以前怎么样?现在呢?为什么会有这样的变化?

2. 根据课文内容填空,并复述课文。Fill in the blanks based on the text and retell it.
   我是_____意大利留学生。我住在_____里,房东是一对_____夫妻,人很热情,对我也非常友好。房东不仅给我的_____打了九折,还常常陪我_____,有时我们也去_____。男主人和我都是_____，我们_____得非常不错，能够_____这么好的房东，我觉得自己是_____的。

_____前，我的汉语程度_____，口语也_____，但是自从和他们_____以后，我的汉语水平_____，因为平时我们之间只用中文_____。现在走在_____，我终于敢跟_____说话了。

虽然我常常想念父母，但是我并不觉得_____，因为身边有非常多热情友好的中国朋友，让我觉得自己的_____挺不错的。

3. 选用下列提示词语和句型，说说你理想中的留学生活是什么样的。
Choose the following prompt words and sentence patterns to describe what your ideal life of studying abroad would be like.

寄宿　主人　相处　整天　程度　难过　反正　相当
大大　不仅……，还……　……是……，不过……

词语2 🎧 19-4

词语	拼音	词性	英文释义
1. 名	míng	量词	used of persons
2. 通过	tōngguò	介词、动词	by; through; pass
3. 找到	zhǎodào		find
4. 寄宿	jìsù	动词	(of students) board
5. 房东	fángdōng	名词	landlord; landlady; house owner; host family
6. 对	duì	量词	pair; couple
7. 中年	zhōngnián	名词	middle age
8. 全年	quánnián	名词	whole year
9. 主人	zhǔrén	名词	host; owner

10. 球迷	qiúmí	名词	(ball game) fan
11. 足球	zúqiú	名词	soccer; football
12. 整天	zhěngtiān	名词	all day long
13. 反正	fǎnzhèng	副词	anyway
14. 相处	xiāngchǔ	动词	get along with
15. 球鞋	qiúxié	名词	sneakers; gym shoes
16. 能够	nénggòu	动词	can; be able to
17. 碰到	pèngdào		come across; meet
18. 相当	xiāngdāng	副词	quite; considerably
19. 程度	chéngdù	名词	level; degree
20. 口语	kǒuyǔ	名词	spoken language
21. 大大	dàdà	副词	greatly

专有名词

| 意大利 | Yìdàlì | | Italy |

重点词

通过

（1）通过这次活动，我认识了很多新朋友。
（2）书上说，只要通过六个人，就可以找到所有想找的人。
（3）你可以通过发邮件的方式交作业。

反正

（1）反正是我自己的事情，你不用管。
（2）你不要再说了，反正我不同意你这么做。
（3）你去不去医院看大卫都行，反正玛丽已经过去了。

能够

（1）妈妈常说，我们家只有我姐姐能够上大学。

（2）我们的愿望一定能够实现。

（3）明天的聚会能不能够带小孩儿去？

相当

（1）今天的天气相当好啊！我们一起出去玩儿吧。

（2）我相当喜欢这里，因为这里可以吃到好多小吃。

（3）我和他的汉语水平相当。

大大

（1）现在，乔治的中文有了大大的进步。

（2）快考试了，最近的作业量大大地多了。

（3）夏天，宿舍里安装了新空调，房间里的温度大大降低了。

练一练

选词填空。Fill in the blanks with the given words.

能够　相处　相当　通过　整天　反正　大大　碰到

（1）_____这几天的努力，我的考试取得了好成绩。

（2）你_____看到自己的缺点，已经很好了。

（3）这个小孩儿太精神了，_____都让我陪她玩儿。

（4）昨天在学校，我_____了一位老同学。

（5）现在音乐会的票是_____贵，而且还很难买到。

（6）在我留学的日子里，我常常想起和国内的朋友们一起_____的日子。

（7）你别说了，_____我不想跟你一起住。

（8）来到中国以后，我的汉语水平也_____地提高了。

语法 GRAMMAR

一、转折复句：……是……，就是 / 不过…… Adversative complex sentence: ……是……，就是 / 不过……

"……是……，就是 / 不过……" 用于承认前一小句的事实，在 "就是 / 不过" 后提出另一个事实或者观点。

"……是……，就是 / 不过……" is used to admit the fact in the preceding clause and bring up another fact or viewpoint after "就是 / 不过".

【A 是 A，就是 / 不过 B。】

A 是 A，	就是 / 不过 B。
好吃是好吃，	就是太贵了。
你的想法好是好，	不过我还是很担心。
网购方便是方便，	就是 / 不过还得等几天才能收到货。

练一练

1. 关于下面这些话题，你有什么想法吗？请用 "……是……，就是 / 不过……" 说说你的观点。Do you have any thoughts on the following topics? Talk about your opinions with "……是……，就是 / 不过……".

    （1）现在的宿舍 _____
    （2）你的同屋 _____
    （3）鱼香肉丝 _____
    （4）你的家乡 _____
    （5）坐火车 _____

2. 请用 "……是……，就是 / 不过……" 改写句子。Rewrite the following sentences with "……是……，就是 / 不过……".

    （1）虽然我的身体挺好的，但是最近经常感冒。

    _____

（2）虽然过节的时候很热闹，但是要花很多钱。

（3）虽然我男朋友对我不错，但是他工作太忙了，没有时间陪我。

（4）虽然她唱歌很好听，但是声音太小了。

（5）虽然你的工资挺高的，但是天天加班，太累了。

（6）虽然北京工作机会多，但是房价比工资高多了。

二、选择复句：不是 A，就是 B Alternative complex sentence: 不是 A, 就是 B

【不是 A，就是 B】表示存在 A、B 两种情况，但两种情况只能或必须选择一项。
Indicating that there are two situations, A and B, but only one of the two situations may or must be chosen.

（1）她每天不是去跳广场舞，就是去唱 KTV，每天都很开心。

（2）他是个大忙人，不是他请别人吃饭，就是别人请他吃饭。

（3）我特别喜欢旅游，春节假期不是去北方，就是去南方。

（4）你真不会买衣服，买的衣服不是大了，就是小了。

练一练

1. 你和你的朋友们找工作时觉得哪些条件很重要？用"不是……，就是……"讨论一下。What conditions matter to you and your friends when looking for a job? Discuss it with "不是……，就是……".

> 同事友好　公司离家近　工资高　老板好　工作轻松　不加班
> 自由　假期多　……

找工作时最看重的两个条件	
工资高	老板好

2. 请用"不是……，就是……"回答问题。Answer the questions with "不是……，就是……".

（1）A：今晚你要做什么？

　　　B：_____。

（2）A：这个月天气不太好啊？

　　　B：_____。

（3）A：你最近怎么买这么多东西？

　　　B：_____。

（4）A：你们家平时谁做饭啊？

　　　B：_____。

（5）A：你知道什么时候放假吗？

　　　B：_____。

三、递进复句：**不仅……，还……**　Progressive complex sentence: 不仅……，还……

"不仅……，还……"连接具有递进关系的两个分句。"不仅"表示"不但"的意思，"还"表示"而且"的意思，连接的分句都表示进一步说明或补充前一分句的内容。

"不仅……，还……" joins two clauses that have a progressive relationship. "不仅" means "not only" and "还" means "and", and the joined clause means further elaboration or supplementation of the preceding clause.

（1）我觉得你们的房间不仅阳光好，布置得还特别漂亮。

（2）我们不仅要好好学习，还要多参加活动。

（3）她不仅长得好看，还很聪明。

练一练

1. 给词语选择合适的位置。Choose the appropriate positions for the words.

   （1）A 明天的会议 B 你 C 要参加，还要 D 早点儿来。（不仅）

   （2）A 老师 B 不仅 C 同意了，D 是很高兴地同意的。（还）

   （3）你的房子不仅 A 位置 B 好，C 房租 D 很便宜。（还）

   （4）A 我们宿舍 B 很干净，C 还很 D 安静。（不仅）

2. 用"不仅……，还……"改写句子。Rewrite the sentences with "不仅……，还……".

   （1）我喜欢跳舞。我喜欢唱歌。
   _____

   （2）他会说法语。她说法语说得很好。
   _____

   （3）她很高。她身材很好。
   _____

   （4）我学习汉语。我学习英语。
   _____

   （5）这件衣服很好看。这件衣服很便宜。
   _____

综合运用 COMPREHENSIVE USE

 语音练习 🎧 19-5

一、听录音选择正确答案。Listen to the recording and choose the correct answers.

1. A. huānyíng   B. huānlíng   2. A. jīngshén   B. jīngshen
3. A. yǒudiǎnr   B. yōudiǎn   4. A. jìsù   B. jīsù
5. A. tōngguò   B. dōngguò   6. A. xiāngchǔ   B. xiàngchù

19 叔叔阿姨看上去真精神！

7. A. chéngdù　　B. chéngtù　　8. A. zhōngnián　　B. zhōnglián

9. A. qiúxié　　B. qiūxié　　10. A. zhěngtiān　　B. zěngtiān

二、听句子给画线词语标声调。Listen to the sentences and mark the tones of the underlined words.

1. 习惯这里的<u>一切</u>了吗？
2. 他们每天不是去唱京剧就是去<u>跳广场舞</u>。
3. 这是我<u>爱人</u>张林，这两位是我<u>父亲</u>和<u>母亲</u>。
4. 有时我也会送给他们一些我从<u>意大利</u>带来的小礼物。
5. 我的汉语水平就<u>大大</u>提高了，因为平时我们之间只用中文<u>交流</u>。

三、听一听，读一读。Listen and read.

望洞庭

〔唐〕 刘禹锡

湖光秋月两相和，潭面无风镜未磨。

遥望洞庭山水翠，白银盘里一青螺。

Wàng Dòngtíng

[Táng]　Liú Yǔxī

Húguāng qiūyuè liǎng xiāng hé, tánmiàn wú fēng jìng wèi mó.

Yáowàng dòngtíng shānshuǐ cuì, báiyínpán li yì qīngluó.

汉字知识

同音字　Homophonous Characters

汉语音节结构简单，不带声调的音节约有400个，带有特定声调的音节约有1300个，常用汉字有三四千个，如果不带声调，平均每个音节要承载7~8个汉字。例如读"shì"的常用字有"是、事、试、士、示、室、市、世、视"等。但是事实上每个音节承载的汉字数量并不是平均分配的，有的音节对应的只有一个汉字，例如：bái 白，

dà 大, dǎ 打, ròu 肉, shǎo 少, shuō 说, tuǐ 腿, zǒu 走, wài 外, yuǎn 远, zěn 怎。在最常用的2500个汉字中，同音字最多的是"shì"，共19个字；其次是"yì"，有16个字；再其次是"xī"，有14个字。尽管汉语中同音字数量很多，但是汉语的词大多数是双音节的，在组成词之后，同音词的现象就大大减少了。例如"士"和"市"是同音字，但是它们组成的词"护士""超市"却不是同音词。另外，同音汉字并不是同形汉字，因此同音现象并不会对阅读造成什么影响。

The structure of Chinese syllables is simple. There are approximately 400 syllables without tones, and about 1,300 syllables with specific tones. There are around 3,000 to 4,000 commonly used Chinese characters. If tones are not considered, each syllable would, on average, represent 7 to 8 characters. For example, the syllable "shì" corresponds to commonly used characters such as 是 (is), 事 (matter), 试 (test), 士 (scholar), 示 (show), 室 (room), 市 (city), 世 (world), 视 (vision), etc. However, in reality, the number of characters represented by each syllable is not evenly distributed. Some syllables correspond to only one character respectively, for instance, bái 白 (white), dà 大 (big), dǎ 打 (hit), ròu 肉 (meat), shǎo 少 (few), shuō 说 (say), tuǐ 腿 (leg), zǒu 走 (walk), wài 外 (outside), yuǎn 远 (far) and zěn 怎 (how).

Among the 2,500 most commonly used characters, the syllable with the most homophonous characters is "shì", with 19 characters. The next is "yì", with 16 characters, followed by "xī", with 14 characters. Despite the large number of homophonous characters in Chinese, most Chinese words are disyllabic, which greatly reduces the occurrence of homophones. For example, "士" (scholar) and "市" (city) are homophonous characters, but the words they form, such as "护士" (nurse) and "超市" (supermarket), are not homophones. Additionally, homophonous characters are not homographic characters, so the phenomenon of homophony does not affect reading significantly.

19 叔叔阿姨看上去真精神！

> 口语表达训练

一、问一问你的同学们上一次去别人家是什么时候。在他们国家，去别人家应该带什么礼物？有什么东西是不可以送的吗？完成调查表。Ask your classmates when was the last time they went to someone else's house. What should one bring with as the visiting gift in their country? Is there anything one shouldn't give as a gift? Complete the questionnaire.

姓名	时间	可以送的礼物	不可以送的礼物

二、你和你的同屋或同学相处得怎么样？你们有什么共同的爱好吗？你觉得他或她有什么优点，有什么缺点？完成调查表。How do you get along with your roommate or classmates? Do you have any hobbies in common? What do you think are their strengths and weaknesses? Complete the questionnaire.

我的同屋/同学				
同屋/同学的名字	你们的关系怎么样？	你们共同的爱好是什么？	他/她的优点	他/她的缺点

文化小贴士 CULTURAL TIPS

岁寒三友
Three Friends of Winter

"岁寒"的意思是天气寒冷的时候,一般指冬天。岁寒三友指的是松树、竹子和梅花三种植物。

中国古代的知识分子喜欢将大自然的事物和人的品质结合在一起,通过这种方式表达自己的理想和追求。

他们认为松树一年四季常绿,再冷的冬天也无法打败松树,而且松树的寿命极长,能成活多年,因此松树象征着倔强、不服输、长寿。

竹子除了一年常绿以外,还因为笔直的竹节被古人认为是正直的代表。竹子内部是空心的,"空"就是"不实","不实"又可以说成"虚";同时,竹子遇风不倒,还能做成各种用品,因此竹子也代表虚心有礼。总的来说,竹子是中国古代君子的形象。

梅花只在万物沉睡的冬天盛开,虽然周围的环境非常寒冷,但梅花依然在此时开放,表现出梅花完全不害怕周围环境的变化,依然要和寒冷抗争的勇敢精神。

除了"岁寒三友",中国人还会把道德品质、理想信念等寄寓在其他植物身上,如:荷代表着出淤泥而不染,桃李代表学生,杏代表讲坛。

"岁寒" means a time of cold weather, generally referring to winter. The phrase "岁寒三友" (Three Friends of Winter) refers to three plants, namely the pine tree, the bamboo, and the plum blossom.

In ancient China, intellectuals liked to link things in nature with human qualities to express their ideals and aspirations.

They think the pine tree remains green throughout the year, even the coldest winter cannot defeat it. Besides, it has a long lifespan and can survive for many years. Therefore, it symbolizes resilience, perseverance, and longevity.

Bamboo is not only evergreen, but also regarded as a representative of integrity by the ancients because of its straight bamboo joints. Bamboo is hollow inside, "hollow" means "insubstantial", "insubstantial" can be interpreted as "modest"; meanwhile, bamboo does not fall down in the wind and can be made into various products. Therefore, bamboo also represents modesty and courtesy. In general, bamboo is the image of the ancient Chinese gentleman.

The plum blossom only blooms in the coldest part of winter when other plants are dormant. Despite the harsh environment, the plum blossom still blooms, demonstrating its fearlessness of changes in its surroundings and determination to thrive in adversity.

Beyond the "Three Friends of Winter", the Chinese people also attribute moral qualities and ideals to other plants. For example, The lotus (荷) represents purity and rising above the mire, the peach and plum trees (桃李) symbolize students, the apricot tree (杏) represents the lectern or platform for teaching.

20 他被一辆出租车撞了
He was hit by a cab

本课学习重点

话题 Topic	谈论一件倒霉事 Talk about a piece of bad luck
重点词 Keywords	结果　赶　直接　等到　全部　简直　突然　必须　白　够
重点句 Key sentences	1. 昨天夜里他被一辆出租车撞了。 2. 左腿受伤，自行车也叫汽车撞坏了。 3. 头被撞破了的话，得赶紧去医院打一种专门的针。 4. 不早不晚，路上又遇到了大雨。
语法 Grammar	1. 被动句1：主语＋被／叫／让＋宾语＋动词（短语）＋其他成分 　　Passive sentence I 2. 被动句2：主语＋被＋动词＋其他成分 　　Passive sentence II
汉字知识 Knowledge of Chinese characters	异体字 Variant Characters in Chinese
文化小贴士 Cultural tips	塞翁失马 A Blessing in Disguise

20 他被一辆出租车撞了

热身 WARM-UP

说一说：他们怎么了？你觉得他们为什么会这样？ Talk about how they feel like and what happened to them.

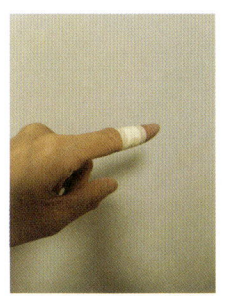　　　　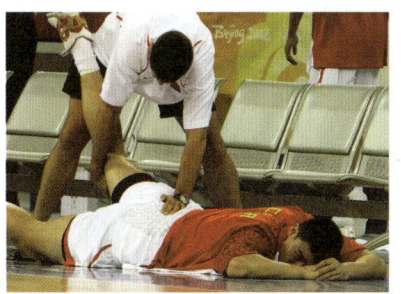

_____　　_____

课文 TEXT

课文 1　🎧 20-1

听前问题：王东的爸爸怎么了？

乔治：喂，王东，我们下午几点练球？

王东：我着急看我爸，今天咱们就先不练球了啊！

乔治：叔叔怎么了？

王东：昨天夜里他被一辆出租车撞了。左腿受伤，自行车也叫汽车撞坏了。

乔治：太可怕了！怎么会发生这样的事？

王东：主要是那段路有点儿黑，路灯也不太亮，出租车司机对路并不太熟，结果就出现了事故。

乔治：那现在叔叔怎么样了？

王东：昨天夜里就住院了。今天上午要被送去进行全身检查。早上接到我妈的电话，我就赶紧往医院赶。

乔治：是司机直接把叔叔送到医院的吗？

王东：对。发生事故后，他就马上送我爸去医院了。

乔治：那叔叔什么时候才能出院呢？

王东：要等到检查结果出来了才知道。

乔治：叔叔的身体什么时候才能全部好了呢？

王东：大概要超过三个月了。我现在快到医院了，咱们有空儿再聊吧！

乔治：好，请代我向叔叔问好！希望他早点儿出院。

课堂练习

1. 根据课文内容回答问题。Answer the questions based on the text.

   （1）乔治为什么给王东打电话？

   （2）王东的爸爸哪条腿受伤了？他住院了吗？

   （3）王东的爸爸大概什么时候身体才能全部好了呢？

2. 分角色表演课文。Act out the text in roles.

3. 如果你是课文中的王东，请根据课文内容向乔治介绍你爸爸是怎么发生的事故。（可参考给出的词语和句型）If you were Wang Dong in the text, please tell George how your father had the accident based on the text. (You can refer to the words and sentence pattern given)

   出租车　自行车　黑　路灯　司机　事故　坏　结果
   被……撞了　腿

词语 1 🎧 20-2

词语	拼音	词性	英文释义
1. 夜里	yèli	名词	night
2. 被	bèi	介词	used in a passive sentence to introduce the agent/doer
3. 辆	liàng	量词	used with vehicles
4. 出租车	chūzūchē	名词	taxi; cab
5. 撞	zhuàng	动词	bump against
6. 腿	tuǐ	名词	leg
7. 受伤	shòu//shāng	动词	get injured
8. 自行车	zìxíngchē	名词	bicycle
9. 叫	jiào	介词	used to introduce the doer of an action
10. 可怕	kěpà	形容词	terrible
11. 发生	fāshēng	动词	happen; occur
12. 黑	hēi	形容词	dark
13. 路灯	lùdēng	名词	street lamp
14. 亮	liàng	形容词、动词	bright; shine
15. 司机	sījī	名词	driver
16. 熟	shú	形容词	familiar
17. 结果	jiéguǒ	连词、名词	thus; consequence
18. 出现	chūxiàn	动词	appear; occur
19. 事故	shìgù	名词	accident
20. 住院	zhù//yuàn	动词	be in hospital; be hospitalized
21. 接到	jiēdào		hear from; receive
22. 赶	gǎn	动词	hurry; rush for
23. 直接	zhíjiē	形容词	immediate; direct
24. 送到	sòngdào		send to

25. 出院	chū//yuàn	动词	be discharged; leave hospital
26. 等到	děngdào	介词	until
27. 全部	quánbù	名词	whole; all
28. 超过	chāoguò	动词	be over; exceed
29. 代	dài	动词、名词	act for; generation
30. 问好	wèn//hǎo	动词	send one's regards to

重点词

结果

（1）我妈妈对这条路不太熟，结果走错了路，迟到了二十分钟。

（2）李娜为了减肥每天都跑步，结果瘦了二十斤。

（3）如果你想做好一件事，就不要担心结果。

赶

（1）接到妈妈的电话，我马上往家赶。

（2）等到我赶过去时，爸爸已经不在公司了。

（3）已经八点多了，现在出发不知道还能不能赶上飞机。

直接

（1）中午下课后，你直接去食堂吃饭了吗？

（2）明天我们打算直接从家出发去看电影。

（3）她这个人说话总是不那么直接，让人有时不知道她的实际想法是什么。

20 他被一辆出租车撞了

等到

（1）等到下周，天气就会慢慢变好的。

（2）等到考试结束，我们就可以好好休息一下了。

（3）等到姐姐回来了，我和妈妈打算和她一起去公园走走。

全部

（1）妈妈一直认为孩子就是她的全部。

（2）等到弟弟做完了全部作业以后，我们就可以一起去打篮球了。

（3）这本书我已经全部看完了。

练一练

选词填空。Fill in the blanks with the given words.

段　赶　直接　事故　等到　发生　全部　撞　可怕　结果

（1）出租车司机开得太快了，结果就发生了_____。

（2）李叔叔昨天被车_____了，我们一起去看看他吧！

（3）你不用问别人了，我可以_____告诉你答案。

（4）今年家里_____了太多的事，他好像变了一个人。

（5）这_____路的风景好美，我特别喜欢看那些绿色的树。

（6）我们太幸运了！终于_____上今天的最后一趟公交车了。

（7）王老师，我们今天能知道考试的_____吗？

（8）小时候，我一直觉得狼（láng, wolf）是一种_____的动物（dòngwù, animal）。

（9）_____天亮了，咱们就出发。

（10）我把_____的钱都给你，请你帮帮我吧！

课文 2   🎧 20-3

听前问题：为什么我的头流血了？

今天，我的运气简直太差了。上午，我打算去自由市场买菜。在路上，我一边走，一边看手机。下台阶时，突然不小心摔了下去。当时头疼极了，摸了一下，发现头流血了。我觉得自己必须马上去医院看看，因为从小妈妈就告诉过我，头被撞破了的话，得赶紧去医院打一种专门的针。不打的话，可能生命都会有危险。

等我到了离我家最近的一家小诊所，大夫告诉我他们那里打不了，我得去医院才行。没办法，白去了，只好又去医院。

不早不晚，路上又遇到了大雨。出门时，我根本没带伞，因此又被淋成了"落汤鸡"。终于到了医院，打针的费用不多不少正好二百块钱。等到交费的时候，才发现自己没带钱包，手机里的钱也不够，又白来了！你说我这一天倒霉不倒霉？

课堂练习

1. 根据课文内容回答问题。Answer the questions based on the text.

   （1）为什么"我"要去打针？
   （2）为什么说去小诊所白去了？
   （3）最后在医院"我"打针了吗？为什么？

2. 根据课文内容填空，并复述课文。Fill in the blanks based on the text and retell it.

   今天，我的运气简直_____。上午，我打算去_____买菜。在路上，我一边走，一边_____。下台阶时，突然不小心_____。当时头_____，摸了一下，发现头_____了。我觉得自己必须马上去医院看看，因为从小妈妈就告诉过我，头被_____的话，得赶紧去医院打一种_____的针。不打的话，可能生命都会_____。

等我到了离我家最近的一家_____，大夫告诉我他们那里_____，我得去医院才行。没办法，白去了，只好又去_____。

不早不晚，路上_____。出门时，我根本_____，因此又被淋成了"_____"。终于到了医院，打针的费用_____正好二百块钱。等到交费的时候，才发现自己没带钱包，手机里的钱也_____，又白来了！你说我这一天倒霉不倒霉？

3. 选用下列提示词语，介绍你的一次倒霉的经历。Choose the following prompt words to describe one of your bad luck experiences.

> 运气　倒霉　不早不晚　突然　必须　白（副词）　够

词语2　🎧 20-4

	词语	拼音	词性	英文释义
1.	运气	yùnqi	名词	luck
2.	简直	jiǎnzhí	副词	simply; literally
3.	自由	zìyóu	形容词、名词	free; freedom
4.	市场	shìchǎng	名词	market
5.	路上	lùshang	名词	way
6.	台阶	táijiē	名词	stairs; steps
7.	时	shí	名词	time
8.	突然	tūrán	形容词	sudden; unexpected; out of the blue
9.	摔	shuāi	动词	fall; lose one's balance
10.	摸	mō	动词	touch
11.	流	liú	动词	flow; stream
12.	血	xiě	名词	blood
13.	必须	bìxū	副词	must; have to

14. 破	pò	形容词	broken
15. 打针	dǎ//zhēn	动词	get/take an injection
16. 生命	shēngmìng	名词	life
17. 危险	wēixiǎn	名词、形容词	danger; dangerous
18. 离	lí	动词	be away from
19. 诊所	zhěnsuǒ	名词	clinic
20. 白	bái	副词	for nothing
21. 淋	lín	动词	drench
22. 落汤鸡	luòtāngjī	名词	someone who is soaked through
23. 费用	fèiyong	名词	cost; expense; charge
24. 交费	jiāofèi	动词	pay fees/charges/rates
25. 钱包	qiánbāo	名词	wallet
26. 够	gòu	动词、副词	be enough; enough
27. 倒霉	dǎo//méi	动词	out of luck

重点词

简直

（1）今天的这场音乐会简直棒极了。

（2）你考了99分，妈妈简直太开心了。

（3）今天我学习了一天的中文，简直累死了。

突然

（1）早上还是晴天，中午就突然开始下大雨了。

（2）我正在家里看电视，突然有人打来了电话。

（3）昨天我还和山本一起吃晚饭，今早他就回国了，这也太突然了。

20 他被一辆出租车撞了

必须

（1）为了成功，我们必须努力工作。

（2）我们必须马上出发，现在已经迟到了。

（3）老师说："明天上课之前，大家必须把作业交上来。"

白

（1）肚子特别饿，到了食堂才发现没有带钱，白来了。

（2）老师说这个作业我们可以不写，昨天白写了。

（3）啊！我的书找到了，白买了一本新的。

够

（1）我们两个人已经点了四个菜了，够吃了。

（2）妈妈，书架太高了，我够不到那本书。

（3）你学习还是不够努力，所以这次考试考得不太好。

练一练

选词填空。Fill in the blanks with the given words.

简直　突然　淋　够　白　危险　倒霉　必须

（1）好大的雨，我们可能要被_____成落汤鸡了。

（2）昨天我写作业写到晚上十二点，可是早上忘记带了，真_____。

（3）开车的时候打电话是很_____的。

（4）这位新老师讲课的声音_____太小了，我坐在教室后边根本听不见。

（5）今天哈尔滨的气温是-25℃，真_____冷的。

（6）今天早上，有一辆车_____撞了过来。

（7）过马路的时候，_____看红绿灯。

（8）我们的作业不是这个，你_____写了，下次一定要好好听课呀。

语 法 GRAMMAR

一、被动句 1 Passive sentence I

在汉语中可以用带"被"的句子表达被动含义,主要用来表示一个受事者受到某种动作行为的影响而有所改变。其结构为"主语+被/叫/让+宾语+动词+其他成分"。其中主语一般是动作的接受者,宾语一般是动作的发出者。"被"字后面的宾语可以省略,"叫"和"让"后面必须有宾语。

In Chinese, passive meaning can be expressed by sentences with "被", mainly used to indicate that a recipient changes under the influence of an action or behavior. The structure is "subject + 被/叫/让 + object + verb + other components". The subject is usually the receiver of the action, and the object is usually the doer/agent of the action. The object after "被" can be omitted, while that after "叫" and "让" cannot.

主语	被/叫/让	宾语	动词(短语)	其他成分
他	被	母亲	影响	了。
树叶	被	大风	吹飞	了。
苹果	让	妹妹	吃完	了。
我的汉语书	叫	谁	拿走	了?

注意,否定副词和能愿动词等应该放在"被"的前边,例如:

Note that negative adverbs and modal verbs should be placed before "被". For example:

(1)这只可爱的小猫还没有被买走。

(2)如果手机不被妈妈发现,你就可以再玩儿30分钟。

(3)他能被大学录取(lùqǔ, admit),是因为他的成绩很优秀。

(4)这位病人要被120送到医院去了。

20 他被一辆出租车撞了

练一练

1. 根据提示词用"被动句"完成对话。Complete the conversations with the passive sentence based on the prompt words.

   （1）A：你的雨伞呢？

   B：_____。（拿）

   （2）A：你怎么没用昨天新买的手机？

   B：_____。（摔）

   （3）A：我刚买的蛋糕呢？

   B：_____。（吃）

   （4）A：他今天怎么没来上课？

   B：_____。（撞）

2. 用"主语＋被/叫/让＋宾语＋动词＋其他成分"描述图片。Describe the pictures with "subject ＋ 被/叫/让 ＋ object ＋ verb ＋ other components".

   A：丽丽，可以_____吗？我想玩儿一会儿游戏。

   B：我的 iPad _____。（被＋摔）

   A：_____？（让＋谁）

   B：_____。（叫＋人）

   A：那现在怎么办？

   B：_____。（让＋人）

二、被动句 2 Passive sentence II

在被动句中，有时做事的人并不出现，用来强调结果，此时句子中的"被"不能用"让"和"叫"替换。

In passive sentences, sometimes the doer is absent to emphasize the result, in which case the character "被" cannot be replaced by "让" or "叫".

主语	被	动词	其他成分
她	被	看见	了。
他	被	打	了。
那本汉语书	被	借	走了。
面包	被	吃	完了。

练一练

1. 用"主语 + 被 + 宾语 + 动词 + 其他成分"完成对话。Complete the conversations with "subject + 被 + object + verb + other components".

   （1）A：你的耳机呢？

   B：_____。

   （2）A：你不是有电脑吗，为什么要用我的电脑呢？

   B：_____。

   （3）A：能借我用用你的手表吗？

   B：_____。

   （4）A：那件挂在外面的衣服呢？

   B：_____。

2. 看图写句子。Look at the pictures and write sentences.

   （1） （2）

_____ _____

（3）

_____

综合运用 COMPREHENSIVE USE

 语音练习   20-5

一、听录音选择正确答案。Listen to the recording and choose the correct answers.

1. A. bìxū   B. bīxū   2. A. kěpà   B. kěbà

3. A. zhíjiē   B. zíjiē   4. A. tūrān   B. tūrán

5. A. lín   B. lìn   6. A. quānbù   B. quánbù

7. A. zìyóu   B. zhìyóu   8. A. síjī   B. sījī

9. A. cháoguò   B. chāoguò   10. A. fāshēng   B. fáshēng

二、听句子给画线词语标声调。Listen to the sentences and mark the tones of the underlined words.

1. 主要那<u>段</u>路有点儿<u>黑</u>，路灯也<u>不太亮</u>。

2. 昨天夜里被<u>一辆出租车</u>撞了。

3. 下台阶时，突然<u>不小心</u>摔了<u>下去</u>。

4. <u>头</u>被撞破了的话，<u>得赶紧</u>去医院打一种专门的<u>针</u>。

5. <u>不早不晚</u>，路上下起了大雨。

三、听一听，读一读。Listen and read.

从军行

［唐］ 王昌龄

青海长云暗雪山，孤城遥望玉门关。

黄沙百战穿金甲，不破楼兰终不还。

Cóngjūnxíng

[Táng]　Wáng Chānglíng

Qīnghǎi cháng yún àn xuěshān, gū chéng yáo wàng Yùmén Guān.

Huáng shā bǎi zhàn chuān jīnjiǎ, bú pò Lóulán zhōng bù huán.

 汉字知识

异体字 Variant Characters in Chinese

历史上汉字数量很多，其中相当一部分是异体字，也就是一个字有几个不同的形体，但是意思并没有什么不同。异体字产生的原因主要有以下几种情况：一是应用不同造字方法而造成的异体字。例如："泪—涙"，"泪"是会意字，"涙"是形声字。二是应用意义相近的不同形旁而造成的异体字。例如："咏—詠"（形旁"口、言"意义相近）。三是应用声音相近的不同声旁而造成的异体字，例如："线—綫"（"戋、㣤"声音相近）。四是偏旁的部位不同而造成的异体字。例如：棋—棊、胸—胷（左右结构和上下结构）。

1955年，中国文化部和文改会公布了《第一批异体字整理表》。2013年6月，中国国务院公布的《通用规范汉字表》对《第一批异体字整理表》进行了调整。虽然现在使用电脑打字，一般不会涉及异体字的问题，但我们应该掌握表中的规范字，不用已淘汰的异体字。

Throughout history, there have been a large number of Chinese characters, with a significant portion being variant characters. These are characters that have different forms but the same meaning. The reasons for the existence of variant characters include: First, variant characters can arise from the use of different methods to create characters. For example, "泪" (tear) is an associative compound, while "涙" is a pictophonetic character. Second, variant characters can also result from using different semantic components that have similar meanings. For example, "咏" (chant) and "詠" use the semantic components "口" (mouth) and "言" (speak), which have similar meanings. Third, variant characters can be created by using different phonetic components that sound similar. For example, "线" (thread) and "線" use the phonetic components "戋" and "泉", which sound similar. Fourth, variant characters can also arise from differences in the position of the radical. For example, "棋" (chess) and "棊" (tea), as well as "胸" (chest) and "曾" (once), have different structures (left-right structure and top-bottom structure).

In 1955, the Chinese Ministry of Culture and the Chinese Language Reform Committee published the *First Batch of Standardized Variant Characters*. In June 2013, the *General Standard Chinese Characters Table* published by the State Council has made some adjustments to the *First Batch of Standardized Variant Characters*.

Nowadays, the use of computers for typing does not usually involve the issue of variant characters. However, we should grasp the standard characters specified in the table and not use the eliminated variant characters.

口语表达训练

一、来中国以后，你生过病吗？身体有什么不舒服的感觉？生病以后，你做了什么？去过医院吗？四位同学一组，互相说说自己的一次生病的经历，并完成表格。
Have you ever fallen ill since coming to China? Do you feel any discomfort in your body? What did you do after you fell ill? Have you been to the hospital? Tell each other about an experience of falling ill in groups of four and complete the table.

姓名	生病后，身体有什么不舒服的感觉？	生病后，你做了什么？

二、最近你的运气怎么样？有没有运气差的时候呢？四人一组，和同学说说最近发生的一件运气差的事情，并完成调查表。Any luck for you lately? Have there been times of bad luck? Tell your classmates about a recent incident of bad luck in groups of four and complete the questionnaire.

同学姓名	最近的运气怎么样	运气差的经历

文化小贴士 CULTURAL TIPS

塞翁失马
A Blessing in Disguise

古时候，有一个住在边塞的老人。有一次，他家的马竟然无缘无故丢失了。遇到这样的不幸，人们都前来安慰他。这个老人却说："这怎么就不能算是一件好事呢？"

过了几个月之后，他家的马带着一匹骏马跑了回来，于是人们都前来祝贺他们一家。可是这个老人却说："这为什么就不能算是一件坏事呢？"

由于家里添了好马，老人的儿子又喜欢骑马，有一次不小心从马上摔了下来，摔断了大腿。人们又都前来安慰他们一家。这个老人却又说："这为什么就不能算是一件好事呢？"

过了一年，有敌人入侵边境，壮年男子都拿起武器去参加战斗。靠近边境一带的人，十有八九都在战斗中战死了。这个老人的儿子由于是个跛子，没有被召参军，免于征战，最终父子双双得以保全生命。

Long ago, there was an old man who lived near the border. One day, his horse inexplicably went missing. Faced with this misfortune, people came to console him. However, the old man said, "How do you know this isn't a good thing?"

A few months later, his horse returned, bringing with a fine stallion. People came to congratulate him. But the old man said, "How do you know this isn't a bad thing?"

With the addition of the fine horse, the old man's son, who loved to ride, ended up falling off the horse one day and breaking his leg. People came to console them again. Yet the old man said, "How do you know this isn't a good thing?"

A year later, enemies invaded the border, and all able-bodied men were called to fight. Nearly all the men from the border region died in battle. The old man's son, however, was spared from conscription because of his broken leg, and thus both father and son survived the war.

21 一天到晚就是手机
All day long, nothing but the mobile phone

本课学习重点	
话题 Topic	谈手机改变生活 Talk about mobile phones changing life
重点词 Keywords	接受　照相　基本上　从……起　整个　满足　无法
重点句 Key sentences	1. 我有空儿，就看看手机。 2. 你一会儿在朋友圈点赞，一会儿微信聊天儿，一天到晚就是手机，我看你没法儿离开手机了。 3. 我不反对你看手机，也不能忘了吃饭睡觉啊！ 4. 春节不带个女朋友回来，你就没我这个妈了！ 5. 从我来到中国的那一天起，就越来越离不开手机了。 6. 他们总是一会儿看看书，一会儿又想拿出手机玩玩儿游戏。
语法 Grammar	1. 不用关联词语的假设复句和转折复句 Hypothetical complex sentences and adversative complex sentences without correlatives 2. 动补式离合词：打开/看见/离开/完成 　Separable verbs of VC (verb-complement) 3. 并列复句：一会儿……，一会儿…… 　Coordinate compound sentence
汉字知识 Knowledge of Chinese characters	形似字 Characters with Similar Shapes
文化小贴士 Cultural tips	中国的"新四大发明" The "Four Great New Inventions" in China

21 一天到晚就是手机

热身 WARM-UP

想一想：平时你会用手机做什么？请选择相应词语填空，并在对应方框里画"√"，然后与同学分享。What do you usually do with your mobile phone? Please choose the appropriate words to fill in the blanks, tick the corresponding boxes, and share them with your classmates.

☐
_____

☐
_____

☐
_____

☐
_____

☐
_____

☐
_____

☐ 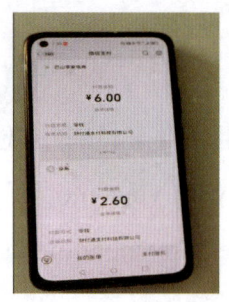　　　　☐

_____　　　　　_____

☐ 　　　　☐

　　　　　　　　　　　　　　……

_____　　　　　_____

付钱　聊天儿　购物　看电视剧　打游戏
看直播(zhíbō, livestream)　听音乐　打视频(shìpín, video)电话　照相
……

课文 TEXT

课文 1　🎧 21-1

听前问题：陈东喜欢用手机做什么？

妈妈：吃饭了！喊了半天，你也不答应。

陈东：妈，来了来了！我正给别人的朋友圈点赞呢！

21 一天到晚就是手机

妈妈：你的手机就没有关机时间，永远都是开机，对不对？

陈东：您太了解我了！我有空儿就看看手机。现在大家喜欢在朋友圈记录自己的美好生活，利用微信和朋友聊聊天儿。

妈妈：你一会儿在朋友圈点赞，一会儿微信聊天儿，一天到晚就是手机。我看你没法儿离开手机了。

陈东：手机确实给我带来了不少欢乐。

妈妈：我不反对你看手机，但也不能忘了吃饭睡觉啊！

陈东：一定接受您的意见！今天做了这么多好吃的啊！等一下，我照张相，发个圈，晒晒您做的美食。

妈妈：有看手机的时间，陪我看看电视多好啊！

陈东：妈，现在已经是二十一世纪啦！基本上人人一部手机。您没发现现在青少年都不怎么看电视了吗？主要是因为手机的功能太强大了。它不光能播放音乐、打电话、照相，还能直播球赛、看电影呢！您平时也多看看手机。

妈妈：那手机能给你找个女朋友？恐怕不行吧？

陈东：妈，您又来了！我现在立刻从手机上找个女朋友给您看看。

妈妈：我还是那句话，春节不带个女朋友回来，你就没我这个妈了！

课堂练习

1. 根据课文内容回答问题。Answer the questions based on the text.
   （1）妈妈喊陈东吃饭，陈东为什么半天不答应？
   （2）陈东看到妈妈做的美食后想做什么？
   （3）为什么现在的青少年都不怎么看电视了？
   （4）陈东现在有女朋友吗？妈妈对他找女朋友是什么态度？

2. 分角色表演课文。Act out the text in roles.

3. 如果你是课文中的陈东，请根据课文内容，向大家说一说现在人们常常用手机做什么。（可参考给出的词语）If you were Chen Dong in the text, tell us what people often do nowadays with their mobile phones based on the text. (You can refer to the words given)

> 朋友圈　点赞　记录　美好　聊天儿　音乐　直播　照相　美食

词语1　🎧 21-2

词语	拼音	词性	英文释义
1. 喊	hǎn	动词	call; shout
2. 答应	dāying	动词	respond; reply
3. 点赞	diǎn//zàn	动词	like (on social media)
4. 关机	guān//jī	动词	switch off
5. 永远	yǒngyuǎn	副词	forever; always
6. 开机	kāi//jī	动词	keep the phone on; switch on
7. 美好	měihǎo	形容词	beautiful; good
8. 利用	lìyòng	动词	use; take advantage of
9. 没法儿	méifǎr		cannot
10. 带来	dàilái		bring
11. 欢乐	huānlè	形容词	joyful
12. 反对	fǎnduì	动词	oppose; object to; be against
13. 接受	jiēshòu	动词	accept
14. 意见	yìjiàn	名词	opinion; view; advice
15. 照相	zhào//xiàng	动词	take a picture
16. 美食	měishí	名词	choice food; gourmet
17. 世纪	shìjì	名词	century
18. 基本上	jīběnshàng	副词	almost; basically; on the whole

21 一天到晚就是手机

19. 青少年	qīng-shàonián	名词	young generation; teenagers; juvenile
20. 功能	gōngnéng	名词	function
21. 强大	qiángdà	形容词	strong; powerful
22. 播放	bōfàng	动词	play
23. 直播	zhíbō	动词	broadcast live
24. 球赛	qiúsài	名词	ball game

专有名词

| 1. 朋友圈 | péngyouquān | | Moments |
| 2. 微信 | Wēixìn | | WeChat |

重点词

接受

（1）昨天李娜很开心地接受了大家送给她的生日礼物。
（2）陈老师接受了乔治的意见，改变了一些上课的方法。
（3）我接受这个任务。

照相

（1）爱华昨天和同学们去参观长城了，她照了很多张相，还把照片发给了爸爸妈妈。
（2）现在的年轻人平时很喜欢用手机照照相，然后发发微信朋友圈。
（3）在外边走了一天，大家都很累了，同学们照了一会儿相就回家休息了。

基本上

（1）这次考试，我们班的同学基本上都取得了很好的成绩。

（2）经过一个星期的休息，我的感冒基本上已经好了。

（3）快放假了，同学们基本上都打算出去玩。

练一练

选词填空。Fill in the blanks with the given words.

| 基本上　接受　照相　利用　美好　答应　永远　强大 |

（1）手机可以拍照、看电视剧、听音乐、聊天儿，功能很_____。

（2）我弟弟学习特别努力，_____每天都要学到晚上十二点才去睡觉。

（3）汉克一看到美食，就想_____几张_____发在朋友圈里给大家看。

（4）我想明年去法国留学，可是爸爸妈妈现在还没_____。

（5）我永远不会忘记我们在一起的那些_____时刻。

（6）大家要好好_____手机学习中文。

（7）同学们都不_____她的意见，所以她很难过。

（8）父母对我们的爱_____都不会改变。

课文2　🎧 21-3

听前问题：手机是怎么改变"我"的生活方式的？

从来到中国的那一天起，我就越来越离不开手机了。手机改变了我以前的生活方式，因为现在很多事都可以在手机上完成。出门的时候，根本不用带现金，只要在手机上动一动手指，就能让处理问题的整个过程变得简单，还能节约我们不少时间。

比如说吃饭，你不想出门，也不想做饭，就可以直接在手机上打开点餐APP，上面可以找到各种价位、满足人们不同口味的美食。选好自己想吃的，然后下单，不一会儿外卖小哥就会把美食送到家门口；想出门吃，可以在手机上找到大家评价最好的饭馆，上面还会显示饭馆的距离、停车信息等。如果正好是吃饭高峰，而你又因为有事无法去饭馆门口排队，那就在APP上先拿个排队的号码，等快轮到你的时候再过去。

手机给老百姓带来了方便，不过也会带来一些问题。手机可能会影响孩子们的学习，因为他们总是一会儿看看书，一会儿又想拿出手机玩玩儿游戏；不少年轻人也总喜欢睡觉前躺着玩手机，有时关灯以后还在玩儿，慢慢地，身体就会出现一些毛病；不少老人对手机上各种APP的使用方法也不太了解，因此他们平时只能用手机打打电话或者看看短信，并不能真正感受到手机给生活带来的很多方便。

课堂练习

1. 根据课文内容回答问题。Answer the questions based on the text.

   （1）如果你不想出门，也不想做饭，可以怎么订外卖？

   （2）如果你想出门吃饭，怎么找到不错的饭馆？

   （3）手机会给人们带来哪些问题？

2. 根据课文内容填空，并复述课文。Fill in the blanks based on the text and retell it.

    手机改变了我以前的_____。现在很多事都可以在手机上完成。出门的时候，根本不用带现金，只要在手机上_____手指，就能让处理问题的_____变得简单，还能节约我们_____。你不想出门，也不想做饭，就可以直接在手机上打开_____APP，上面可以找到_____、满足人们_____的美食。选好自己想吃的，然后下单，不一会儿外卖小哥就会把美食送到_____；想出门吃，可以在手机上找到大家_____的饭馆，上面还会显示饭馆的_____、_____等。如果正好是吃饭_____，而你又因为有事无法去饭馆门口_____，那就在APP上先拿个_____，等快轮到你的时候再过去。

手机给老百姓带来了_____，不过也会带来_____。手机可能会影响孩子们的_____，因为他们总是一会儿看看书，一会儿又想拿出手机_____；不少年轻人也总喜欢睡觉前_____玩手机，有时关灯以后还在玩儿，慢慢地，身体就会出现一些_____；不少老人对手机上各种APP的使用方法也_____，因此他们平时只能用手机_____或者_____，并不能真正_____手机给生活带来的很多方便。

3. 选用下列提示词语和句型，说说手机给我们的生活带来了什么。Choose the following prompt words to talk about what mobile phones have brought into our lives.

> 离不开 完成 现金 处理 简单 节约 满足 无法 排队
> 影响 躺 了解 一会儿……，一会儿……

词语 2 🎧 21-4

词语	拼音	词性	英文释义
1. 来到	láidào	动词	come to
2. 离不开	lí bu kāi		cannot do without
3. 现金	xiànjīn	名词	cash
4. 处理	chǔlǐ	动词	deal with; manage
5. 整个	zhěnggè	形容词	whole; all; entire
6. 过程	guòchéng	名词	process
7. 节约	jiéyuē	动词	economize; save
8. 餐	cān	名词	meal
9. 上面	shàngmiàn	名词	used to indicate the scope of sth.

21 一天到晚就是手机

10. 价位	jiàwèi	名词	price
11. 满足	mǎnzú	动词	satisfy; please
12. 人们	rénmen	名词	people
13. 口味	kǒuwèi	名词	taste
14. 下单	xià//dān	动词	place an order
15. 评价	píngjià	名词、动词	evaluation; evaluate
16. 距离	jùlí	名词、动词	distance; be away from
17. 停车	tíng//chē	动词	park the car
18. 信息	xìnxī	名词	information
19. 高峰	gāofēng	名词	peak
20. 无法	wúfǎ	动词	unable
21. 轮	lún	动词、名词、量词	take turns; wheel; *used of things/actions that rotate*
22. 老百姓	lǎobǎixìng	名词	common people
23. 拿出	náchū		take out
24. 灯	dēng	名词	light
25. 慢慢	mànmàn		slowly; gradually
26. 使用	shǐyòng	动词	use
27. 感受	gǎnshòu	动词	feel

专有名词

APP　　　　　　　　　　　　　　　　　Application

重点词

从……起

（1）从来到中国起，我就越来越喜欢中国的美食了。

（2）从下周起，我们班每个同学都要参加这个活动。

（3）从上个星期五起，我就没有去过学校了。

整个

（1）整个中秋节假期，我都和家人在一起。

（2）上个月的活动，整个学校的学生都参加了。

（3）工作了一天，我整个人都快累死了。

满足

（1）这次考试如果能取得好一点儿的成绩，我就满足了。

（2）妈妈说我过生日那天，可以满足我的一个愿望。

（3）不好意思，你不满足我对男朋友的要求。

无法

（1）对不起，我无法满足你的这些要求。

（2）2022年以前，由于有很多工作要做，因此我无法来中国留学。

（3）刚来北京的时候，我无法接受中国人喊我"老外"。

练一练

选词填空。Fill in the blanks with the given words.

> 整个　满足　无法　感受　使用　评价　离不开　从……起

（1）你已经有那么多钱了，还不_____？

（2）你知道怎么_____这台新电脑吗？如果不知道，我可以教你。

（3）_____中学_____，妹妹就开始学游泳了。

（4）来中国已经半年了，请大家说一说你们的_____。

（5）大卫很喜欢交朋友，_____篮球队的人都认识他。

（6）最近我们公司很多人都没买到火车票，所以春节前_____回家了。

（7）现在，网络越来越重要了，我们也越来越_____它。

（8）这位老师在学校里很受欢迎，学生们对她的_____都很高。

语法 GRAMMAR

一、不用关联词语的假设复句和转折复句　Hypothetical complex sentences and adversative complex sentences without correlatives

在复句中，如果小句本身的意义足够体现它们之间的意义联系，那么复句中的关联词语通常可省略。

In a complex sentence, if the meaning of the clauses themselves is sufficient to reflect the association of meaning between them, the correlatives in the complex sentence can usually be omitted.

在不用关联词语的假设复句中，表示假设的关联词语，如"如果""的话"等，或表示相应结果或反应的词语在句中省略，前后小句的假设关系由小句本身的意义体现。以"如果……，就……"为例：

In a hypothetical complex sentence without correlatives, the correlatives of hypothesis, such as "如果", "的话", etc., or the words indicating the corresponding result or reflection are omitted, and the hypothetical relationship between the preceding and following clauses is reflected by the meaning of the clauses themselves. Take "如果……，就……" as an example:

	小句1	小句2
（如果）	我有空儿，	就看看手机。
	你愿意，	我们这个周末（就）去爬山。
	晚高峰交通不太好，	你（就）坐地铁来。

在不用关联词的转折复句中，表示转折的关联词语，如"不过""但（是）""可（是）"等可省略，前后小句的转折关系由小句意义体现。例如：

In an adversative complex sentence without correlatives, the correlatives indicating the transition, such as "不过", "但（是）", "可（是）", etc., can be omitted, and the adversative relationship between the preceding and following clauses is reflected by the meaning of the clauses. For example:

我不反对你看手机，	（不过/但/但是/可/可是……）	也不能忘了吃饭睡觉啊。
这个饭馆的饭菜好吃，		有点儿贵。
我的邻居在花园里种了很多花，		显得有点儿乱。

练一练

1. 请在下列句子中画出可以省略的关联词语。Underline the correlatives that can be omitted in the following sentences.

   （1）如果房间里太挤，就把书架搬出去。

   （2）旅行可以丰富我们的经历，但有的时候也会遇到麻烦。

   （3）如果你愿意参加这次跳高比赛，我们可能就会赢。

   （4）虽然屋子里开了暖气，但是她还穿着厚厚的羽绒服。

2. 请仿照例句，根据句子后的意义要求，完成句子。Please complete the sentences after the example according to the requirements of meaning.

例：手机给我们带来了很多欢乐，<u>也带来了很多问题</u>。

（转折关系 adversative relation）

（1）爸爸做饭很好吃，_____。

（转折关系 adversative relation）

（2）大家很喜欢给我的朋友圈点赞，_____。

（假设关系 hypothetical relation）

（3）这套房子的位置很好，_____。

（转折关系 adversative relation）

（4）"双十一"你不下单，_____。

（假设关系 hypothetical relation）

二、动补式离合词：打开 / 看见 / 离开 / 完成 Separable verbs of VC (verb-complement): 打开 / 看见 / 离开 / 完成

动补结构的"打开 / 看见 / 离开 / 完成"表示动作完成的结果，这类离合词的中间通常可以加入"得"或"不"来表示动作实现的可能性。

The verb-complement structures "打开 / 看见 / 离开 / 完成" indicate the result of the completion of an action, and "得" or "不" can usually be inserted in the middle of this kind of separable verbs to indicate the possibility of the realization of the action.

1. 打开

（1）屋里太热了，请把窗户打开。

（2）这台电脑打得开吗？如果打不开，就让师傅来修（xiū, repair）一下。

（3）我没有遥控器（yáokòngqì, remote control），打不开空调。

2. 看见

（1）爸爸，你看见我的书了吗？我刚刚看见过，但现在找不到了。

（2）那辆公交车太远了，我根本看不见它是几路车。

（3）这个座位很好，整个电影屏幕（píngmù, screen）我都看得见。

3. 离开

（1）她下个星期开始在上海工作，但今天早上就坐高铁离开了。

（2）现在基本上做什么事情都需要手机，你觉得我们还离得开它吗？

（3）我们现在取得的成功，离不开父母和朋友们的帮助。

4. 完成

（1）如果按照这个效率工作，一天就能完成任务。

（2）这个星期的作业太多了，我可能完不成了。

（3）只要我们互相帮助，就完得成这项任务（rènwù, task）！

练一练

1. 选择合适的词语，并用适当形式填空。Choose the appropriate words and fill in the blanks with the appropriate forms.

> 打开　　看见　　离开　　完成

（1）这门的前面和后面都放了很多东西，根本_____。

（2）他很聪明，这几道题肯定（kěndìng, definitely）_____。

（3）如果努努力，我们也许离得开电脑，但我们永远都_____空气和水。

（4）我的视力（shìlì, eyesight）不好，戴上眼镜，我就_____那栋（dòng, a measure word）楼，不戴就看不见。

2. 完成句子。Complete the sentences.

（1）这么小的差别你都看得见？不过，反正我眼睛不好，_____。

（2）城市的发展_____发达的交通。

（3）冰箱的门坏了，_____东西。

（4）这件事情很简单，我_____。

三、并列复句：一会儿……，一会儿……　Coordinate compound sentence: 一会儿……，一会儿……

"一会儿……，一会儿……"表示动作交替进行或依次发生，也可表示事物依次出现或其属性不断变化。有时，会有三个及以上"一会儿"出现，形成较长的并列复句。例：

"一会儿……，一会儿……" indicates that actions take place alternately or sequentially, and can also indicate that things appear sequentially or that their attributes change continuously. Sometimes there are three or more "一会儿" forming a longer coordinate compound sentence. For example:

（1）考试的时候，安琪一会儿拿起笔，一会儿又放下，显得很紧张。

（2）这几天，我的运气一会儿好，一会儿差。

（3）鲍比拿着新买的手机，一会儿照相，一会儿看直播，一会儿听音乐，很兴奋。

练一练

1. 连线。Match the columns.

（1）这个月的天气很奇怪 (qíguài, strange)，一会儿冷，

（2）他们在聚会上一会儿唱歌，

（3）我做菜很随便，一会儿加盐，

（4）我感冒了，一会儿发烧，

（5）乔治学习的时候不太认真，一会儿玩手机，

一会儿加糖，结果味道都不太好。

一会儿不发烧，身体真不舒服。

一会儿热，不知道该穿什么衣服。

一会儿听音乐，一会儿看电视，到现在都还没写完作业。

一会儿跳舞，玩得很开心。

2. 看图完成句子。Look at the pictures and complete the sentences.

（1）

在超市_____，_____，最后也没决定买什么。

（2）

周末的时候，＿＿＿＿＿＿，＿＿＿＿＿＿，一天到晚都很开心。

（3）

这个星期的天气很不好，＿＿＿＿＿＿，＿＿＿＿＿＿，非常冷。

（4）

她去了餐厅，＿＿＿＿，＿＿＿＿，＿＿＿＿，吃得很开心。

21 一天到晚就是手机

 综合运用 COMPREHENSIVE USE

 语音练习　🎧 21-5

一、听录音选择正确答案。Listen to the recording and choose the correct answers.

1. A. jiéshòu　　B. jiēshòu　　2. A. zhào//xiàng　　B. jiàoxiàng
3. A. huānlè　　B. huānyuè　　4. A. wúfǎ　　B. wǔfǎ
5. A. mǎnzú　　B. mǎnzhú　　6. A. zhěnggè　　B. zhěngè
7. A. pōfàng　　B. bōfàng　　8. A. chǔlǐ　　B. qǔlǐ
9. A. píngjià　　B. pínjià　　10. A. gòuchéng　　B. guòchéng

二、听句子给画线词语标声调。Listen to the sentences and mark the tones of the underlined words.

1. 我<u>有空</u>儿，就<u>看看</u>手机。
2. 我不<u>反对</u>你看手机，但也不能忘了吃饭<u>睡觉</u>啊！
3. <u>春节</u>不带个女朋友<u>回来</u>，你就没我这个妈了！
4. 从我来到中国起，就越来越<u>离不开</u>手机了。
5. 手机可能会影响孩子们的学习，因为他们<u>总是一会儿看看</u>书，一会儿又想拿出手机<u>玩玩儿</u>游戏。

三、听一听，读一读。Listen and read.

绝句

［唐］　杜甫

两个黄鹂鸣翠柳，一行白鹭上青天。

窗含西岭千秋雪，门泊东吴万里船。

Juéjù

[Táng] Dù Fǔ

Liǎng gè huánglí míng cuì liǔ, yì háng báilù shàng qīngtiān.

Chuāng hán Xī Lǐng qiānqiū xuě, mén bó Dōng Wú wàn lǐ chuán.

 汉字知识

形似字 Characters with Similar Shapes

汉字是由点、横、竖、撇、捺、提等笔画构成的，一个字一个样子。但有些字，形体相近，差别很细微。这些字称为形似字。形似字容易造成误读、误写。有一些笔画数目少但字形相似的汉字，例如：干、千、平、乎、土、士；儿、几、八、人、入；大、太、天、夫、元、无。这些汉字的差别主要在于笔形及其关系。这些字只是形近，读音和意义差别很大，可以通过强化音义关系来帮助记忆。随着汉字量的增加，那些声旁相同、形旁相似的汉字会成为容易混淆的汉字，例如：晴、睛；蓝、篮；辩、辨；练、炼；裁、栽、载。这些字不仅字形会对识字、写字产生干扰，有时字音也会产生干扰。区分这些字，可以通过强化形旁来掌握。

Chinese characters are composed of strokes such as dots, horizontal strokes, vertical strokes, left-falling strokes, right-falling strokes, and rising strokes. Each character has a unique shape. However, some characters have similar shapes with very subtle differences. These characters are called "形似字" (characters with similar shapes). Characters with similar shapes can easily lead to misreading and miswriting.

There are some characters with few strokes but similar shapes, such as: 干, 千, 平, 乎, 土 (tǔ), 士 (shì); 儿 (ér), 几 (jǐ), 八 (bā), 人 (rén), 入 (rù); 大 (dà), 太 (tài), 天 (tiān), 夫 (fū), 元 (yuán), 无 (wú). The differences among these characters mainly lie in the shape of the strokes and their relationships. These characters are only similar in shape, their pronunciations and meanings are very different. You can memorize them by strengthening the sound-meaning relationship. As the number of characters you know increases, characters with the same phonetic component and similar semantic components can become easily confused, such as 晴 and 睛, 蓝 and 篮, 辩 and 辨, 练 and 炼, 裁, 栽 and 载. Not only do the shapes of these characters can interfere with recognition and writing but also the pronunciations at times. To distinguish these characters, you can focus on the semantic components to better grasp them.

21 一天到晚就是手机

口语表达训练

一、你的同学们每天使用手机多长时间？他们平时喜欢用手机做什么？请三位同学介绍一下他们使用手机的情况，完成调查表。How much time do your classmates spend on their mobile phones each day? What do they like to do with their mobile phones? Ask three of your classmates to introduce their use of mobile phones and complete the questionnaire.

姓名	使用时间	喜欢用手机做什么

二、同学们每天都使用手机，那么手机给我们带来的欢乐多还是问题多呢？请和你的同学们讨论一下并举例说明。You use mobile phones every day. Does mobile phone bring us more joy or more problems? Discuss this with your classmates and explain with examples.

欢乐多	问题多

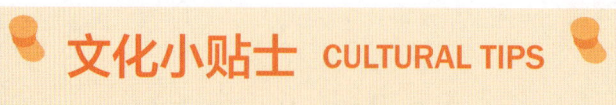

中国的"新四大发明"
The "Four Great New Inventions" in China

造纸术、指南针、印刷术、火药（zàozhǐshù、zhǐnánzhēn、yìnshuāshù、huǒyào）是中国古代的四大发明。2017年5月，来自"一带一路"沿线的20国青年评选出了"中国的新四大发明"：高铁（gāotiě）、扫码支付（sǎomǎ zhīfù）、共享单车（gòngxiǎng dānchē）和网购（wǎnggòu）。事实上，这四项并非由中国发明，只是在中国推广应用较为领先、对国外影响较大。

中国高铁近些年来发展迅猛。中国将高铁技术和产品用到了极致（jízhì）。

电子支付、移动支付、扫码支付改变了消费者的消费方式，在中国得到了很好的发展，短短数年间就改变了中国消费市场的整体环境，并因为大量的普及（pǔjí），使得消费者在进行支付时能够享受到更便捷（biànjié）的生活。

共享单车是指企业与政府合作，在公共服务区、地铁站点、公交站点、商业区、居民区、校园等地方提供共享服务，是共享经济（gòngxiǎng jīngjì）的一种新形态。这种出行方式十分环保节能，是当下共享经济大环境下的产物。到目前为止，全国共享单车的应用软件已经有三十多个。

21 一天到晚就是手机

　　网购在中国深入了人们的生活，不论老小基本都有过网上购物的经历。网购节省了大量时间，十分方便，深受国民喜爱，"6·18"和"双十一"等都是中国特有的购物狂欢节。网购的便利依托于强大的物流系统（wùliú xìtǒng），中国的物流行业十分发达，覆盖（fùgài）面积十分广大。

　　Papermaking technology, the compass, printing, and gunpowder (zàozhǐshù, zhǐnánzhēn, yìnshuāshù, huǒyào) are the four great inventions in ancient China. In May 2017, young people from 20 countries along the "Belt and Road Initiative" voted for the "Four Great New Inventions in China": high-speed rail (gāotiě), QR code payment (sǎomǎ zhīfù), shared bicycles (gòngxiǎng dānchē), and online shopping (wǎnggòu). In fact, these four items were not invented by China but have been widely promoted and adopted in China and have had a significant impact globally.

　　China's high-speed rail has developed rapidly in recent years. China has taken high-speed rail technology and products to their highest attainments.

　　Electronic payment, mobile payment, and QR code payment have changed consumers' way of spending and have developed well in China. In just a few years, they have transformed the entire environment of China's consumer market. Because of their massive popularization, consumers are able to enjoy a more convenient life when they make payments.

　　Shared bicycles involve enterprises and governments cooperating to provide shared bicycle services in public areas, metro stations, bus stops, commercial districts, residential areas, and campuses. It is a new form of sharing economy. This mode of transportation is environmental-friendly and energy-efficient, reflecting the current trend of the sharing economy. So far, there are over 30 shared bicycle apps available nationwide.

　　Online shopping has become an integral part of people's lives in China, with almost everyone having experienced it. Online shopping saves a lot of time and is very convenient, making it popular among the people. Events like "6·18" and "Double Eleven" are unique shopping festivals in China. The convenience of online shopping relies on a strong logistics system, and China's logistics industry is highly developed, covering a vast area.

22 买房还是租房？
Buying a house or rent one?

本课学习重点

话题 Topic	谈消费 Talk about consumption
重点词 Keywords	有的是　仍然　值　按　决心　相同　建议　提前　足够
重点句 Key sentences	1. 您坐飞机来，坐高铁来？ 2. 要是衣服没穿破，就能一直穿。 3. 一看到喜欢的东西就买，把钱都花在吃吃喝喝上真不值。 4. 他们认为除了买房这件事以外，其他的事情都不是最重要的。 5. 买房除了要有足够的资金，还要考虑工作的地点，这是个现实问题。 6. 每个月除了付房租，我还可以过自己喜欢的日子。
语法 Grammar	1. 不用关联词语的选择复句 Alternative complex sentences without correlatives 2. 假设复句：要是……，（主语）就…… Hypothetical complex sentence 3. 紧缩复句：一……，就…… Compressed complex sentence 4. 固定格式：除了……（以外），……还/也/都…… Fixed pattern
汉字知识 Knowledge of Chinese characters	汉字的字体演变 The Evolution of Chinese Characters
文化小贴士 Cultural tips	中国行政区划 Administrative Divisions of China

热 身 WARM-UP

说一说：你去旅行时是坐火车、高铁还是飞机？为什么？ When going traveling, what do you prefer to take for the ride? The train, high-speed rail, or airplane? Why?

课 文 TEXT

课文 1　🎧 22-1

听前问题：为什么陈东爸爸不坐飞机来找陈东？

陈东：爸，您坐飞机来，坐高铁来？

爸爸：我坐卧铺过去，能便宜好几百呢！

陈东：十几个小时，多慢啊！

爸爸：没事儿。我退休了，有的是时间。

陈东：爸，退休等于人生的一个新开始，您得更好地过才行。别跟以前一样，一件衬衫穿了十多年还仍然穿着。前年给您买了件上衣，您还批评了我半天。

爸爸：买这买那的不花钱啊？要是衣服没穿破，就能一直穿，不能浪费。一看到喜欢的东西就买，把钱都花在吃吃喝喝上真不值。

陈东：按您的想法，国家经济还发展不发展了？要是大家的想法都跟您一样，那我们的生活还有什么意思？时代变了，您的消费观念也得改一改了。

爸爸： 我一买东西就要买最好的，这样能用好多年。你看咱家那台电视机，买的时候可是花了大价钱的，看了十几年了还是挺好的。

陈东： 爸，科技推动时代发展，现在人们家里都是家庭影院了。让生活变得有趣又舒服才是个人努力的重点目标，而且您儿子我已经工作了，收入也不算低，您没有理由不过过现代生活，您说呢？

爸爸： 好，听你的。我决心开始过一过退休后的新生活！那就坐高铁吧！机票太贵，能省一点儿是一点儿！

课堂练习

1. 根据课文内容回答问题。Answer the questions based on the text.
   （1）陈东爸爸打算怎么去找陈东？为什么？
   （2）陈东爸爸是一个浪费钱的人吗？
   （3）陈东的消费观念和他爸爸的一样吗？哪里不同？

2. 分角色表演课文。Act out the text in roles.

3. 如果你是课文中的陈东，请根据课文内容向大家介绍你爸爸的消费观念。（可参考给出的词语和句型）If you were Chen Dong in the text, please tell us about your father's idea of consumption based on the text. (You can refer to the words and sentence patterns given)

> 高铁　卧铺　便宜　穿破　浪费　不值
> 要是……，就……　一……，就……

22 买房还是租房？

词语 1 🎧 22-2

	词语	拼音	词性	英文释义
1.	高铁	gāotiě	名词	high-speed rail
2.	卧铺	wòpù	名词	berth
3.	便宜	piányi	动词	cheap
4.	有的是	yǒudeshì		have plenty of
5.	等于	děngyú	动词	be the same as
6.	人生	rénshēng	名词	life
7.	衬衫	chènshān	名词	shirt
8.	仍然	réngrán	副词	still
9.	前年	qiánnián	名词	the year before last
10.	上衣	shàngyī	名词	jacket
11.	批评	pīpíng	动词	blame; criticize
12.	浪费	làngfèi	动词	waste
13.	值	zhí	动词	be worthwhile
14.	按	àn	介词	according to
15.	经济	jīngjì	名词	economy
16.	消费	xiāofèi	动词	consume
17.	改	gǎi	动词	change
18.	咱	zán	代词	we; us
19.	价钱	jiàqián	名词	price
20.	科技	kējì	名词	science and technology
21.	推动	tuī//dòng	动词	push; promote; drive
22.	影院	yǐngyuàn	名词	cinema
23.	个人	gèrén	名词	individual
24.	努力	nǔlì	动词	make an effort

25.	重点	zhòngdiǎn	名词	emphasis; focus; key
26.	目标	mùbiāo	名词	target; aim; goal
27.	理由	lǐyóu	名词	reason
28.	决心	juéxīn	动词、名词	be determined; determination
29.	一点儿	yìdiǎnr		a little bit

重点词

有的是

（1）你看我们的马路上，共享单车有的是。

（2）我们篮球队有的是打球水平高的男孩子。

（3）中国有的是美丽的地方，我们可以多去各地旅旅游。

仍然

（1）我妈妈仍然和以前一样，爱买衣服。

（2）这件事已经过去十多年了，但是我仍然记得很清楚。

（3）这个男孩儿的父亲和母亲找了他那么久，仍然没有找到。

值

（1）我认为把钱都花在学习上非常值。

（2）这件衬衫这么普通还花了1000块钱，真不值。

（3）能够来北京和大家一起在学校学习，准备这么久也值了。

按

（1）按以前的说法，女孩子根本无法掌控自己的人生。
（2）按你的想法，所有人都要帮助你，对吗？
（3）按电影院的要求，我们不能在这里大喊。

决心

（1）我决心下个学期好好准备准备HSK五级考试。
（2）弟弟是不是有决心不再玩儿手机了？
（3）你让爸爸下决心不抽烟，这事他一定做不到。

练一练

选词填空。Fill in the blanks with the given words.

> 仍然　值　浪费　按　理由　改　有的是　决心

（1）王老师，请您看一下，我的这个题是不是_____错了？
（2）你有和他分手的_____吗？
（3）_____我爸的想法，我们应该把钱花在有用的地方。
（4）那些坏事还没有发生，你却一直在想，其实就是在_____时间。
（5）虽然你说美食会让人变胖，但是我_____认为美食可以让我们生活变得更美好。
（6）这台电脑刚买不久就坏了，还这么贵，一点也不_____。
（7）你多吃点儿，饺子_____。
（8）你每次迟到，都有不一样的_____。

课文 2 🎧 22-3

听前问题:"我"爸妈建议买房还是租房?

买房还是租房?这个话题我们全家讨论了一个晚上。

爸妈的观点是相同的,他们主张一定要买房,认为房子才是生存的根本。要是没房子,就不会有稳定的生活。买了房的话,工作会有更大的动力,还能防止被房东赶走。只有房子才是最可靠的,才是最应该买的。他们的建议是越早买房越好,争取三十岁前就把房子买好了。他们认为除了买房这件事以外,其他的事情都不是最重要的。

我理解爸妈的想法,可是我的想法跟他们不太一样。如果计算一下现在房子的价格,那可是一大笔钱。我现在可没那么多钱,只能向银行借。这表明我一买房,就要定期向银行还钱,而且至少要还二十年。当然,要是有足够的钱,也可以提前还完。买房除了要有足够的资金,还要考虑工作的地点,这是个现实问题。房子离单位太远,那每天上下班在路上可能就要花四五个小时。要是租房,那就不用担心单位和家的距离了,因为我可以随时搬家。每个月除了付房租,我还可以过自己喜欢的日子,因为租房压力远远比买房要小得多。我一直认为人不应该只为房子活着。除了房子,心中还要有更多的人生愿望去实现。

课堂练习

1. 根据课文内容回答问题。Answer the questions based on the text.

 (1)"我们"家在讨论什么话题?

 (2)爸妈对这个话题的观点是什么?

 (3)"我"的想法和爸妈的相同吗?如果不同,有什么不同?

2. 根据课文内容填空，并复述课文。Fill in the blanks based on the text and retell it.

对于买房还是租房这个_____，我们全家讨论了一个晚上。我和我爸妈的观点不_____，我的爸妈_____一定要买房，越早买房越好，争取_____前就把房子买好了。要是没房子，就没有_____的生活。但是我的想法和我爸妈的想法不同，我现在没有_____的资金买房子，而且还要考虑_____，这是个现实问题。要是租房，那就不用担心单位和家的_____了，因为我可以_____搬家。我一直认为人不应该只为房子活着，除了_____，心中还要有更多的_____。

3. 你认为年轻人应该买房还是租房，参考下面给出的词语和句型说一说你的想法。Should young people buy a house of their own, or just rent one? Talk about your thoughts referring to the words and sentence pattern given below.

| 主张 | 稳定 | 动力 | 可靠 | 资金 | 足够 | 房租 |
| 随时 | 除了……，还/也…… |

词语 2 🎧 22-4

词语	拼音	词性	英文释义
1. 租	zū	动词	rent
2. 话题	huàtí	名词	topic; subject
3. 观点	guāndiǎn	名词	opinion; viewpoint
4. 相同	xiāngtóng	形容词	same
5. 主张	zhǔzhāng	动词、名词	advocate; position
6. 生存	shēngcún	动词	make a living
7. 稳定	wěndìng	形容词	stable
8. 动力	dònglì	名词	drive; motivation
9. 防止	fángzhǐ	动词	prevent; avoid
10. 可靠	kěkào	形容词	reliable; credible; trustworthy

11.	建议	jiànyì	动词、名词	propose; suggestion
12.	争取	zhēngqǔ	动词	strive for
13.	除了	chúle	介词	besides
14.	以外	yǐwài	名词	beyond
15.	不太	bú tài		not too
16.	笔	bǐ	量词	used to indicate sums of money or business
17.	只能	zhǐ néng		have no other choice but; can only
18.	表明	biǎomíng	动词	make clear; show
19.	定期	dìngqī	形容词	at fixed period; regular
20.	足够	zúgòu	动词	be enough; be sufficient; be adequate
21.	提前	tíqián	动词	do sth. ahead of schedule; do sth. in advance
22.	资金	zījīn	名词	fund; money
23.	地点	dìdiǎn	名词	location
24.	现实	xiànshí	名词	reality
25.	上下班	shàng-xiàbān		go to and get off work
26.	不用	búyòng	副词	need not
27.	远远	yuǎnyuǎn		by far
28.	心中	xīnzhōng	名词	(in) one's heart/mind

重点词

相同

（1）我爸妈都认为我应该早点儿买房，他们的观点是相同的。

（2）他们两个有相同的兴趣和爱好。

（3）妈妈对我和弟弟的要求完全不相同。

建议

（1）我爸妈都建议我早点儿回国。

（2）我不建议你一个人去国外旅游。

（3）怎么学好汉语？王老师已经给了我们不少建议。

提前

（1）王老师每天都提前五分钟到学校。

（2）今年我想提前回国。

（3）因为下周他要去法国，所以我们这周提前给他过了生日。

足够

（1）我们有足够的食物和水，一个星期不出门也没问题。

（2）我已经有这么多衣服了，足够了。

（3）这些钱足够你买一部新手机了。

练一练

选词填空。Fill in the blanks with the given words.

相同　主张　防止　生存　可靠　建议　争取　表明　提前　足够

（1）有些人_____男生和女生一样，但是却对女生有各种要求。

（2）你现在就把明天上课的东西都准备好，_____明天早上你忘记了。

（3）王老师今天_____十分钟就下课了，因为他身体不太舒服。

（4）今年的考试内容和去年的不太_____，请大家好好复习。

（5）如果没有水和空气，人们就无法_____。

（6）如果观点不相同，你仍然可以_____自己的看法，我们都很欢迎。

（7）有多少钱才算_____？每个人都有不同的答案。

（8）只要还有一点儿希望，我们都应该努力_____。

（9）我的_____是你好好休息一天，别工作了。

（10）我觉得他这个人不太_____，你小心一点儿。

语法 GRAMMAR

一、不用关联词语的选择复句　Alternative complex sentences without correlatives

表示说出两种或几种可能的情况，让人从中选择，但是全句不出现表示选择关系的关联词语。

It means that two or more possible scenarios are listed, and a person may choose from them, but there is no correlatives indicating the alternative relationship in the sentence.

"S（主语）+……（选择$_1$），……（选择$_2$）？" "S (Subject) + ... + (Choice$_1$), ... (Choice$_2$)?"

（1）A：我们今天喝红酒，喝白酒？

　　　B：喝红酒吧，白酒喝太多对身体不好。

（2）A：你等会儿骑自行车去，坐地铁去？

　　　B：我想坐地铁去，现在时间不早了。

（3）A：他们想出去吃，在家吃？

　　　B：他们想一起出去吃中国菜。

练一练

1. 看图，用选择复句（不用关联词语）写句子。Look at the pictures and write alternative complex sentences without correlatives.

 or

 or

_____

 or

_____

 or

_____

2. 用选择复句（不用关联词语）完成下列对话。Complete the following conversations with alternative complex sentences without correlatives.

（1）A：_____？

B：我想以后去，现在一月份，哈尔滨还是很冷，等到夏天再去吧。

（2）A：_____？

B：我以后想当一名小学老师。

（3）A：_____？

B：我打算周二去，周三去太晚了。

（4）A：_____？

B：我和大卫一起去吧，安琪现在已经不去游泳了。

（5）A：_____?

B：我昨天是坐飞机来的，坐高铁的时间太长了。

二、假设复句：要是……，（主语）就…… Hypothetical complex sentence: 要是……, (Subject) 就……

假设复句，"要是"后面的分句表示一种假设，"就"后面的分句是在这种假设情况下产生的结果。注意，第二个分句的主语要放在"就"的前边。例如：

In a hypothetical complex sentence, the clause after "要是" indicates a hypothesis, and the clause after "就" is the result that would occur under that hypothetical situation. Note that the subject of the second clause should be placed before "就". For example:

（1）要是你太累了，就休息一会儿。

（2）要是你喜欢，我就给你买一件。

（3）要是你不舒服，就去医院检查一下吧。

练一练

1. 选词填空。Fill in the blanks with the given words.

> 重要   主要   只要   要是

（1）A：我正想找你呢，你说让他去哪儿留学好？

B：这_____还得看孩子自己的想法。

（2）A：上次的事太谢谢您了，_____别人，这事可能就办不了了。

B：别客气。

（3）A：明天的考试很_____，你一定要早点儿出门。

B：我知道，你别担心了！

（4）A：我本来也想当一名医生，但是最后却成了一名英语老师。

B：其实做什么都一样，_____认真努力，都能做好。

2. 连线。Match the columns.

（1）老同学聚会真不容易，要是去年，　　　　我们就去西湖玩儿吧。

（2）要是有人问，　　　　　　　　　　　　咱们都还在国外呢！

（3）要是时间还早，　　　　　　　　　　　请帮我买一本。

（4）要是他不去，　　　　　　　　　　　　你就说我在老王家。

（5）要是看见《英汉词典》，　　　　　　　你还会去吗？

三、紧缩复句：一……，就…… Compressed complex sentence: 一……，就……

紧缩复句"一……，就……"主要表示前后两个动作或状态紧接着发生，间隔时间非常短，甚至中间没有停顿；还可以表示当具备某种条件时就一定会出现某种结果，前一动作是条件和原因，后一动作是结果。前后两个分句可以有同一主语，放在"一"的前面；也可以分别有一个主语，分别放在"一"和"就"的前面。

The compressed complex sentence "一……，就……" mainly indicates that two actions or states occur immediately after each other, with a very short interval, or even without any pause in between; it can also indicate that when a certain condition is met, there will be a certain result, with the former action being the condition and cause, and the latter action being the result. The former and latter clauses can share the same subject, placed in front of "一"; they can also have a subject respectively, placed in front of "一" and "就".

1.【主语＋一＋动词1/形容词1（短语），就＋动词2/形容词2（短语）】

[Subject＋一＋Verb 1/Adjective 1 (Phrase), 就＋Verb 2/Adjective 2 (Phrase)]

（1）我一难过，就想吃东西。

（2）王东一考试，就紧张。

（3）大卫一来北京，就去了故宫。

2.【主语1＋一＋动词1/形容词1（短语），主语2＋就＋动词2/形容词2（短语）】

[Subject 1＋一＋Verb 1/Adjective 1 (Phrase), Subject 2＋就＋Verb 2/Adjective 2 (Phrase)]

（1）老师一讲，我们就理解了。

（2）天气一热，雪就化（huà, melt）了。

（3）爸爸一说话，妈妈就不高兴。

练一练

1. 连词成句。String the words together into appropriate sentences.

（1）一 到 就 我 上海 学校 去 了

_____

（2）丽美 去 东西 买 一 就 商场 很多

_____

（3）女孩儿们 夏天 一 减肥 到 就

_____

（4）上……课 一 就 口语 紧张 乔治

_____

2. 用"一……，就……"完成下列句子。Complete the following sentences with "一……，就……".

（1）小孩子很怕医生，_____。

（2）丽美很喜欢回答问题，_____。

（3）我很喜欢夏天，_____。

（4）听力课太难了，_____。

（5）这个生词不太难，_____。

四、固定格式：除了……（以外），……还/也/都…… Fixed pattern: 除了……（以外），……还/也/都……

1.【除了 A（以外），(B) 还/也 (B) ……】

表示在 A 之外，还有别的，即排除一部分（如 A），补充其他的（如 B），A 和 B 相同。句子的主语放在句首，或者放在"还/也"前。例如：

It indicates that in addition to A, there is something else, that is, to exclude some (such as A) and add others (such as B), A and B are the same. The subject of the sentence is placed at the very beginning of the sentence, or before "还" or "也". For example:

（1）在中国，除了春节以外，端午节和中秋节也是很重要的节日。

（2）上网除了看新闻以外，还可以听音乐。

（3）除了安娜以外，别的同学也去了舞会。

2.【除了 A（以外），B 都……】

表示所说的不计算在内，即在某个特定的范围内，排除一部分（如 A），其他部分（如 B）都有相同的情况，A 和 B 不同。其中"以外"可以省略。例如：

It indicates that what is said is not included, that is, within a certain range, excluding one part (such as A), the other part (such as B) has the same situation, A and B are different. The word "以外" can be omitted. For example:

（1）除了中国以外，其他国家我都没去过。

（2）除了榴梿以外，其他水果我都爱吃。

（3）除了大卫以外，其他人都来了。

练一练

1. 用"除了……（以外），……也/还/都……"改写句子。Rewrite the sentences with "除了……（以外），……也/还/都……".

  例如：我喜欢春天，也喜欢夏天。

  ——除了春天以外，我也喜欢夏天。

  （1）我们班只有王老师是中国人，其他人是外国人。

  （2）我只想吃烤鸭，别的菜我都不想吃。

  （3）我会说汉语，也会说英语。

  （4）我认识这个汉字，别的汉字我也认识。

  （5）我想去东北旅行，还想去南方旅行。

2. 看图说话。Talk about the pictures.

例如：

A：除了踢足球以外，你还喜欢什么运动？

B：除了踢足球以外，我还喜欢游泳。

（1）

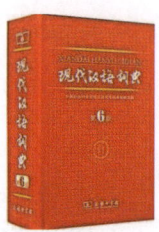 

___

（2）

___

（3）

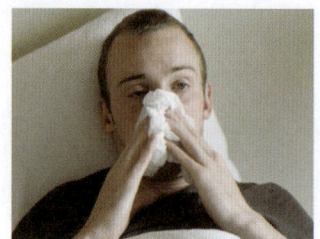 

___

22 买房还是租房？

综合运用 COMPREHENSIVE USE

 语音练习   🎧 22-5

一、听录音选择正确答案。Listen to the recording and choose the correct answers.

1. A. qiánnián   B. jiánnán   2. A. jīngjì   B. jīngjí
3. A. wòpù   B. wǒpù   4. A. sīxiǎng   B. shīxiǎng
5. A. xiāofèi   B. jiāohèi   6. A. guāndiǎn   B. kuāntiǎn
7. A. pīpíng   B. pīnpín   8. A. gējì   B. kējì
9. A. tìngjī   B. dìngqī   10. A. zhòngdiǎn B. chòngtiǎn

二、听句子给画线词语标声调。Listen to the sentences and mark the tones of the underlined words.

1. 您坐<u>飞机</u>来，坐<u>高铁</u>来？
2. 退休<u>等于</u>人生的一个新<u>开始</u>，您得更好地过才行。
3. 要是衣服没穿<u>破</u>，就能<u>一直</u>穿，不能<u>浪费</u>。
4. 只有房子才是最<u>可靠</u>的，才是最<u>值得</u>买的。
5. 我一直认为人不应该只为房子<u>活着</u>，除了房子，<u>心中</u>还要有更多的人生<u>愿望</u>去实现。

三、听一听，读一读。Listen and read.

寻隐者不遇	Xún Yǐnzhě Bú Yù
[唐] 贾岛	[Táng] Jiǎ Dǎo
松下问童子，言师采药去。	Sōng xià wèn tóngzǐ, yán shī cǎi yào qù.
只在此山中，云深不知处。	Zhǐ zài cǐ shān zhōng, yún shēn bù zhī chù.

汉字知识

汉字的字体演变 The Evolution of Chinese Characters

汉字产生于原始社会末期，至今已有五千多年的历史。从比较成熟的甲骨文算起，也有三千多年的历史了。从甲骨文产生至今，汉字字体发展经历了古文字和今文字两大阶段。古文字阶段可分为甲骨文、金文、大篆、小篆四个阶段。今文字以汉隶为开端，到汉末魏晋出现楷书，文字形体完成定型，迄今没有大的变化。甲骨文图画特征明显，由于是用刀在龟甲、兽骨上刻写的，因此线条比较细瘦，字形大小不一。金文笔画肥大厚实，结构、行款趋向整齐，图画特征明显减少，文字符号特征有所加强；大篆字形整齐匀称，笔画粗细一致，趋于线条化；小篆笔画、结构简易规范，字体、字形高度统一；隶书完全打破了小篆的结构，形成了点、横、竖、撇、捺等基本笔画，结构匀称、字形扁方，图画性完全消失，字体完全符号化；隶书是汉字发展史上的一个转折点，是古今文字的分水岭；草书是为提高书写速度在隶书的基础上形成的一种字体；楷书去掉了隶书的波势挑法，笔画十分平直，字形比较方正，结构显得紧凑。行书是介于草书和楷书之间的一种字体。行书的书写比楷书灵活流畅，辨认比较容易，已成为与楷书的各种变体印刷体相对的一种字体——手写体，人们日常书写，一般都使用行书。

甲骨文	金文	大篆	小篆	隶书	草书	楷书	行书	简化字

Chinese characters originated in the late primitive society and have a history of over 5,000 years. Even counting from the more mature Oracle Bone Script, they have a history of over 3,000 years. From the emergence of Oracle Bone Script to the present, the development of Chinese characters has gone through two major stages: ancient scripts and modern scripts. The ancient script stage can be divided into four phases: Oracle Bone Script, Bronze Script, Large Seal Script, and Small Seal Script. The modern script stage began with Clerical Script in the Han Dynasty, and by the end of the Han Dynasty and the Wei and Jin Periods, Regular Script emerged, marking the final standardization of the form of the characters, which has not undergone significant changes since. Oracle Bone Script has prominent pictographic features, and since it was carved with a knife on tortoise shells and animal bones, the lines are relatively thin, and the characters vary in size. Bronze Script has thicker and more substantial strokes, with a more uniform structure and layout, reducing pictographic features and enhancing symbolic characteristics. Large Seal Script has uniform and symmetrical character forms, with consistent stroke thickness, tending towards linearity. Small Seal Script has simple and standardized strokes and structure, with highly unified character form. Clerical Script completely broke away from the structure of Small Seal Script, forming basic strokes such as the dot, horizontal stroke, vertical stroke, left-falling stroke, and right-falling stroke. The structure is symmetrical, and the character form is flatter and squarer, completely losing the pictographic nature and becoming fully symbolic. Clerical Script is a turning point in the history of Chinese characters, and a watershed between ancient and modern scripts. Cursive Script developed from Clerical Script to increase the speed of writing. Regular Script eliminated the wave-like strokes of Clerical Script, with very straight strokes and squarer character forms, resulting in a compact structure. Semi-Cursive Script is a style between Cursive Script and Regular Script. It is more flexible and fluid to write than Regular Script and easier to recognize, and has become a handwritten style in contrary to various variants and printing styles of Regular Script. In daily writing, people generally use Semi-Cursive Script.

口语表达训练

一、问问同学们以后想买房还是租房。为什么？他们的家人同意不同意他们买房子？支撑他们观点的论据有哪些？ Ask your classmates if they want to buy a house or rent one in the future. Why? Do their families agree or disagree with them buying a house? What are the arguments that support their viewpoints?

同学姓名	买房 / 租房	理由

二、你和你父母的消费观点分别是什么？你认为你和父母在哪些方面消费观点相同？在哪些方面（如购房、择校、日常花销、爱好和娱乐等）不同？What are your and your parents' perspectives on consumption? In what ways do you think you and your parents share the same perspectives on consumption? And in what ways (e.g., buying a house, choosing a school, daily spending, hobbies and entertainment, etc.) do you differ?

我的观点	父母的观点	相同/不相同

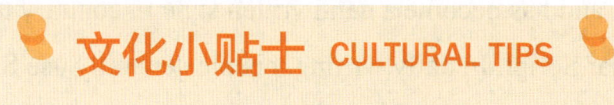

中国行政区划
Administrative Divisions of China

中国位于亚洲大陆的东部，陆地总面积为960万平方千米，幅员辽阔，疆域广大，为了对国家进行有效的管理，把国家疆域划分为不同的行政区域，这在中国有着悠久的历史。

春秋时期，开始设置"县"或"郡"；从秦汉到隋朝，中国大体实行"郡县制"；唐宋至辽金，则是实行"道路制"；元明清三代基本实行"行省制"；新中国成立后，全国的行政区划不断发展完善。

目前，中国有23个省、5个自治区、4个直辖市和2个特别行政区，共34个省级行政区域。直辖市是指由中国中央人民政府直接管辖的大城市，中国4个直辖市分别是北京市、上海市、天津市、重庆市，其中北京是中国的首都。自治区是省级民族自治地方，5个自治区分别是内蒙古自治区、广西壮族自治区、宁夏回族自治区、新疆维吾尔自治区、西藏自治区。2个特别行政区是香港特别行政区、澳门特别行政区。

我们可以通过顺口溜"两湖两广两河山，五江二宁青陕甘，云贵西四北上天，内重台海福吉安，还有港澳好河山"，来记住中国的行政区域。

China is located in the eastern part of the Asian continent, with a total land area of 9.6 million square kilometers. It is vast and expansive, and to effectively manage the country, its territory is divided into different administrative regions, a practice with a long history in China.

During the Spring and Autumn Period, various states began to establish "county" or "prefecture"; from the Qin and Han dynasties to the Sui Dynasty, China generally implemented the "prefecture and county system"; during the Tang, Song, Liao, and Jin dynasties, the "Dao-Lu system" was implemented; the Yuan, Ming, and Qing dynasties basically implemented the "Province system"; after the founding of the People's Republic of China, the country's administrative divisions have been continuously developing and improving.

Currently, China has 23 provinces, 5 autonomous regions, 4 municipalities, and 2 special administrative regions, totaling 34 provincial-level administrative regions. Municipalities are large cities directly administered by the State Council of the People's Republic of China. The 4 municipalities are Beijing, Shanghai, Tianjin, and Chongqing, with Beijing being the capital of China. Autonomous regions are provincial-level ethnic autonomous areas. The 5 autonomous regions are Inner Mongolia Autonomous Region, Guangxi Zhuang Autonomous Region, Ningxia Hui Autonomous Region, Xinjiang Uygur Autonomous Region, and Xizang Autonomous Region. The 2 special administrative regions are Hong Kong Special Administrative Region and Macau Special Administrative Region.

We can remember the administrative regions of China by the jingle "Two *Hu*, two *Guang*, two *He* and *Shan*, five *Jiang* and two *Ning*, *Qing*, *Shaan* and *Gan*, *Yun*, *Gui*, *Zang*, *Chuan*, *Jing*, *Hu*, and *Jin*, *Nei*, *Chong*, *Tai*, *Hai*, *Fu*, *Ji* and *An*, as well as Hong Kong and Macau".

23 我一点儿计划都没有
I don't have any plans at all

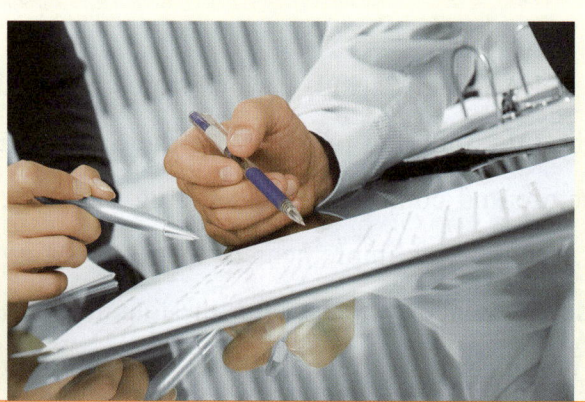

本课学习重点	
话题 Topic	谈假期计划 Talk about vacation plans
重点词 Keywords	早已 反复 决定 到达 深刻 演出 印象 保存 集中 必然
重点句 Key sentences	1. 我一点儿计划都没有。 2. 我还一个都没去过呢! 3. 我找了几家,反复比较,最后决定选网友评价最好的这家,网友们都说他们的服务特别好。 4. 想吃什么吃什么,想多慢就多慢。 5. 大熊猫们在那里想做什么就做什么。
语法 Grammar	1. 固定格式:一……也/都+不/没(有)…… Fixed pattern 2. 不用关联词语的承接复句 Successive complex sentences without correlatives 3. 疑问代词任指用法(2):疑问代词(+就)+疑问代词 Arbitrary reference of interrogative pronouns II
汉字知识 Knowledge of Chinese characters	中国书法艺术 The Art of Chinese Calligraphy
文化小贴士 Cultural tips	西南双城记 A Tale of Two Cities in the Southwest

23 我一点儿计划都没有

热身 WARM-UP

你去过中国的这些地方吗？请给下列景点选择对应的图片。Have you ever been to any of these places in China? Choose the corresponding pictures for the following scenic spots.

（1）黄山_____   （2）西湖_____
（3）杜甫草堂_____   （4）武侯祠_____
（5）四川大熊猫自然保护区_____   （6）宽窄巷子_____

A.

B.

C.

D.

E.

F.

课文 TEXT

课文 1 🎧 23-1

听前问题：安琪是一个人去旅行吗？

安琪：汉克，放假以后你有什么打算？

汉克：我一点儿计划都没有。你呢？

安琪：我早已计划好了。我想到各地旅旅游，打听了一下，黄山、西湖、成都都很不错。

汉克：你说的这些地方，我还一个都没去过呢！

安琪：那咱们一起去吧。

汉克：近期我有点儿忙，以后吧。不过，我很好奇你是一个人去旅行吗？

安琪：当然不是啦！我是跟团游。

汉克：从哪儿找的旅行社？

安琪：从网上。我找了几家，反复比较，最后决定选网友评价最好的这家，网友们都说他们的服务特别好。

汉克：这样你就不用亲自去办理各种手续了。

安琪：对啊！导游带领游客们坐飞机、前往酒店和景点，特别省心。

汉克：看来你只要带着行李，拿好证件，早点儿到达机场就行了。

安琪：是的。

汉克：那你预计旅行多久呢？

安琪：半个月吧。当中有一天是自由活动，正好可以去看我最喜欢的一位歌手的演唱会。能在现场看他的舞台演出，一直是我的愿望。

汉克：这样完美的旅行，一定会给你留下深刻的印象。

23 我一点儿计划都没有

> 课堂练习

1. 根据课文内容回答问题。Answer the questions based on the text.

    （1）汉克放假后有计划吗？安琪呢？

    （2）安琪从哪儿找的旅行社？她为什么选择跟团游？

    （3）安琪预计旅行多久？

2. 分角色表演课文。Act out the text in roles.

3. 如果你是课文中的安琪，请根据课文内容向大家介绍你的假期旅行计划。（可参考给出的词语）If you were Angie in the text, please introduce your travel plan for the vacation to the class based on the text. (You can refer to the words given)

各地	打听	旅行社	反复	办理	带领	前往
预计	当中	现场	完美	印象		

词语 1 🎧 23-2

	词语	拼音	词性	英文释义
1.	早已	zǎoyǐ	副词	already
2.	各地	gèdì	名词	everywhere; various places
3.	打听	dǎting	动词	inquire about
4.	近期	jìnqī	名词	near future
5.	好奇	hàoqí	形容词	curious
6.	团	tuán	名词	group
7.	旅行社	lǚxíngshè	名词	travel agency
8.	网上	wǎng shang		on the Internet
9.	反复	fǎnfù	副词、名词	over and over again; repeatedly; reversal
10.	决定	juédìng	动词、名词	decide; decision
11.	服务	fúwù	动词	serve

12. 办理	bànlǐ	动词	handle; deal
13. 手续	shǒuxù	名词	formalities; procedure
14. 带领	dàilǐng	动词	guide; lead
15. 游客	yóukè	名词	tourist
16. 前往	qiánwǎng	动词	head for; go up to
17. 酒店	jiǔdiàn	名词	hotel
18. 景点	jǐngdiǎn	名词	tourist attraction; scenic spot
19. 省心	shěng//xīn	动词	free from worry
20. 证件	zhèngjiàn	名词	certificate; credentials
21. 到达	dàodá	动词	arrive
22. 预计	yùjì	动词	estimate
23. 当中	dāngzhōng	名词	the midst
24. 演唱会	yǎnchànghuì	名词	concert
25. 现场	xiànchǎng	名词	site
26. 舞台	wǔtái	名词	stage
27. 演出	yǎnchū	动词、名词	perform; performance
28. 完美	wánměi	形容词	perfect
29. 留下	liúxia		leave
30. 深刻	shēnkè	形容词	deep; profound
31. 印象	yìnxiàng	名词	impression

专有名词

1. 黄山	Huáng Shān		Mount Huang
2. 西湖	Xī Hú		West Lake
3. 成都	Chéngdū		Chengdu

重点词

早已

（1）马上到假期了，我早已计划好了，我打算去法国旅行。
（2）演出还有一个小时开始，我们早已准备好了。
（3）很多年过去了，我早已忘了她了。

反复

（1）他反复问我明天的计划。
（2）最近太冷了，我一直反复感冒。
（3）妈妈病情的反复，让我们全家人都很担心她。

决定

（1）他决定明年出国留学。
（2）我还没决定这个周末要不要和他再见一面。
（3）公司这么重要的决定你怎么不告诉我呢？

到达

（1）我比他早二十分钟到达机场。
（2）他们两个人一起到达了演出现场。
（3）我家离学校很远，但坐地铁一个小时就能到达。

深刻

（1）这次演出给我留下了深刻的印象。
（2）这本书是他送给我的，对我有深刻的意义。
（3）这是一个深刻的话题，说到这个话题，大家都不说话了。

演出

（1）这个周末他去国家大剧院演出。

（2）昨天俄罗斯芭蕾舞团的演出太精彩了。

（3）你问问小陈，他可能知道明天的演出时间和地点。

印象

（1）A：你对中国的第一印象怎么样？

　　B：中国给我的第一印象是人多。

（2）她给我留下了非常深刻的印象。

（3）这件事我没有印象了，你问问别人吧。

练一练

选词填空。Fill in the blanks with the given words.

反复　深刻　到达　决定　预计　打听　完美　演出　早已　印象

（1）今天晚上是我的毕业_____，你有时间来看吗？

（2）我们预计还有两分钟_____学校。

（3）我们只见过一次，但他给我留下了非常不错的_____。

（4）这部电影有非常_____的教育意义，中小学生都应该去看一看。

（5）我觉得这次旅行很_____，已经开始计划下一次了。

（6）到现在你还不清楚我的_____是什么。

（7）下大雪了，火车晚点，我_____明天中午才能到家。

（8）我_____想好这个假期去哪儿玩儿了。

（9）经过他们_____研究，终于找到了问题的原因。

（10）你去别的班_____一下，我们是不是明天不上课？

课文 2 🎧 23-3

听前问题：成都有哪些旅游景点？

成都，是中国西南部一座美丽的城市，它已有2300多年的历史了。去成都旅行的话，首先要去的就是宽窄巷子，它是一条保存完整的清朝古街道。那里既有清朝民间建筑，又有民国时期的西式洋楼，集中体现了中西方古代建筑的美。除了观察古代传统建筑，你在那里还能明显感受到当地人的慢生活。喝茶、吃正宗的四川火锅，想吃什么吃什么，想多慢就多慢。

如果喜欢中国古代历史和文学，那么武侯祠和杜甫草堂是你必然要选择的两个地方。当你在那里看到眼前的一切时，可能会想到诸葛亮的故事和他写的文章，也可能会突然说出几句伟大诗人杜甫写的诗。

去成都，你不能不去看一看形象特别可爱的大熊猫。迎接你的不是一只两只，是很多很多只。成都是大熊猫的故乡，那儿有专门的自然保护区和繁育研究基地。大熊猫们在那里想做什么就做什么，它们被照顾得非常好。

第一次去成都是三年前，现在我想重游那里。因为还有好多地方没去过，好多美食没吃过。听我介绍了这么多，你会不会也想赶紧订张机票，和我一起出发？

课堂练习

1. 根据课文内容回答问题。Answer the questions based on the text.
   （1）成都在哪里？它有多少年的历史？
   （2）在宽窄巷子里你能看到什么？在武侯祠和杜甫草堂呢？
   （3）为什么去成都不能不去看大熊猫？

2. 根据课文内容填空，并复述课文。Fill in the blanks based on the text and retell it.

　　成都，是中国_____部一座_____的城市，它已有_____年的历史了。去成都旅行的话，首先要去的就是宽窄巷子，它是一条_____的清朝古街道。那里既有清朝_____，又有_____的西式洋楼，_____了中西方古代建筑的美。除了_____古代传统建筑，你在那里还能明显感受到当地人的慢生活。喝茶、吃正宗的_____，想吃什么吃什么，想多慢就多慢。

　　如果喜欢中国古代_____和_____，那么武侯祠和杜甫草堂是你_____要选择的两个地方。当你在那里看到眼前的_____时，可能会想到诸葛亮的故事和他写的_____，也可能会突然说出几句伟大诗人杜甫写的_____。

　　去成都，你不能不去看一看形象特别可爱的大熊猫。迎接你的不是一只两只，是很多很多只。成都是大熊猫的故乡，那儿有专门的自然保护区和_____。大熊猫们在那里想做什么就做什么，它们被_____得非常好。

　　第一次去成都是三年前，现在我想_____。因为还有好多地方没去过，好多美食没吃过。听我介绍了这么多，你会不会也想_____，和我一起出发？

3. 选用下列词语和句型，介绍一下中国的成都。Choose the following words and sentence patterns to introduce Chengdu, China.

西南　美丽　历史　首先　既……，又……　集中　体现
除了……，还……　疑问代词＋就＋疑问代词　必然　选择
不能不去

词语 2 🎧 23-4

词语	拼音	词性	英文释义
1. 西南	xīnán	名词	southwest
2. 保存	bǎocún	动词	conserve; save
3. 完整	wánzhěng	形容词	complete; whole
4. 清朝	Qīngcháo		Qing Dynasty
5. 古	gǔ	形容词	ancient
6. 街道	jiēdào	名词	street; avenue
7. 民间	mínjiān	名词	folk; the people
8. 建筑	jiànzhù	名词	architecture
9. 时期	shíqī	名词	period
10. 西式	xīshì		Western-style
11. 洋楼	yánglóu	名词	Western-style building of two storeys or more
12. 集中	jízhōng	形容词、动词	concentrated; concentrate
13. 体现	tǐxiàn	动词	embody; incarnate
14. 中西方	Zhōng-Xīfāng		China and the West
15. 美	měi	形容词	beautiful
16. 观察	guānchá	动词	observe
17. 火锅	huǒguō	名词	hotpot
18. 文学	wénxué	名词	literature
19. 必然	bìrán	形容词	certain; necessary; inevitable
20. 眼前	yǎnqián	名词	being before one's eyes
21. 文章	wénzhāng	名词	article; essay
22. 伟大	wěidà	形容词	great
23. 诗人	shīrén	名词	poet
24. 诗	shī	名词	poem

25.	熊猫	xióngmāo	名词	panda
26.	迎接	yíngjiē	动词	welcome
27.	繁育	fányù	动词	breed
28.	基地	jīdì	名词	base
29.	重	chóng	副词	once again
30.	订	dìng	动词	book; order

专有名词

1.	宽窄巷子	Kuān-zhǎi Xiàngzi	Wide and Narrow Alley
2.	民国时期	Mínguó shíqī	the Republic of China era
3.	四川	Sìchuān	Sichuan
4.	武侯祠	Wǔhóu Cí	Wuhou Shrine
5.	杜甫草堂	Dù Fǔ Cǎotáng	Du Fu Thatched Cottage
6.	诸葛亮	Zhūgě Liàng	Zhuge Liang, a character in the *Romance of the Three Kingdoms*, is a real historical figure who lived during the Three Kingdoms period in Chinese history. He is a person of great wisdom and resourcefulness.
7.	杜甫	Dù Fǔ	one of the greatest poets in Tang Dynasty

重点词

保存

（1）A：这是演出门票，请您保存好。

　　B：好的，谢谢。

（2）这几天太热了，水果保存不了很长时间。

（3）他送给我的这本书，我一直保存到现在。

23 我一点儿计划都没有

集中

（1）A：妈妈，这些衣服放在哪里？
　　　B：你把它们集中放在衣柜里吧。
（2）同学们，今天咱们集中复习一下前20课的语法。
（3）今天工作的时候，他总是不能集中注意力。

必然

（1）我们在学习中文时必然会有很多困难。
（2）成功必然属于努力的人。
（3）她学习很认真，这次考试取得第一名的好成绩是必然的。

练一练

选词填空。Fill in the blanks with the given words.

> 集中　必然　体现　保存　迎接　完整　重

（1）这部电影太好看了，我打算周末再_____看一遍。
（2）公司让我们几个人去机场_____法国旅游团。
（3）请您_____介绍一下这本书的内容。
（4）虽然弟弟只有三岁，但是他能把相同的玩具（wánjù, toy）_____放在一起。
（5）你写的这篇小作文，并没有_____父母对孩子的爱。
（6）期末考试要来了，大家_____会好好复习的。
（7）这本书对我来说很重要，我一定会好好_____。

语法 GRAMMAR

一、固定格式：一……也 / 都 + 不 / 没（有）…… Fixed pattern: 一……也 / 都 + 不 / 没（有）……

固定格式，表示完全否定，意思是"完全没有……"或者"完全不……"。"一"的后面常跟"量词 + 名词"或只跟名量词或动量词；"不"和"没"的后面常跟动词或形容词性成分。例如：

A fixed pattern that indicates complete negation, meaning "not having...at all" or "not at all". "一" is often followed by "quantifier + noun" or only a nominal or verbal quantifier; "不" and "没" are often followed by a verbal or adjectival element. For example:

（1）我一点儿计划都没有。

（2）我还一个都没去过呢！

（3）他一个人都不认识。

（4）北京他一次也没有来过。

练一练

1. 看图回答问题。Look at the pictures and answer the questions.

（1）健身房有人吗？

_____

（2）他们累吗？

_____

（3）她想吃饭吗？

_____

（4）她的手机有电吗？

_____

（5）杯子里有水吗？

_____

2. 用"一……也/都+不/没（有）……"改写句子。Rewrite the sentences with "一……也/都+不/没（有）……".

例如：我今天很累。→ 我今天一点儿都不累。

（1）教室里很热。

_____

（2）以前我去过成都。

_____

（3）她拿来了几本汉语书。

_____

（4）我会说英语。

_____

（5）妈妈吃了早饭。

_____

二、不用关联词语的承接复句　Successive complex sentences without correlatives

承接复句中,分句间的关系是时间或动作上的顺承。分句间可以不加关联词,通过动作发生的先后顺序排列分句,分句的排列顺序不可颠倒。

In a successive complex sentence, the relationship between the clauses is one of succession in time or action. The clauses can be arranged in the order in which the actions take place without correlatives, and the order of the clauses cannot be reversed.

例如:

(1) 我找了几家,反复比较,最后决定选网友评价最好的这家。

(2) 吃了晚饭,我们出去走走。

(3) 他回房间拿了衣服,去教室上课了。

练一练

1. 看图,用承接复句(不用关联词语)写句子。Look at the pictures and write successive complex sentences without correlatives.

(1)

_____

(2)

_____

（3）

_____

（4）

_____

（5）

_____

2. 连线。Match the columns.

（1）王老师打开门，　　　　　　　　我们在教室里继续学习一会儿。

（2）我们爬上了山，　　　　　　　　加入辣椒。

（3）下了课，　　　　　　　　　　　走进了教室。

（4）把肉丝放到锅里，　　　　　　　在山上照相。

三、疑问代词任指用法（2）：疑问代词（+就）+疑问代词 Arbitrary reference of interrogative pronouns II: Interrogative pronoun (+ 就) + Interrogative pronoun

疑问代词在这个句型中，不表示疑问，而表示任指。格式为：疑问代词（+就）+疑问代词，其中"就"也可以省略。用两个同样的疑问代词，前后呼应，指同一个人、同一件事物、同一种方式、同一个时间、同一个地点等。第一个疑问代词是任指的，第二个疑问代词表示的人或事物以第一个疑问代词为转移，与第一个疑问代词指称同样的人或事物。例如：

When an interrogative pronoun is used in the this sentence pattern, not to indicate doubt, but to indicate an arbitrary reference. The pattern is interrogative pronoun (+ 就) + interrogative pronoun, where "就" can also be omitted. Two same interrogative pronouns are used to refer to the same person, the same thing, the same way, the same time, the same place, etc. The first interrogative pronoun is arbitrary, and the second interrogative pronoun refers to the same person or thing as the first interrogative pronoun. For example:

1. 我们 想 (吃什么) (吃什么)。
2. 大熊猫在那里 想 (做什么) (做什么)。
3. 他们 (几点来) 就 (几点开始)。
4. 你喜欢 (哪个)，我就送你 (哪个)。
5. 你愿意 (怎么去) 就 (怎么去)。

练一练

1. 根据提示词，用疑问代词的任指用法完成句子。Complete the sentences with the arbitrary reference of interrogative pronouns based on the prompt words.

（1）我想_____ _____。（说）

（2）你喜欢_____ _____。（去）

（3）你_____，我就_____。（做）

（4）你们想_____ _____。（玩）

（5）这本书我想_____ _____。（给）

2. 请用"疑问代词+疑问代词"回答问题。Answer the questions with "interrogative pronoun + interrogative pronoun".

（1）这有很多饮料，我们买哪个？
_____

（2）这些人你喜欢谁？
_____

（3）我们怎么去机场？
_____

（4）这个比赛谁可以参加？
_____

（5）生日晚会几点开始？
_____

综合运用 COMPREHENSIVE USE

 语音练习 🎧 23-5

一、听录音选择正确答案。Listen to the recording and choose the correct answers.

1. A. zǎojǐ　　B. zǎoyǐ　　2. A. jìnqī　　B. jìnqí

3. A. fǎnfù　　B. fǎnfǔ　　4. A. dàilǐng　　B. dàilíng

5. A. bànlǐ　　B. pànlǐ　　6. A. bǎochún　　B. bǎocún

7. A. jiédào　　B. jiēdào　　8. A. jízhōng　　B. jízhòng

9. A. guānchá　　B. guāncā　　10. A. wénzāng　　B. wénzhāng

二、听句子给画线词语标声调。Listen to the sentences and mark the tones of the underlined words.

1. 我早已计划好了，我想到各地旅旅游。
2. 导游会带领游客们坐飞机、前往酒店和景点，特别省心。
3. 想吃什么吃什么，想多慢就多慢。
4. 大熊猫们在那里想做什么就做什么，它们被照顾得非常好。
5. 能在现场看他的舞台演出，一直是我的愿望。

三、听一听，读一读。Listen and read.

蜀相

[唐] 杜甫

丞相祠堂何处寻？锦官城外柏森森。

映阶碧草自春色，隔叶黄鹂空好音。

三顾频烦天下计，两朝开济老臣心。

出师未捷身先死，长使英雄泪满襟。

Shǔ Xiàng

[Táng] Dù Fǔ

Chéngxiàng cítáng hé chù xún? Jǐnguān Chéng wài bǎi sēnsēn.

Yìng jiē bìcǎo zì chūnsè, gé yè huánglí kōng hǎo yīn.

Sān gù pín fán tiānxià jì, liǎng cháo kāijì lǎo chén xīn.

Chūshī wèi jié shēn xiān sǐ, cháng shǐ yīngxióng lèi mǎn jīn.

汉字知识

中国书法艺术 The Art of Chinese Calligraphy

书法本来是指用毛笔书写汉字的方法和规律，在此基础上形成了汉字书法艺术。商代时，甲骨文部分文字书写全用曲线，线条圆转流利，应当是毛笔所书。战国时期毛笔书写已经非常普遍，现在可以见到当时写在竹简上的文字。汉代造纸技术的成熟使得纸张成为毛笔书写的主要材料，并逐渐取代了丝帛、竹简。毛笔和纸张的普遍使用使书法艺术进入了迅速发展的阶段，涌现出了大量著名的书法家。如魏晋时期的钟繇、王羲之，唐代的颜真卿、柳公权、欧阳询等。

毛笔书法用得比较多的书体主要有五种，即楷书、行书、草书、隶书、篆书。毛笔书法作品常常用作家庭和公共场所的装饰品。硬笔书法用得比较多的主要是楷书和行书两种实用性的字体。

传统的中文书写格式是从上到下一个字一个字地书写，从右到左一列一列地书写，现在很多书法作品还是采用这样的传统书写方式。

Calligraphy originally referred to the method and rules of writing Chinese characters with a writing brush. Based on this, the art of Chinese calligraphy was formed. During the Shang Dynasty, some Oracle Bone Script characters were written entirely with curves, featuring smooth and flowing lines, likely written with a writing brush. By the Warring States Period, brush writing had become very common, and we can still see characters written on bamboo slips from that time. The maturation of papermaking technology in the Han Dynasty made paper the primary material for brush writing, gradually replacing silk and bamboo slips. The widespread use of brushes and paper led to a rapid development phase for the art of calligraphy, producing many famous calligraphers. Notable examples include Zhong Yao and Wang Xizhi from the Wei and Jin Periods, and Yan Zhenqing, Liu Gongquan, and Ouyang Xun from the Tang Dynasty.

There are mainly five styles of brush calligraphy, namely Regular Script (Kǎishū), Semi-Cursive Script (Xíngshū), Cursive Script (Cǎoshū), Clerical Script (Lìshū), and Seal Script (Zhuànshū). Brush calligraphy works are often used as decorative pieces in homes and public spaces. Hard-pen calligraphy mainly uses the practical styles of Regular Script and Semi-Cursive Script.

The traditional format for writing Chinese is from top to bottom, one character at a time, and from right to left, one column at a time. Many calligraphy works still adopt this traditional writing method today.

口语表达训练

一、这个假期你有什么计划？请三位同学介绍一下他们的假期旅游计划，并完成调查表。What is your plan for this vacation? Ask three of your classmates to introduce their travel plans for the vacation and complete the questionnaire.

同学姓名	假期旅游计划		
	去哪儿？	为什么去那里？	打算怎么去？为什么选这种方式去？

二、你去过哪些景点？那些景点给你留下了什么印象深刻的人或事？请给大家介绍一下。What scenic spots have you been to? Who or what impressed you deeply? Please tell us about them.

我的旅游经历		
景点名	景点介绍	印象深刻的人 / 事

西南双城记

A Tale of Two Cities in the Southwest

巴蜀一家亲，川渝一盘棋。

成都，四川省省会，别称"蓉城、锦城"，处于四川盆地西部，地势平坦、河网纵横、物产丰富、农业发达。成都是中国历史文化名城、古蜀文明发祥地、中国十大古都之一，自古便有"天府之国"的美誉。重庆原为四川省辖市（地级），1997年设为直辖市、重庆是中国西南地区最大的工商业城市，有"中国火锅之都"的称号。

成都与重庆两个城市有着深厚的历史渊源。作为中国西部两个重要的中心城市，两个城市之间既有竞争，也有合作。两个城市在竞争中打破地域界限，加强城市间的经济合作和一体化建设，极大地促进了巴蜀大地乃至整个西部地区的经济发展。

Bashu as one family, Chuan and Yu as one chessboard.

Chengdu, the capital of Sichuan Province, is also known as "Rongcheng" and "Jincheng". Located in the western part of the Sichuan Basin, Chengdu has flat terrain, an extensive network of rivers, abundant resources, and developed agriculture. Chengdu is a famous historical and cultural city in China, the birthplace of the ancient Shu civilization, and one of China's ten ancient capitals. It has long been praised as the "Land of Abundance". Chongqing was originally a prefecture-level city under Sichuan Province but was established as a municipality in 1997. Chongqing is the largest commercial and industrial city in southwestern China and is known as the "Hot Pot Capital of China".

Chengdu and Chongqing share deep historical ties. As two important central cities in western China, there are both competition and cooperation between the two cities. Through competition, they have broken down regional boundaries, strengthened economic cooperation, and promoted integrated development, which greatly advanced the economic growth of the Bashu region and the entire western area.

24 你不是要读研究生吗?
Aren't you going to graduate school?

本课学习重点	
话题 Topic	谈理想 Talk about ideals
重点词 Keywords	如何　理想　专业　想象　到底　果然　进步　不断　值得
重点句 Key sentences	1. 你不是要读研究生吗? 2. 我期待以后可以在什么公司做汉语翻译。 3. 我是还没有想好到底要做什么,不过我一点儿也不担心,到时候总会有安排的。 4. 你越着急,就越不知道怎么办才好。 5. 我早已想好了,就希望二十年以后我还好好的。 6. 课堂上老师让我给大家说点儿什么,说真的,我是有点儿激动。
语法 Grammar	1. 强调的方法 Ways to emphasize 　(1) 用反问句表示强调:不是……吗? / 难道……吗? 　(2) 用"一点儿也不……"表示强调 　(3) 用"是"表示强调 　(4) 用"就"表示强调 2. 疑问代词的不定指用法 Indefinite reference of interrogative pronouns 3. 固定格式:Fixed pattern: 　越……,越……
汉字知识 Knowledge of Chinese characters	常见印刷字体 Common Printing Fonts
文化小贴士 Cultural tips	理想也会变化 Ideals Will Also Change

24 你不是要读研究生吗？

热 身 WARM-UP

给下面的词语选择对应的图片。Choose the corresponding pictures for the following words.

A.

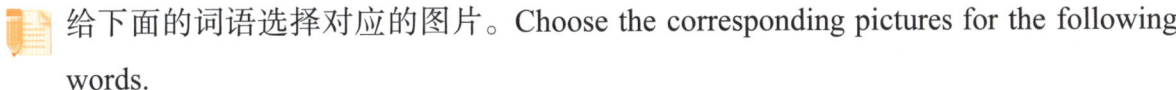
B.

C.

D.

E.

F.

（1）做鬼脸 zuò guǐliǎn _____　　（2）支持 zhīchí _____

（3）教授 jiàoshòu _____　　（4）告别 gàobié _____

（5）增加 zēngjiā _____　　（6）勇敢 yǒnggǎn _____

课文 TEXT

课文 1 🎧 24-1

听前问题：二十年后，乔治可能会是什么样子？

老师： 毕业以后你们如何打算啊？来，说说你们的理想。

大卫： 我是想先回国生活一段时间，最好先找个满意的工作，然后再考虑接着做什么。

爱华： 大卫，你不是要读研究生吗？

大卫： 原来确实是这个打算，不过现在变了。你呢？爱华。

爱华： 我想读研究生，但是还没想好选什么专业。

安琪： 我期待以后可以在什么公司做汉语翻译，工作地点可能会在不同的国家。

野田： 你难道不想读研究生？

安琪： 当然想了。不过有好的工作机会，我就会先工作。

乔治： 我是还没有想好到底要做什么，不过我一点儿也不担心，到时候总会有安排的。你越着急，就越不知道怎么办才好。

老师： 想象一下，二十年以后再回学校来，你们会是个什么样子？

大卫： 二十年以后我希望自己成为一个作家，把我写的作品送给老师。

爱华： 我希望当一名教授，二十年以后把我教过的学生也送到这里来学习汉语。

野田： 我在校园里种了一棵树，二十年以后，我会带着我的孩子来看看这棵树长成什么样子了。

安琪： 我希望以后我能当一个大老板，赚很多钱，到那时我请大家在哪儿吃烤鸭。

24 你不是要读研究生吗?

乔治：我早已想好了，就希望二十年以后我还好好的。（做鬼脸）

老师：乔治，大家都说你是越来越有意思了，果然是这样。

课堂练习

1. 根据课文内容回答问题。Answer the questions based on the text.

   （1）毕业后大卫会做什么？

   （2）安琪打算毕业以后做什么？

   （3）想象中，二十年后爱华会是什么样子？

2. 分角色表演课文。Act out the text in roles.

3. 如果你是课文中的乔治，请根据课文内容向大家介绍你和你的同学们的理想。（可参考给出的词语和句型）If you were George in the text, please tell us about the ideals of you and your classmates based on the text. (You may refer to the words and sentence patterns given)

> 先……，然后……　　研究生　　专业　　期待　　机会
> 一点儿也不　　越……，越……

词语 1 🎧 24-2

	词语	拼音	词性	英文释义
1.	如何	rúhé	代词	how; what
2.	理想	lǐxiǎng	名词、形容词	ideal; dream
3.	研究生	yánjiūshēng	名词	graduate student; postgraduate
4.	专业	zhuānyè	名词、形容词	major; profession; professional
5.	期待	qīdài	动词	look forward to; expect
6.	难道	nándào	副词	*used in a rhetorical question for emphasis*
7.	到底	dàodǐ	副词	finally; in the end

8. 想象	xiǎngxiàng	动词、名词	imagine; imagination
9. 作家	zuòjiā	名词	writer
10. 作品	zuòpǐn	名词	works
11. 教授	jiàoshòu	名词	professor
12. 校园	xiàoyuán	名词	campus
13. 老板	lǎobǎn	名词	boss; business owner
14. 赚	zhuàn	动词	gain; make a profit
15. 那时	nà shí		then
16. 烤鸭	kǎoyā	名词	roast duck
17. 做鬼脸	zuò guǐliǎn		make faces
18. 果然	guǒrán	副词	as expected

重点词

如何

（1）请问，留学生如何在网上买火车票？

（2）我一点儿也不关心你是如何找到手机的。

（3）我很好奇他们是如何学会四川话的。

理想

（1）娜娜的理想是成为一位成功的英汉翻译。

（2）我们要做有理想的年轻人。

（3）他学习非常努力，但是成绩并不理想。

24 你不是要读研究生吗?

专业

（1）大学我打算选择汉语专业。
（2）我们学校教小学生篮球的都是专业的篮球教练。
（3）我们公司这次请来的翻译非常专业。

想象

（1）很难想象，一个人不会说英语，怎么在说英语的国家生活。
（2）请想象一下，你以后会在哪里工作。
（3）这都只是你自己的想象，根本不是真的。

到底

（1）他看起来这么年轻，到底是老师还是学生？
（2）他沉默了半天，到底还是说出了自己的观点。
（3）南方到底是南方，三月已经很热了。

果然

（1）听说这部电影很好，看了以后果然不错。
（2）天气预报说今天要下雨，果然下雨了。
（3）那里果然像你说的那么冷，我出门的时候要多穿点儿衣服。

练一练

选词填空。Fill in the blanks with the given words.

> 期待　到底　赚　果然　如何　理想　专业　想象

（1）真没想到，咱俩选的_____一样。
（2）我们可以去北京学习了，我们都很_____北京的生活。

（3）小时候，他的_____是成为一名老师。
（4）你教会了我_____更好地学习中文。
（5）我_____不到自己结婚以后的样子。
（6）认真学习后，安娜的成绩_____提高了。
（7）如果_____了很多钱，我想买个房子自己住。
（8）他说这话_____是什么意思？我不太明白。

课文 2 24-3

听前问题：我因为什么事情有点儿激动？

这个学期马上就要结束了，我也马上就独自回国继续上大学了。课堂上老师让我给大家说点儿什么，说真的，我是有点儿激动。

在这个学期，我学到了许多有用的知识，也取得了不少进步。我通过了HSK五级，也获得了学校的奖学金，今年还成了优秀留学生。在这一年中，有成功，也有失败；有快乐，也有难过。我认识了许多来自不同国家的朋友，虽然大家的国籍不同，但是老师、同学，还有生活中碰到的那些普普通通的人，大家都对我很友好，也很热情。

在这个时候，我特别想表达我对他们的感谢。感谢各位老师对我的培养，让我学会了这么多的知识，让我能成为一名合格的留学生；感谢同学和朋友的关心和照顾，让我在中国也找到了家的感觉；感谢爸妈对我的支持和信任，他们不断地鼓励我努力学习；我还要感谢大学生活中遇到的每一个人，给我的生活增加了这么多不一样的色彩。

二十二岁的我，将来还要面对很多新的挑战。以后遇到什么情况，我相信我都会勇敢地去面对，用乐观的态度对待一切。我相信，越是困难的事，越值得我们去做。

马上就跟老师和同学们告别了，我心中有点儿难过，希望以后还

24 你不是要读研究生吗？

能再回到中国，在这里继续工作和生活。

课堂练习

1. 根据课文内容回答问题。Answer the questions based on the text.

   （1）这个学期"我"过得怎么样？

   （2）"我"感谢了哪些人？为什么感谢他们？

   （3）说这些话的时候"我"的心情是怎样的？为什么会有这样的心情？

2. 根据课文内容填空，并复述课文。Fill in the blanks based on the text and retell it.

   这个学期_____就要结束了，我也马上就_____回国继续上大学了。课堂上老师让我给大家_____，说真的，我是有点儿_____。

   在这个学期，我学到了许多_____，也取得了不少_____。我通过了HSK五级，也获得了学校的_____，今年还成了_____留学生。在这一年中，有成功，也有_____；有_____，也有难过。我认识了许多来自不同国家的朋友，虽然大家的_____不同，但是老师、同学，还有生活中碰到的那些_____的人，大家都对我很友好，也很_____。

   在这个时候，我特别想表达我对他们的_____。感谢各位老师对我的_____，让我学会了这么多的知识，让我能成为一名合格的留学生；感谢同学和朋友的_____和照顾，让我在中国也找到了家的_____；感谢爸妈对我的支持和_____，他们不断地_____我努力学习；我还要感谢大学生活中遇到的每一个人，给我的生活增加了这么多不一样的_____。

   二十二岁的我，将来还要面对很多新的_____。遇到什么情况，我相信我都会_____地去面对，用_____的态度对待一切。我相信，越是困难的事，越_____我们去做。

   马上就跟老师和同学们_____了，我心中有点儿难过，希望以后还能再回到中国，在这里继续工作和_____。

229

3. 这个学期马上就结束了，你想对你的老师和同学们说点儿什么？请选用下列提示词语和句型说一说。This semester is coming to an end soon. What would you like to say to your teachers and classmates? Please say something using the following prompt words and sentence pattern.

| 激动 | 进步 | 获得 | 失败 | 合格 | 支持 | 培养 |
| 信任 | 不断 | 将来 | 值得 | 越……越…… | | |

词语 2 🎧 24-4

	词语	拼音	词性	英文释义
1.	独自	dúzì	副词	by oneself
2.	课堂	kètáng	名词	classroom
3.	激动	jīdòng	形容词	excited; thrilled
4.	获得	huòdé	动词	acquire; obtain; gain
5.	奖学金	jiǎngxuéjīn	名词	scholarship
6.	失败	shībài	动词、形容词	fail; lose; failed
7.	国籍	guójí	名词	nationality
8.	表达	biǎodá	动词	express
9.	各位	gèwèi	代词	everyone
10.	培养	péiyǎng	动词	train; cultivate; nurture
11.	合格	hégé	形容词	qualified
12.	支持	zhīchí	动词	support
13.	信任	xìnrèn	动词	trust
14.	不断	búduàn	副词、动词	constantly; not stop
15.	色彩	sècǎi	名词	color
16.	将来	jiānglái	名词	future
17.	勇敢	yǒnggǎn	形容词	brave; courageous

24 你不是要读研究生吗？

18. 值得	zhí//dé	动词	be worthwhile
19. 告别	gào//bié	动词	say farewell to

重点词

进步

（1）这个学期，他的汉语口语进步很大。
（2）虽然他每天很努力地工作，但是却觉得自己一点儿进步也没有。
（3）弟弟最近的学习成绩已经有了不小的进步。

不断

（1）这条路上的红绿灯总是不断地出现问题。
（2）妈妈希望你新的学期不断取得进步。
（3）不知道为什么，最近我总是麻烦不断。

值得

（1）这么好的音乐会，值得去。
（2）花了这么多钱只买了一个小碗，真不值得。
（3）这点儿小事也值得你哭？

练一练

选词填空。Fill in the blanks with the given words.

表达　增加　支持　告别　激动　进步　不断　值得

（1）你想得到大家的_____，就得先清楚地表达你的观点。
（2）我们可以把她的观点_____进来。

（3）他怎么这么_____？发生什么事情了吗？

（4）上课的时候，他总是_____地影响我听课。

（5）长大以后，我们都要学会和小时候的自己_____。

（6）他说了很多，可是我不知道他想_____什么。

（7）他这样一个人，还_____你去爱他？

（8）科技_____了，我们的生活也发生了很大的改变。

语法 GRAMMAR

一、强调的方法　Ways to emphasize

1. 用反问句表示强调　Emphasize with a rhetorical question

"不是……吗？"该格式强调肯定，提醒注意某种明显的事实。

This pattern emphasizes affirmation, drawing attention to an obvious fact.

（1）你不是要读研究生吗？——我认为你要读研究生。

（2）天气预报不是说今天有雨吗？——天气预报说今天有雨。

（3）她不是你的好朋友吗？——我觉得她是你的好朋友。

"难道……吗？"该格式中的"吗"也可换为"不成"，或者直接用"难道……"表示反问，句中往往有副词"还"及能愿动词"能""会""得"等，全句有"不会""不可能""不一定"的意思，常含有不容辩驳的语气。

The character "吗" in this pattern can also be replaced with "不成" or simply using "难道……" to express a rhetorical question. There are often adverbs such as "还" and modal verbs such as "能", "会" and "得" in the sentence. The whole sentence contains the meaning of "won't", "can't", "not sure", and often contains an irrefutable tone.

（1）你难道不想上研究生？——我认为你肯定想上研究生。

（2）这么简单的题，她难道不会做吗？——这么简单的题，我觉得她一定会做。

（3）都这么晚了，难道还要奶奶亲自去不成？——这么晚了，不应该让奶奶亲自去了。

2. 用"一点儿也不……"表示强调 Emphasize with "一点儿也不……"

"一点儿也 / 都 + 不 + 形容词 / 动词"格式表示完全否定。

The pattern "一点儿也 / 都 + 不 + adjective/verb" indicates complete negation.

(1) 中文一点儿也不简单。

(2) 妈妈昨天买的西瓜一点儿都不甜。

(3) 法语太难了，我一点儿都不会。

(4) 她最近在减肥，晚饭一点儿也不吃。

3. 用"是"表示强调 Emphasize with "是"

用在动词（短语）、形容词（短语）前表示强调，所强调的往往具有较高的程度，或肯定前边的话，所肯定的是已知信息。

It is used before verbs (verb phrases) and adjectives (adjective phrases) to emphasize and what is emphasized is often of a higher degree or to affirm what has been said before, which is known information.

(1) 课堂上老师让我给大家说点儿什么，说真的，我是有点儿激动。

(2) 你说得没错，中国人口是挺多的。

(3) 学生们是又唱歌又跳舞，特别高兴。

(4) A：这个电影是不是很不错？

B：这个电影是很不错。

4. 用"就"表示强调 Emphasize with "就"

"就"可以表示肯定的语气，一般放在谓语前。

"就" can express an affirmative tone and is usually placed before the predicate.

(1) 我早已想好了，就希望二十年以后我还好好的。

(2) 你看，这就是我们上课的教室。

(3) 她家就在前面的医院旁边。

(4) 你别问了，我就不知道这件事。

> 练一练

1. 根据提示词，改写句子。Rewrite the sentences with the prompt words.

　（1）这双鞋穿着很舒服。

　　　_____。（一点儿也/都不）

　（2）你来北京这么久了，一定去过长城吧。

　　　_____？（难道……吗）

　（3）你汉语说得很好，学了很长时间吧。

　　　_____？（不是……吗）

　（4）你说得对，那家饭馆的饭菜很好吃。

　　　_____。（是）

　（5）我家在学校旁边，离学校很近。

　　　_____。（就）

2. 完成对话。Complete the conversations.

　（1）A：你喜欢看电影吗？

　　　B：_____。（一点儿也不）

　（2）A：_____？（难道……吗）

　　　B：没想到吧，汉语我真的没学多久。

　（3）A：_____？（不是……吗）

　　　B：你记错了，今天不是星期天。

　（4）A：大卫，我昨天给你推荐的书很好看吧。

　　　B：_____。（是）

　（5）A：电影院离车站很近吗？

　　　B：对，_____。（就）

24 你不是要读研究生吗？

二、疑问代词的不定指用法　Indefinite reference of interrogative pronouns

疑问代词用于不定指时，表示不知道、说不出来或者不想说的人或事物。例如：

When used as the indefinite, interrogative pronouns refer to something or someone that one doesn't know, or that one cannot say, or that one doesn't want to talk about. For example:

（1）这件事好像谁告诉过我。

（2）你看起来很眼熟，我们好像在什么地方见过面。

（3）我把东西落在宿舍了，你坐哪儿等我一下。

（4）你哪天有时间，来我家玩儿吧。

练一练

1. 根据提示，完成对话。Complete the conversations with the prompts.

　（1）A：_____吧。（什么）

　　　　B：好，我也有点儿渴了。

　（2）A：_____吧。（哪儿）

　　　　B：今天天气很好，我们去公园吧。

　（3）A：_____。（谁）

　　　　B：附近没有人，怎么问路呢？

　（4）A：_____。（什么时候）

　　　　B：等考完试，周末再去吧。

　（5）A：太累了。

　　　　B：_____。（怎么）

2. 用疑问代词完成下面的句子。Complete the sentences with interrogative pronouns.

　（1）只要去了商店，_____。

　（2）看她的嘴在动，好像_____。

　（3）这么多东西你一个人搬不了，_____。

　（4）王老师刚买了车，_____。

　（5）一个人旅行真没意思，_____。

235

三、固定格式：越……，越…… Fixed pattern: 越……，越……

固定格式"越……，越……"，表示在程度上后者随着前者的变化而变化。有以下两种情况：

The fixed pattern "越……，越……" indicates that the latter changes with the former in terms of degree. There are two cases:

1. 前后主语相同。例如：The former and the latter have the same subject. For example:

（1）汉语越学越有意思。

（2）雨越下越大。

（3）鸟儿越飞越高，最后看不见了。

2. 前后主语不同。例如：The former and the latter have different subjects. For example:

（1）衣服越好看，价格越贵。

（2）人的压力越大，身体越容易出现问题。

（3）十多岁的孩子不愿意听父母的话，父母越说，他们越不听。

练一练

1. 根据下列情况，用"越……，越……"造句。Write sentences with "越……，越……" based on the following situations.

（1）昨天的雨：小雨→中雨→大雨

_____。

（2）大卫的睡觉时间：11:00pm → 12:00pm → 1:00am

_____。

（3）汉语：没意思→有点儿意思→很有意思

_____。

（4）跑步：很慢，不累→不快，有点儿累→很快，很累

_____。

（5）妈妈不批评，孩子很听话→妈妈批评，孩子不听话

_____。

2. 用"越……，越……"完成句子或对话。Complete the sentences or conversations with "越……，越……".

（1）考试的时候不要紧张，因为_____。

（2）买这种苹果要买红一点儿的，因为_____。

（3）A：你喝饮料喜欢喝冰的还是热的？
　　　B：_____。

（4）A：你为什么总是买这么贵的衣服？
　　　B：_____。

（5）A：你听到家乡的音乐就想家了吧？
　　　B：_____。

综合运用 COMPREHENSIVE USE

语音练习 24-5

一、听录音选择正确答案。Listen to the recording and choose the correct answers.

1. A. jiānglái　　　B. jiànglái　　　2. A. guōrān　　　B. guǒrán
3. A. xiǎngxiàng　　B. xiǎngxiang　　4. A. biǎodā　　　B. biǎodá
5. A. dúzì　　　　　B. dúzhì　　　　6. A. péiyǎng　　　B. béiyǎng
7. A. gǎobié　　　　B. gào//bié　　　8. A. lǐxiǎng　　　B. lǐxiàng
9. A. sècǎi　　　　 B. sèchǎi　　　 10. A. dāodǐ　　　　B. dàodǐ

二、听句子给画线词语标声调。Listen to the sentences and mark the tones of the underlined words.

1. 我想读<u>研究生</u>，但是还没想好选什么<u>专业</u>。

2. 你越<u>着急</u>，就越不知道<u>怎么办</u>才好。

3. <u>课堂</u>上老师让我给大家说点儿什么，我是有点儿<u>激动</u>。

4. 我还要感谢大学生活中遇到的每一个人，给我的生活增加了这么多不一样的色彩。

5. 我相信，越是困难的事，越值得我们去做。

三、听一听，读一读。Listen and read.

忆江南　　　　　　　　　　　　Yì Jiāngnán

[唐]　白居易　　　　　　　　　[Táng]　Bái Jūyì

江南好，风景旧曾谙。　　　　　Jiāngnán hǎo, fēngjǐng jiù céng ān.

日出江花红胜火，春来江水绿如蓝。　Rì chū jiānghuā hóng shèng huǒ, chūn lái jiāngshuǐ lǜ rú lán.

能不忆江南？　　　　　　　　　Néng bú yì Jiāngnán?

 汉字知识

常见印刷字体 Common Printing Fonts

　　唐代末期，中国开始印刷书籍。最初的印刷字体是雕版印刷用的字体。雕版印刷是中国发明的印刷方法，先将写好的文字反贴于木板上，然后雕刻成反体凸字，制成印版。因此，雕版印刷的字体是手写的楷书。到了宋代，印刷数量和品种大大增加，出现了专职写版的人员，他们和刻版工匠合作，设计了一种美观而较易雕刻的字体，这就是初期的宋体。宋体是在楷书的基础上形成的，最大的特点是横细竖粗、结体方正严谨。除了宋体外，常用的印刷字体还有仿宋体、楷体、黑体等。

　　印刷体字体的大小分不同的字号，中文印刷字体常用字号与磅数的对应关系可以上网查询。

　　Towards the end of Tang Dynasty, China began printing books. The earliest printing font was that used for woodblock printing, a printing method invented in China. This involved pasting the written text face down onto a wooden board, and then carving out the reversed text to create a raised printing block. Therefore, the font used in woodblock printing was handwritten Regular Script (Kǎishū). During the Song Dynasty, the volume and variety of printed materials had greatly increased, leading to the emergence of specialized block writers who worked with carvers and designed a font that was both aesthetically pleasing and relatively easy to carve. This resulted in the early form of Song typeface (Sòngtǐ). Song typeface is formed based on Regular Script and is characterized by thin horizontal strokes and thick vertical strokes, with a formal and square structure. In addition to Song typeface, other commonly used printing fonts include Fangsong (Imitation Song), Kaishu (Regular Script), and Heiti (Black Body).

The size of printing fonts is measured in different point sizes. The correspondence between common Chinese printing font sizes and point sizes can be found online.

口语表达训练

一、请问一问同学们的理想是什么。请三位同学介绍一下他们的理想，完成调查表。
Ask your classmates about their ideals. Ask three of your classmates to describe their ideals and complete the questionnaire.

同学姓名	理想 / 将来想做的事	为什么

二、你的理想是什么？为什么？你打算怎么做？ What is your ideal? Why? What do you plan to do?

我的理想：
为什么：
怎么实现： 1. 2. 3. ……

文化小贴士 CULTURAL TIPS

理想也会变化
Ideals Will Also Change

理想是照亮人生道路的一盏灯,指引着每个人向前走下去。如果没有理想,人在前进的过程中很容易失去方向,很容易变得迷茫。每个人的经历和性格都不相同,每个人的理想也都不一样,但不变的是为了实现自己的理想,每个人都需要付出很多的努力。

实际上,随着时代的变化,年轻人的理想也在发生变化。

有些年轻人希望自己可以做出很大的贡献,比如成为一名科学家,发明出了不起的东西,改善大家的生活;或者成为一名航天员,到九天之上为人类探索宇宙的奥秘。也有些年轻人希望在平凡的岗位上做出不平凡的事。比如成为一名医生,学好一身本领,在医院挽救无数病人的生命;或者成为一名教师,在学校里培养国家未来的花朵。

社会一直在发展,社会分工也日益细致。现在很多年轻人的理想已经变"小"了很多,只要能做好一件事就行,哪怕要花一辈子的时间。这种精益求精、精雕细琢的精神被称为"匠人精神"。比如在故宫修复文物的文物修复师们,靠自己的双手让宝贵的文物获得新生。除此之外,甚至有的年轻人的理想仅仅是平凡地过好自己的生活,不让工作占据所有的时间,拥有劳逸结合的生活。

理想不分高低贵贱,不管是什么样的理想,都会在我们前行的路上带来光和希望。

Ideals are like a lamp that illuminates the path of life, guiding each person forward. Without ideals, people can easily lose their way and become confused during their journey. Everyone's experience and personality is different, so is his/her ideal. However, what remains constant is that everyone needs to put in a lot of effort to achieve his/her ideal.

In fact, as times change, the ideals of young people are also changing.

Some young people aspire to make significant contributions, such as becoming scientists and inventing remarkable things to improve everyone's life, or becoming astronauts and exploring the mysteries of the universe for mankind. Some young people hope to do extraordinary things in ordinary positions, such as becoming doctors and saving countless lives in hospitals, or becoming teachers and nurturing the future of the nation in schools.

Society is constantly developing, and social divisions of labor are becoming increasingly refined. Nowadays, many young people's ideals have become more modest. They aim to do one thing well, even if it takes a lifetime. This spirit of pursuing perfection and meticulous craftsmanship is known as the "spirit of craftsmanship". For example, the artisans who restore cultural artefacts in the Imperial Palace use their hands to breathe new life into precious cultural relics. Beyond that, some young people's ideals are simply to live a peaceful life, not letting work consume all their time, and achieving a balance between work and leisure.

Ideals are not ranked by nobility. No matter what kind of ideal it is, it will bring light and hope to our journey.

生词表

		A		
阿姨	āyí	名词	auntie	19
爱人	àiren	名词	my love; sweetheart; spouse	19
按	àn	介词	according to	22
按照	ànzhào	介词	according to	13
		B		
把	bǎ	介词	*used to put the object before the verb*	16
把握	bǎwò	动词、名词	grasp; seize; assurance	18
白	bái	副词	for nothing	20
办法	bànfǎ	名词	way; approach	14
办理	bànlǐ	动词	handle; deal	23
半天	bàntiān	数量词	quite a while	17
伴奏	bànzòu	动词	musical accompaniment	15
帮忙	bāng//máng	动词	help	16
保持	bǎochí	动词	keep	18
保存	bǎocún	动词	conserve; save	23
保护	bǎohù	动词	protect; preserve	14
被	bèi	介词	*used in a passive sentence to introduce the agent/doer*	20
本来	běnlái	副词	originally; at first	15
笔	bǐ	量词	*used to indicate sums of money or business*	22
必然	bìrán	形容词	certain; necessary; inevitable	23
必须	bìxū	副词	must; have to	20
变化	biànhuà	动词、名词	change	18
表达	biǎodá	动词	express	24

表明	biǎomíng	动词	make clear; show	22
并且	bìngqiě	连词	and; what's more	17
播放	bōfàng	动词	play	21
不断	búduàn	副词、动词	constantly; not stop	24
不太	bú tài		not too	22
不用	búyòng	副词	need not	22
不再	búzài	动词	no more	18
补	bǔ	动词	make up for	17
不得不	bùdébù		have to; cannot but	18
不光	bùguāng	连词	not only	17
不仅	bùjǐn	连词	not only	19
不少	bù shǎo		quite a few	18
不行	bùxíng	动词	not allow	14
不一定	bùyídìng	副词	not certainly	15
不一会儿	bù yíhuìr		a while	13
C					
材料	cáiliào	名词	material; ingredient	16
菜谱	càipǔ	名词	recipe; cookbook	16
餐	cān	名词	meal	21
拆	chāi	动词	unpack; unwrap	13
长期	chángqī	名词	long term; a long period of time	18
尝	cháng	动词	taste	17
常见	cháng jiàn		common	14
常用	cháng yòng		frequently used; in common use	16
超过	chāoguò	动词	be over; exceed	20
朝	cháo	介词、动词	towards; face	14
炒	chǎo	动词	stir fry	16
陈	Chén	名词	a surname	17
衬衫	chènshān	名词	shirt	22

称为	chēngwéi		be called as	18
成就	chéngjiù	名词、动词	achievement; accomplish	18
成长	chéngzhǎng	动词	grow	18
程度	chéngdù	名词	level; degree	19
池塘	chítáng	名词	pond	14
重	chóng	副词	once again	23
重新	chóngxīn	副词	again	13
抽烟	chōu//yān	动词	smoke	13
出来	chū//lái	动词	used after a verb to indicate the completion of an action	14
出现	chūxiàn	动词	appear; occur	20
出院	chū//yuàn	动词	be discharged; leave hospital	20
出租车	chūzūchē	名词	taxi; cab	20
除了	chúle	介词	besides	22
处理	chǔlǐ	动词	deal with; manage	21
从此	cóngcǐ	副词	from then on; henceforth	13
从没	cóng méi		never ever	15
促销	cùxiāo	动词	promote sales	13
醋	cù	名词	vinegar	16
D					
答应	dāying	动词	respond; reply	21
达到	dá//dào	动词	reach; come up to	13
打听	dǎting	动词	inquire about	23
打折	dǎ//zhé	动词	give a discount	13
打针	dǎ//zhēn	动词	get/take an injection	20
大大	dàdà	副词	greatly	19
大多数	dàduōshù	名词	vast majority	18
代	dài	动词、名词	act for; generation	20
代表	dàibiǎo	动词、名词	mean; stand for; representative	18

带来	dàilái		bring	21
带领	dàilǐng	动词	guide; lead	23
戴	dài	动词	wear	15
当中	dāngzhōng	名词	the midst	23
导游	dǎoyóu	名词	tour guide	14
倒霉	dǎo//méi	形容词	out of luck	20
到达	dàodá	动词	arrive	23
到底	dàodǐ	副词	finally; in the end	24
倒	dào	动词	pour	16
的话	dehuà	助词	used at the end of a conditional clause	18
灯	dēng	名词	light	21
灯笼	dēnglong	名词	lantern	17
等到	děngdào	介词	until	20
等于	děngyú	动词	be the same as	22
地点	dìdiǎn	名词	location	22
点赞	diǎn//zàn	动词	like (on social media)	21
电子	diànzǐ	名词	electron	15
调查	diàochá	名词、动词	survey; investigate	18
掉	diào	动词	fall (into)	14
订	dìng	动词	book; order	23
定期	dìngqī	形容词	at fixed period; regular	22
东北菜	dōngběicài	名词	Northeastern Chinese cuisine	19
动	dòng	动词	move	13
动力	dònglì	名词	drive; motivation	22
独自	dúzì	副词	by oneself	24
读音	dúyīn	名词	pronunciation	17
段	duàn	量词	used to indicate time/distance	15
对	duì	量词	pair; couple	19

		E		
额	é	后缀	volume; amount	13
儿	ér	名词	son; child	18
耳机	ěrjī	名词	earphone; headset	15
		F		
发生	fāshēng	动词	happen; occur	20
发展	fāzhǎn	名词、动词	development; develop	18
繁体字	fántǐzì	名词	traditional Chinese character	17
繁育	fányù	动词	breed	23
反对	fǎnduì	动词	oppose; object to; be against	21
反复	fǎnfù	副词、名词	over and over again; repeatedly; reversal	23
反正	fǎnzhèng	副词	anyway	19
方向	fāngxiàng	名词	direction	14
防	fáng	动词	prepare for; prevent	18
防止	fángzhǐ	动词	prevent; avoid	22
房东	fángdōng	名词	landlord; landlady; house owner; host family	19
房租	fángzū	名词	rent	19
放	fàng	动词	put	16
放心	fàng//xīn	动词	feel relieved; rest assured; be relaxed	18
非物质文化遗产	Fēiwùzhì wénhuà yíchǎn		intangible cultural heritage	15
费用	fèiyong	名词	cost; expense; charge	20
分	fēn	动词	tell... from...; distinguish	16
风俗	fēngsú	名词	custom	17
夫妻	fūqī	名词	wife and husband; couple	18
扶	fú	动词	adjust; support with the hand	17
服务	fúwù	动词	serve	23
幅	fú	量词	*used for cloth, pictures, scrolls, etc.*	17

父亲	fùqīn	名词	father	19
付	fù	动词	pay	13
G				
改	gǎi	动词	change	22
赶	gǎn	动词	hurry; rush for	20
赶紧	gǎnjǐn	副词	without delay; as soon as possible	16
赶快	gǎnkuài	副词	hurriedly; at once	18
感受	gǎnshòu	动词	feel	21
高	gāo	形容词	high; above average	18
高低	gāodī	名词	height	18
高峰	gāofēng	名词	peak	21
高铁	gāotiě	名词	high-speed rail	22
告别	gào//bié	动词	say farewell to	24
歌手	gēshǒu	名词	singer	15
个人	gèrén	名词	individual	22
各地	gèdì	名词	everywhere; various places	23
各位	gèwèi	代词	everyone	24
根本	gēnběn	副词、名词	at all; base	18
工艺品	gōngyìpǐn	名词	handiwork	13
功能	gōngnéng	名词	function	21
购买	gòumǎi	动词	buy; purchase	13
购物	gòuwù	动词	go shopping	13
够	gòu	动词、副词	be enough; enough	20
古	gǔ	形容词	ancient	23
古代	gǔdài	名词	ancient times	15
古诗	gǔshī	名词	ancient poetry	15
故乡	gùxiāng	名词	hometown	18
故意	gùyì	副词	on purpose; deliberately	13
挂	guà	动词	hang	17

关机	guān//jī	动词	switch off	21
关系	guānxì	名词	relationship	17
关心	guānxīn	动词	care for; be concerned with	14
关注	guānzhù	动词	pay attention to; concern	18
观察	guānchá	动词	observe	23
观点	guāndiǎn	名词	opinion; viewpoint	22
观念	guānniàn	名词	idea; concept	17
管	guǎn	动词	take care of	18
光	guāng	副词	only	15
广场	guǎngchǎng	名词	square	19
广式月饼	Guǎngshì Yuèbing		Cantonese-style moon cake	17
规定	guīdìng	名词、动词	specification; stipulate	13
锅	guō	名词	pot; pan	16
国籍	guójí	名词	nationality	24
果然	guǒrán	副词	as expected	24
果汁	guǒzhī	名词	juice	19
过程	guòchéng	名词	process	21
过来	guò//lái	动词	come over	14
H				
喊	hǎn	动词	call; shout	21
好听	hǎotīng	形容词	easy on the ear	15
好奇	hàoqí	形容词	curious	23
合格	hégé	形容词	qualified	24
合理	hélǐ	形容词	sensible; reasonable	18
合适	héshì	形容词	suitable; appropriate	16
和	hé	形容词	harmonious	17
和平	hépíng	名词	peace	17
黑	hēi	形容词	dark	20
哼	hēng	动词	hum; croon	15

红	hóng	形容词	red	17
红茶	hóngchá	名词	black tea	19
红酒	hóngjiǔ	名词	red wine	19
忽然	hūrán	副词	unexpectedly; all of a sudden; suddenly	13
化	huà	后缀	*used as a suffix to turn a noun or an adjective into a verb*	16
化妆品	huàzhuāngpǐn	名词	cosmetics	13
话	huà	名词	words	18
话题	huàtí	名词	topic; subject	22
坏	huài	形容词	bad	17
欢乐	huānlè	形容词	joyful	21
欢迎	huānyíng	动词	welcome	19
回来	huí//lái	动词	come back	14
婚礼	hūnlǐ	名词	wedding	13
火锅	huǒguō	名词	hotpot	23
获得	huòdé	动词	acquire; obtain; gain	24
J				
基本	jīběn	副词、形容词	almost; by and large; on the whole; basic	19
基本上	jīběnshàng	副词	almost; basically; on the whole	21
基地	jīdì	名词	base	23
激动	jīdòng	形容词	excited; thrilled	24
集	jí	量词	episode	15
集中	jízhōng	形容词、动词	concentrated; concentrate	23
计算	jìsuàn	动词	calculate; measure	16
寄宿	jìsù	动词	(of students) board	19
加	jiā	动词	add	16
家	jiā	量词	*used of families/enterprises*	17
家和万事兴	jiā hé wànshì xīng		Harmony in the family leads to success in everything.	17

价格	jiàgé	名词	price	13
价钱	jiàqián	名词	price	22
价位	jiàwèi	名词	price	21
简直	jiǎnzhí	副词	simply; literally	20
见到	jiàndào		meet	19
建议	jiànyì	动词、名词	propose; suggestion	22
建筑	jiànzhù	名词	architecture	23
将来	jiānglái	名词	future	24
讲究	jiǎngjiu	动词、形容词	be particular about; tasteful	16
奖学金	jiǎngxuéjīn	名词	scholarship	24
交费	jiāofèi	动词	pay fees/charges/rates	20
交易	jiāoyì	名词	transaction	13
叫	jiào	介词	*used to introduce the doer of an action*	20
教授	jiàoshòu	名词	professor	24
教育	jiàoyù	动词、名词	educate; education	18
接到	jiēdào		hear from; receive	20
接近	jiējìn	动词	approach; be close to; approximate	14
接受	jiēshòu	动词	accept	21
接下来	jiē xiàlái		next; then; after that	15
街道	jiēdào	名词	street; avenue	23
节约	jiéyuē	动词	economize; save	21
结果	jiéguǒ	连词、名词	thus; consequence	20
解释	jiěshì	动词	explain	17
今后	jīnhòu	名词	future; days to come	16
仅仅	jǐnjǐn	副词	just; only	16
尽量	jǐnliàng	副词	as... as possible	16
进行	jìnxíng	动词	conduct; carry on	14
近	jìn	形容词	close	14
近期	jìnqī	名词	near future	23

京胡	jīnghú	名词	*jinghu*	15
京戏	jīngxì	名词	Peking/Beijing opera	15
经济	jīngjì	名词	economy	22
精神	jīngshen	形容词、名词	energetic; energy	19
景点	jǐngdiǎn	名词	tourist attraction; scenic spot	23
酒店	jiǔdiàn	名词	hotel	23
菊花	júhuā	名词	chrysanthemum	14
举	jǔ	动词	raise; hold up	17
举行	jǔxíng	动词	hold	17
句	jù	量词	*used of language*	18
距离	jùlí	名词、动词	distance; be away from	21
聚会	jùhuì	名词、动词	gathering; get together	17
决定	juédìng	动词、名词	decide; decision	23
决心	juéxīn	动词、名词	be determined; determination	22
K				
开机	kāi//jī	动词	keep the phone on; switch on	21
看来	kànlái	动词	it looks; it seems	15
看起来	kàn qǐlái		it looks	19
看上去	kàn shàngqù		it seems	19
考虑	kǎolǜ	动词	think about; consider	13
烤	kǎo	动词	roast	16
烤鸭	kǎoyā	名词	roast duck	24
靠	kào	动词	rely on; count on	18
科技	kējì	名词	science and technology	22
科学	kēxué	名词	science	14
可	kě	副词	*used for emphasis*	15
可不是	kěbúshi	副词	exactly	18
可靠	kěkào	形容词	reliable; credible; trustworthy	22
可怕	kěpà	形容词	terrible	20

课堂	kètáng	名词	classroom	24
空巢老人	kōngcháo lǎorén		empty nester	18
口味	kǒuwèi	名词	taste	21
口语	kǒuyǔ	名词	spoken language	19
快递	kuàidì	名词	express	13

L

辣椒	làjiāo	名词	chilli	16
啦	la	助词	combination of 了 and 啊, expressing exclamation, interrogation, etc.	19
来到	láidào	动词	come to	21
浪费	làngfèi	动词	waste	22
老	lǎo	形容词	old	18
老百姓	lǎobǎixìng	名词	common people	21
老板	lǎobǎn	名词	boss; business owner	24
离	lí	动词	be away from	20
离不开	lí bu kāi		cannot do without	21
离开	lí//kāi	动词	leave	15
里	lǐ	名词	inside	15
里面	lǐmiàn	名词	inside	17
理解	lǐjiě	动词	understand; comprehend	14
理想	lǐxiǎng	名词、形容词	ideal; dream	24
理由	lǐyóu	名词	reason	22
立刻	lìkè	副词	immediately; right away	13
利用	lìyòng	动词	use; take advantage of	21
例如	lìrú	动词	take for example	15
亮	liàng	形容词、动词	bright; shine	20
辆	liàng	量词	used with vehicles	20
列入	lièrù	动词	be included in; be listed in	15
临时	línshí	形容词、副词	temporary; at the last moment	17

淋	lín	动词	drench	20
留下	liúxia		leave	23
流	liú	动词	flow; stream	20
流行	liúxíng	动词	be popular	13
路灯	lùdēng	名词	street lamp	20
路上	lùshang	名词	way	20
旅行社	lǚxíngshè	名词	travel agency	23
绿茶	lǜchá	名词	green tea	16
轮	lún	动词、名词、量词	take turns; wheel; *used of things/actions that rotate*	21
锣鼓	luógǔ	名词	gongs and drums	15
落汤鸡	luòtāngjī	名词	someone who is soaked through	20
M				
麻烦	máfan	形容词、动词	troublesome; trouble	15
满足	mǎnzú	动词	satisfy; please	21
慢慢	mànmàn		slowly; gradually	21
毛病	máobìng	名词	health problem; disease	19
没法儿	méifǎr		cannot	21
美	měi	形容词	beautiful	23
美好	měihǎo	形容词	beautiful; good	21
美食	měishí	名词	choice food; gourmet	21
迷	mí	后缀	fan; enthusiast	13
米	mǐ	量词	meter	14
免税店	miǎnshuìdiàn	名词	duty-free shop	13
民间	mínjiān	名词	folk; the people	23
名	míng	量词	*used of persons*	19
名录	mínglù	名词	list; directory	15
名牌	míngpái	名词	famous brand	13
明年	míngnián	名词	next year	19

明显	míngxiǎn	形容词	obvious; distinct	16
命运	mìngyùn	名词	fate; destiny; fortune	18
摸	mō	动词	touch	20
母亲	mǔqīn	名词	mother	19
目标	mùbiāo	名词	target; aim; goal	22
N				
拿出	náchū		take out	21
哪些	nǎxiē	代词	which	15
那个	nàge	代词	that	14
那时	nà shí		then	24
那些	nàxiē	代词	those	15
奶茶	nǎichá	名词	milk tea	16
南	nán	名词	south	14
难道	nándào	副词	used in a rhetorical question for emphasis	24
能够	nénggòu	动词	can; be able to	19
能力	nénglì	名词	capability; competence	18
年初	niánchū	名词	beginning of the year	19
弄	nòng	动词	make; do	14
努力	nǔlì	动词	make an effort	22
P				
拍	pāi	动词	purchase (online)	13
培养	péiyǎng	动词	train; cultivate; nurture	24
碰到	pèngdào	动词	come across; meet	19
批评	pīpíng	动词	blame; criticize	22
便宜	piányi	动词	cheap	22
票友	piàoyǒu	名词	amateur performer	15
评价	píngjià	名词、动词	evaluation; evaluate	21
破	pò	形容词	broken	20

		Q		
期	qī	量词	*referring to things done periodically*	15
期待	qīdài	动词	look forward to; expect	24
期中	qīzhōng	名词	midterm	17
起来	qǐ//lái	动词	stand up	14
千万	qiānwàn	副词	must; be sure to	18
前年	qiánnián	名词	the year before last	22
前往	qiánwǎng	动词	head for; go up to	23
钱包	qiánbāo	名词	wallet	20
强	qiáng	形容词	strong; high-standard	18
强大	qiángdà	形容词	strong; powerful	21
墙	qiáng	名词	wall	17
敲	qiāo	动词	knock; beat	15
亲人	qīnrén	名词	one's family	18
亲子	qīnzǐ	名词	parent-child	18
亲自	qīnzì	副词	in person; personally	16
青少年	qīng-shàonián	名词	young generation; teenagers; juvenile	21
情况	qíngkuàng	名词	situation; circumstances	18
请进	qǐng jìn		please come in	19
请坐	qǐng zuò		please take a seat	19
庆祝	qìngzhù	动词	celebrate	17
秋游	qiūyóu	动词	autumn outing	14
球迷	qiúmí	名词	(ball game) fan	19
球赛	qiúsài	名词	ball game	21
球鞋	qiúxié	名词	sneakers; gym shoes	19
区	qū	名词	section; area; zone	14
去年	qùnián	名词	last year	17
全部	quánbù	名词	whole; all	20
全国	quánguó	名词	whole country	17

全年	quánnián	名词	whole year	19
全球	quánqiú	名词	whole world	16
全身	quánshēn	名词	whole body	15
全职	quánzhí	形容词	full-time	18
缺点	quēdiǎn	名词	disadvantage	19
缺少	quēshǎo	动词	lack; be short of	13
却	què	副词	however	16
群	qún	量词	cluster; group; flock	15
R				
让	ràng	动词	let	15
人们	rénmen	名词	people	21
人生	rénshēng	名词	life	22
仍然	réngrán	副词	still	22
日常	rìcháng	形容词	day-to-day; daily	18
如何	rúhé	代词	how; what	24
S				
色彩	sècǎi	名词	color	24
晒	shài	动词	post online	13
商量	shāngliang	动词	talk over; discuss	17
商品	shāngpǐn	名词	goods; merchandise	13
赏	shǎng	动词	appreciate; enjoy; admire	17
上来	shàng//lái	动词	come up	14
上面	shàngmiàn	名词	used to indicate the scope of sth.	21
上去	shàng//qù	动词	go up	14
上下班	shàng-xiàbān		go to and get off work	22
上衣	shàngyī	名词	jacket	22
少许	shǎoxǔ	形容词	a little; a bit	16
社会	shèhuì	名词	society	18
伸	shēn	动词	stretch	14

深	shēn	形容词	deep	14
深刻	shēnkè	形容词	deep; profound	23
生存	shēngcún	动词	make a living	22
生命	shēngmìng	名词	life	20
声	shēng	名词、量词	tone; *used for sounds*	17
省心	shěng//xīn	动词	free from worry	23
失败	shībài	动词、形容词	fail; lose; failed	24
诗	shī	名词	poem	23
诗人	shīrén	名词	poet	23
湿	shī	形容词	wet	14
时	shí	名词	time	20
时代	shídài	名词	time; era; age	16
时期	shíqī	名词	period	23
实力	shílì	名词	strength; power; competence	18
实现	shíxiàn	动词	realize	17
使用	shǐyòng	动词	use	21
始终	shǐzhōng	副词	always; from beginning to end	15
世纪	shìjì	名词	century	21
市场	shìchǎng	名词	market	20
市花	shìhuā	名词	city flower	14
事故	shìgù	名词	accident	20
事实	shìshí	名词	fact	18
试	shì	动词	try	15
适量	shìliàng	形容词	just proper in amount; appropriate; moderate	16
适应	shìyìng	动词	adjust to; adapt; fit	18
收	shōu	动词	keep	13
手	shǒu	名词	hand	14
手表	shǒubiǎo	名词	(wrist) watch	13

手续	shǒuxù	名词	formalities; procedure	23
手指	shǒuzhǐ	名词	finger	13
首先	shǒuxiān	副词	first	16
受不了	shòubuliǎo	动词	can't stand; can't take it anymore	15
受伤	shòu//shāng	动词	get injured	20
输入	shūrù	动词	input	16
熟	shú	形容词	familiar	20
摔	shuāi	动词	fall; lose one's balance	20
双	shuāng	量词	pair	19
睡着	shuìzháo		fall asleep	13
说法	shuōfǎ	名词	expression; saying	17
司机	sījī	名词	driver	20
送到	sòngdào		send to	20
随便	suíbiàn	形容词、动词	at random; do as one pleases	16
随便	suíbiàn	动词	do at one's convenience	19
所有	suǒyǒu	形容词	all	17

T

台阶	táijiē	名词	stairs; steps	20
太太	tàitai	名词	wife	18
讨论	tǎolùn	动词	discuss	16
套	tào	量词	*used of series/sets of things*	19
特点	tèdiǎn	名词	distinguishing feature; characteristic	17
提前	tíqián	动词	do sth. ahead of schedule; do sth. in advance	22
提醒	tí//xǐng	动词	remind	13
体现	tǐxiàn	动词	embody; incarnate	23
天	tiān	名词	day	15
甜	tián	形容词	sweet	16
挑战	tiǎo//zhàn	动词	challenge	15

跳舞	tiào//wǔ	动词	dance	19
听到	tīngdào		hear	18
停车	tíng//chē	动词	park the car	21
通过	tōngguò	介词、动词	by; through; pass	19
同时	tóngshí	连词、名词	meanwhile; same time	14
统一	tǒngyī	形容词、动词	uniform; unify	16
突然	tūrán	形容词	sudden; unexpected; out of the blue	20
团	tuán	名词	group	23
推	tuī	动词	push; give a hand from behind	14
推动	tuī//dòng	动词	push; promote; drive	22
腿	tuǐ	名词	leg	20
退休	tuì//xiū	动词	retire	15
拖鞋	tuōxié	名词	slippers	19
W				
完成	wán//chéng	动词	complete; accomplish	13
完美	wánměi	形容词	perfect	23
完整	wánzhěng	形容词	complete; whole	23
碗	wǎn	名词	bowl	16
万	wàn	数词	ten thousand	17
网上	wǎng shang		on the Internet	23
危险	wēixiǎn	名词、形容词	danger; dangerous	20
伟大	wěidà	形容词	great	23
为了	wèile	介词	for; so as to	18
位置	wèizhì	名词	location; place	14
文学	wénxué	名词	literature	23
文章	wénzhāng	名词	article; essay	23
文字	wénzì	名词	writing	23
稳定	wěndìng	形容词	stable	22
问好	wèn//hǎo	动词	send one's regards to	20

问候	wènhòu	动词	send one's regards to	18
卧铺	wòpù	名词	berth	22
无法	wúfǎ	动词	unable	21
舞台	wǔtái	名词	stage	23
		X		
西方	Xīfāng	名词	the West	16
西南	xīnán	名词	southwest	23
西式	xīshì		Western-style	23
戏	xì	名词	traditional Chinese opera	15
下单	xià//dān	动词	place an order	21
下去	xià//qù	动词	go down	14
闲	xián	形容词	idle	16
显示	xiǎnshì	动词	reveal; show	18
现场	xiànchǎng	名词	site	23
现代	xiàndài	名词	modern times	13
现金	xiànjīn	名词	cash	21
现实	xiànshí	名词	reality	22
馅儿	xiànr	名词	filling; stuffing	17
相处	xiāngchǔ	动词	get along with	19
相当	xiāngdāng	副词	quite; considerably	19
相互	xiānghù	副词	mutually	14
相同	xiāngtóng	形容词	same	22
相信	xiāngxìn	动词	believe	13
享受	xiǎngshòu	名词、动词	enjoyment; enjoy	15
想象	xiǎngxiàng	动词、名词	imagine; imagination	24
项	xiàng	量词	*used of itemized things*	18
消费	xiāofèi	动词	consume	22
消息	xiāoxi	名词	news	17
小	xiǎo	形容词	small	15

小心	xiǎoxīn	动词、形容词	be careful; careful	14
校园	xiàoyuán	名词	campus	24
鞋	xié	名词	shoe	14
血	xiě	名词	blood	20
心中	xīnzhōng	名词	(in) one's heart/mind	22
信任	xìnrèn	动词	trust	24
信息	xìnxī	名词	information	21
信用卡	xìnyòngkǎ	名词	credit card	13
行李	xíngli	名词	luggage; baggage	13
形象	xíngxiàng	名词	image; imagery	15
形状	xíngzhuàng	名词	shape	16
幸运	xìngyùn	形容词	lucky; fortunate	19
熊猫	xióngmāo	名词	panda	23
Y				
压力	yālì	名词	pressure; stress	18
鸭蛋黄	yādànhuáng		duck's egg yolk	17
烟	yān	名词	cigarette	13
研究	yánjiū	动词	research	14
研究生	yánjiūshēng	名词	graduate student; postgraduate	24
盐	yán	名词	salt	16
眼镜	yǎnjìng	名词	spectacles; glasses	17
眼前	yǎnqián	名词	being before one's eyes	23
演	yǎn	动词	play; act; perform	15
演唱	yǎnchàng	动词	sing; chant	15
演唱会	yǎnchànghuì	名词	concert	23
演出	yǎnchū	动词、名词	perform; performance	23
阳光	yángguāng	名词	sunshine	19
洋楼	yánglóu	名词	Western-style building of two storeys or more	23

261

养	yǎng	动词	raise	18
夜里	yèli	名词	night	20
一切	yíqiè	代词	everything; all	19
以外	yǐwài	名词	beyond	22
一点儿	yìdiǎnr		a little bit	22
一方面	yì fāngmiàn		on the one hand	18
亿	yì	数词	a hundred million	13
艺术	yìshù	名词	art	15
意见	yìjiàn	名词	opinion; view; advice	21
意思	yìsi	名词	meaning	17
意外	yìwài	形容词、名词	unexpected; accident	13
因此	yīncǐ	连词	therefore; thus	15
音响	yīnxiǎng	名词	stereo equipment	15
饮料	yǐnliào	名词	drink; beverage	16
印象	yìnxiàng	名词	impression	23
应该	yīnggāi	动词	be supposed to; should	13
迎接	yíngjiē	动词	welcome	23
营养	yíngyǎng	名词	nutrition	16
影院	yǐngyuàn	名词	cinema	22
永远	yǒngyuǎn	副词	forever; always	21
勇敢	yǒnggǎn	形容词	brave; courageous	24
优点	yōudiǎn	名词	advantage	19
由	yóu	介词	by	14
由于	yóuyú	连词、介词	since; because of	15
油腻	yóunì	形容词	oily; taste greasy	17
游	yóu	动词	go visiting; tour; go sightseeing	14
游客	yóukè	名词	tourist	23
有的是	yǒudeshì		have plenty of	22
有时	yǒushí	副词	sometimes	19

鱼香肉丝	yúxiāng ròusī		Shredded Pork with Garlic Sauce	16
娱乐	yúlè	名词、动词	recreation and entertainment; amuse	15
预计	yùjì	动词	estimate	23
遇到	yùdào		come across; encounter	18
原来	yuánlái	名词、形容词、副词	the past; original, former; originally	15
圆	yuán	形容词	round	17
圆满	yuánmǎn	形容词	perfect; satisfactory	17
远远	yuǎnyuǎn		by far	22
愿望	yuànwàng	名词	wish; dream; aspiration	17
月饼	yuèbing	名词	moon cake	17
月份	yuèfèn	名词	month	19
月亮	yuèliang	名词	moon	17
运气	yùnqi	名词	luck	20

Z

咱	zán	代词	we; us	22
早已	zǎoyǐ	副词	already	23
增加	zēngjiā	动词	increase	14
展览	zhǎnlǎn	动词、名词	exhibit; exhibition	14
站	zhàn	动词	stand	14
长大	zhǎngdà		grow up	15
找到	zhǎodào		find	19
照顾	zhàogù	动词	look after	14
照相	zhào//xiàng	动词	take a picture	21
这个	zhège	代词	this	14
真的	zhēn de		real	18
诊所	zhěnsuǒ	名词	clinic	20
争取	zhēngqǔ	动词	strive for	22
整	zhěng	形容词	whole; complete	19

整个	zhěnggè	形容词	whole; all; entire	21
整理	zhěnglǐ	动词	clear up; sort out	13
整天	zhěngtiān	名词	all day long	19
正宗	zhèngzōng	形容词	authentic and original	16
证件	zhèngjiàn	名词	certificate; credentials	23
之一	zhīyī	名词	one of	14
支持	zhīchí	动词	support	24
汁	zhī	名词	sauce; gravy	16
直播	zhíbō	动词	broadcast live	21
直接	zhíjiē	形容词	immediate; direct	20
值	zhí	动词	be worthwhile	22
值得	zhí//dé	动词	be worthwhile	24
植物园	zhíwùyuán		botanical garden; arboretum	14
只能	zhǐ néng		have no other choice but; can only	22
只要	zhǐyào	连词	as long as; if only	16
只有	zhǐyǒu	连词	only	18
指	zhǐ	动词	point at; identify	14
至少	zhìshǎo	副词	at least	14
中餐馆	zhōngcānguǎn	名词	Chinese restaurant	16
中年	zhōngnián	名词	middle age	19
中西方	Zhōng-Xīfāng		China and the West	23
中心	zhōngxīn	名词	center; hub	14
终于	zhōngyú	副词	finally; eventually; in the end	19
种类	zhǒnglèi	名词	class; kind; category	16
重	zhòng	形容词	heavy	13
重点	zhòngdiǎn	名词	emphasis; focus; key	22
重要	zhòngyào	形容词	important	17
主人	zhǔrén	名词	host; owner	19
主张	zhǔzhāng	动词、名词	advocate; position	22

住院	zhù//yuàn	动词	be in hospital; be hospitalized	20
专业	zhuānyè	名词、形容词	major; profession; professional	24
赚	zhuàn	动词	gain; make a profit	24
撞	zhuàng	动词	bump against	20
资金	zījīn	名词	fund; money	22
子女	zǐnǚ	名词	sons and daughters; children; offspring	18
自从	zìcóng	介词	since	15
自然	zìrán	名词	nature	14
自行车	zìxíngchē	名词	bicycle	20
自由	zìyóu	形容词、名词	free; freedom	20
自娱自乐	zìyú-zìlè		amuse oneself	15
字画	zìhuà	名词	calligraphy and painting	17
租	zū	动词	rent	22
足够	zúgòu	动词	be enough; be sufficient; be adequate	22
足球	zúqiú	名词	soccer; football	19
组成	zǔchéng	动词	form; compose; constitute	14
组织	zǔzhī	动词、名词	organize; organization	14
作家	zuòjiā	名词	writer	24
作品	zuòpǐn	名词	works	24
做法	zuòfǎ	名词	way of doing sth.	16
做鬼脸	zuò guǐliǎn		make faces	24

专有名词			
成都	Chéngdū	Chengdu	23
杜甫	Dù Fǔ	one of the greatest poets in Tang Dynasty	23
杜甫草堂	Dù Fǔ Cǎotáng	Du Fu Thatched Cottage	23
黄山	Huáng Shān	Mount Huang	23
可口可乐	Kěkǒu Kělè	Coca-Cola	16
肯德基	Kěndéjī	KFC	16

宽窄巷子	Kuān-zhǎi Xiàngzi	Wide and Narrow Alley	23
联合国教科文组织	Liánhéguó Jiào-kē-wén Zǔzhī	United Nations Educational, Scientific and Cultural Organization (UNESCO)	15
麦当劳	Màidāngláo	McDonald's	16
民国时期	Mínguó shíqī	the Republic of China era	23
朋友圈	péngyouquān	Moments	21
清朝	Qīngcháo	Qing Dynasty	23
四川	Sìchuān	Sichuan	23
天猫商城	Tiānmāo Shāngchéng	Tmall	13
微信	Wēixìn	WeChat	21
卧佛寺	Wòfó Sì	Temple of the Reclining Buddha	14
武侯祠	Wǔhóu Cí	Wuhou Shrine	23
西湖	Xī Hú	West Lake	23
香山	Xiāng Shān	Fragrant Hill	14
星巴克	Xīngbākè	Starbucks	16
意大利	Yìdàlì	Italy	19
张林	Zhāng Lín	Zhang Lin	19
《中国好声音》	《Zhōngguó Hǎo Shēngyīn》	*The Voice of China*	15
《中国诗词大会》	《Zhōngguó Shīcí Dàhuì》	*Chinese Poetry Conference*	15
中秋节	Zhōngqiū Jié	Mid-Autumn Festival	17
诸葛亮	Zhūgě Liàng	Zhuge Liang, a character in the *Romance of the Three Kingdoms*, is a real historical figure who lived during the Three Kingdoms period in Chinese history. He is a person of great wisdom and resourcefulness.	23
APP		Application	21